# *Your Best Speech Ever*

The ultimate public speaking "How To Guide" featuring the
Speech Formula—a proven design and delivery system.

## J.R. Steele

Published by, The International Public Speaking
Institute, Fort Lauderdale, FL 2017

The International
Public
Speaking
Institute

# Dedication

To my students who have opened themselves to learn the life lessons speech provides; I have learned so much from you.

# Acknowledgements

Many people helped make this book a reality. From the beginning, Julie Haan, Micki Johnson, and Marcia McPherson have supported my vision and provided tremendous morale support. As that vision morphed into Your Best Speech Ever, I am so grateful for the careful edit provided by James Lange. Nolan Haan never fails to have the courage to provide honest, meaningful feedback and has availed himself for many creative consultations. Mitchell, your input made a big difference! My support system includes a long list of cherished people who have listened, encouraged, admonished and offered patience throughout this project. Thank you! Amy Parker has painstakingly designed every page. She has the patience of a saint and has earned my deepest gratitude. Finally, Lloyd Cosby, my rock, thank you for your patience and so much more.

For information contact www.yourbestspeechever.com

Cover and graphic design by Amy Parker
www.apdesignworks.com

ISBN: 978-1-947450-00-4 (Black and White Edition)

First Edition: September 2017

"Feel free to share this – just don't try to pass it off as your own!
If you enjoy this book, I really hope you'll do me the favor of leaving a review.
You can connect with me jr@yourbestspeechever.com

10 9 8 7 6 5 4 3 2 1

# Reviews

Finally! As a speech instructor who has used three different speech course textbooks over the past seven years in hopes of finding a book that would both awaken and enlighten my students, I view *Your Best Speech Ever* as, forgive the corny pun, the best speech text ever. Steele incorporates new, relevant research like that of Amy Cuddy's on power poses, deals with students' most palpable fears about public speaking while offering specific strategies to overcome them (unlike the overly-generalized tips that most books give), includes tools of engagement like self-awareness quizzes, numbered lists, cognitive exercises and surveys all while punctuating it with a unique sense of humor and wit—the type that students love in both a textbook and a teacher. Furthermore, I have asked my students to use the online engagement platforms for two other speech textbooks and they found them incomplete with a confusing user experience. I am eager to have my students use the online speech formula tool that Steele has developed to accompany her text. I'm beyond excited to get started!

*Tiffani Knowles*, Author of HOLA AMERICA: Guts, Grit, Grind and Further Traits in the Successful American Immigrant, Speech Instructor, City University of New York, NYC Public Schools, Barry University

*Your Best Speech Ever* helped me be the speaker I always wished I could be!

*Katherine Espinosa,* Athlete

Turns a frustrating and anxiety ridden experience into a journey of self-discovery and actualization.

*John Leyden III,* Student

A great and simple way to create a phenomenal speech.

*Adam Dean,* Ph.D.

No other book guides you through a logical process that allows you to clearly express your ideas, keeping the audience's needs foremost throughout each step.

*Sam De Jesus,* Nurse Practitioner

*Your Best Speech Ever* is a fantastic way to advance leadership skills with my staff. Each has their own copy on their desk."

**Marcia McPherson**, Owner Employment Resources

I have grown so much as a speaker. At first, I was too nervous to speak in front of an audience, mainly because I didn't know how to prepare. By mastering the Delivery Principles and then learning how to organize my ideas better, I now write worthwhile speeches that I'm excited to deliver.

**Ninnosca Reyes,** Radio Personality

Wow, this is the most organized way I have ever written a speech, even a paper. It forces you to thoroughly know your research, cite ethically, and organize your speech the best way.

**Shaylis Guerrero**

Awesome use for any form of presentation on any subject.

**Kyle Schulze,** Deaf Ninja Warrior

Works as great gift! My sons in college loved it as much as my colleagues!

**Kathleen Casey,** Esquire

*Your Best Speech Ever* is a no nonsense text for new or experienced public speakers. Each chapter is filled with checklists and strategies which can easily be revisited whenever tasked with delivering a speech. So grateful this tool is in my repertoire to enhance my leadership skills, which will allow me to succeed within my team, in the classroom and in the workplace!

**Hanna Durocher,** Student-Athlete

*Your Best Speech Ever* gives those of us who find public speaking terrifying permission to embrace our anxiety while providing us with the tools to overcome that fear. It accomplishes this by guiding us through the public speaking process using humor and practical structured approaches.

**Darla J. Slicton,** Ph.D. Clinical Psychologist

# Table of Contents

*F*or many people, the thought of speaking in public makes them tremble, sweat and stutter. I felt just this way when I taught my first college course. Imagine being the instructor for a group of 25 freshman college students and having to tell the group, "You have a speech to deliver." At first, the speeches were painful to hear—for both students and the instructor! I soon realized that while there were some great textbooks out there, they did little to help students improve. I carefully analyzed each speech, each student, and each class. My instructional design background came in handy to identify a better way to ease the pain and anxiety and help each student deliver a dynamic speech.

After time, a Speech Formula emerged. As each student in each class applied the Speech Formula, a remarkable thing happened—their speeches became worth hearing, and their peers looked forward to speech day! Students began to develop a feeling of excitement at the idea of presenting their ideas because they had a message worth hearing and the confidence to do so. The Speech Formula provided a systematic way for them to improve. It was exciting to see the students enter the classroom terrified during their first presentation and soaring with confidence by their last. This confidence extended beyond the classroom. It penetrated their daily lives. Many reported receiving an array of compliments ranging from simple acknowledgment for having shared their ideas to salary raises, and many expressed enjoying healthier relationships with their friends and family. Public speaking is said to be the language of leadership for a reason. As student after student, class after class experienced the same improvement, the Speech Formula clearly showed it could help people reach their full potential by becoming better, more conscious communicators.

For the past several years, I've shared these principles with an array of individuals from the neighbor compelled to speak at the city commissioner's meeting to business executives preparing for a company product launch and even an artist presenting a workshop about their life's work. In each instance, it helped these individuals deliver their best speech. Recently, I had a speech to deliver. I followed the Speech Formula exactly. The process was so simple and fast. The speech could not have gone better. It fills my heart to know the Speech Formula works to help me deliver my best speech too! I am delighted to share the entire process of creating "Your Best Speech Ever." Each chapter offers an array of probing questions; interactions and practice speeches that will help you build the specific skill addressed. This process helps you think differently when you communicate. You may notice that your dialog will become more precise—before long, you will be able to choose the right strategy for each audience. I refer to this transformation as being "Speech Actualized." I encourage you to reach your full potential through the lessons learned from speech. I invite you to join those of us who have used the Speech Formula to become "Speech Actualized." Let's begin the journey to discover "Your Best Speech Ever"…

SPEECH COACH

*J.R.Steele,* M.S.

# How to Read this Book

This book can be read differently depending upon your experience as a speaker and how you learn best. Allow me to explain.

**Inexperienced Speakers:** Your best approach to reading this book is to read the book straight through, begin with Chapter 1 and end with Chapter 8. Be sure to slow down as you go through the chapters and complete the activities provided throughout as they are designed to help you explore the ideas introduced in the chapter and build your ability to design and deliver a speech with confidence. At the end of every chapter, except the last, practice speeches are provided, do every one, as they will help you deliver your best speech ever!

**Experienced Speakers:** The beginning chapters go into depth explaining the fear and ways to conquer your fear. If you have already confronted your fear, you may want to advance through these ideas quickly and focus more on the chapters that focus on strategies to enhance your skill set as a speaker: Chapter 3 Transform Your Delivery, Chapter 4: Make Visuals Count, Chapter 7: The Speech Formula and Chapter 8: Putting It All Together

**Sequential vs. Global Learners:** The ideas in this book culminate in the final two chapters of this book. Readers have their own learning style. Some are more global and others sequential. For the global learners, taking a look at the "big picture" first is how you learn best. If this describes you, read Chapter 8 before you read Chapter 7. For sequential learners who prefer the details first and then the big picture just read the book as written.

**Key Ideas Are Addressed from Different Angles:** As you progress through the book, you will explore some ideas multiple times. Thoroughly understanding what goes into a speech and the process of creating a speech is complex. It involves an itinerant (back and forth motion) process. Therefore, elements must be addressed more than once. Let's use "Source" as an example. Isn't information important to insert in a speech? Of course, the information literally drives the speech; it is the reason for it. However, what is the best place to discuss it at length? There is no one specific place; in fact we address the significance and the use of a source in five different chapters from five different perspectives.

Chapter 1: Public Speaking Freaks us Out

- Not knowing your information increases anxiety.

Chapter 2: Conquer your Fear

- Knowing your information helps reduce anxiety.
- Quality, credible information gets speakers excited about delivering, thus reducing anxiety.

Chapter 4: Make Visuals Count

- Why it is crucial to break down research on your slides.
- How to keep your audience engaged as you present the content.
- How to cite sources correctly.

Chapter 7: Speech Formula

- The driving part of the Body is the Source.

- How to evaluate, identify and implement credible source content.

Chapter 8: Putting it All Together

- Description of when, where and how to conduct research.

- When, where and how to incorporate it correctly into the speech.

Yes, we discuss "Source" content quite a bit and given it's significance in the speech, we should. Writing a speech involves an itinerant process. Don't be surprised when significant elements of the speech are addressed within different chapters shedding new light on it's importance. If you fully complete the process, you will master each element therein.

# Chapter 1:
# Forget Spiders, Snakes and Claustrophobia, Public Speaking Freaks Us Out

## Objectives

By the end of this chapter you should be able to:

1. Describe how Dorothy and her friends facing the Great Oz can help us face an audience with control.

2. Identify your physical response to speaking in public.

3. Explain how what we feel differs from how we react and respond.

4. Identify methods to reduce the use of filler words when speaking in public.

5. Evaluate two communication theories that help explain why the fear/anxiety exists.

> There are two types of speakers: those that are nervous and those that are liars.
> – Mark Twain

**FEAR**

## Chapter 1
# Forget Spiders, Snakes and Claustrophobia, Public Speaking Freaks Us Out

Imagine that you have a message and you have to share this message with one person. How does that make you feel? Now imagine that it is five people. Okay...50? 500? What instinctual thoughts come to mind if I told you that you had to speak in front of 5000 people? Did your level of anxiety change with the number of people? People's anxiety level often correlates directly with the number of people in the audience. Why?

## Part 1: Lessons from Oz

Do you remember watching the movie classic, The Wizard of Oz (1939)? Dorothy and her friends travelled on an incredible journey in the hopes of meeting the Great Oz. When they arrived, the less than enthusiastic greeting ended with Oz declining their request for an audience. The group insisted, and eventually the Great Oz appeared. The heartless Tin Man, the brainless Scarecrow, the cowardly Lion, and the distraught Dorothy all stood shaking and terrified by the vast powers they imagined him to have.

Smoke and light billowed from the room as Oz spoke words that seemed to make the earth tremble. However, the smallest member of the team took no heed of the others. Little

> ## No one can make you feel intimidated except yourself.
>
> *– Eleanor Roosevelt*

Toto, Dorothy's dog, ran over and peeled back the curtain, revealing the control booth where a mortal man stood, anxiously grasping and clutching various buttons and levers, attempting to maintain the facade.

My clients often experience the same terror Dorothy and her friends displayed as they stand before an audience. Like the characters in the Wizard of Oz, the anxiety-shaken speaker allows irrational fear to interfere with performance—in essence, they disempower themselves. Often, just moments before, these trembling individuals addressed the same group from their seats, raised their hands, participated, and boldly shared their ideas only to shrink in stature, reduced to a bumbling sack of nerves when they stand before the same group to deliver a presentation. What changed? How does the difference between a seat "within" the group to the space "in front" of the audience change a person's entire demeanor and state of mind?

One of my favorite quotes by Eleanor Roosevelt (O'Toole, 2012), warns us of falling prey to insecurities. She stated, "No one can make you feel intimidated except yourself."

An audience has no more magical powers than the Wizard of Oz. Our perception of the experience fuels the terror. The mere thought of standing before an audience is more than most can stand, leading to fear and avoidance. So, claim personal power and don't follow Dorothy's example of ceding control to your audience.

### Interaction 1.1: A Lesson From Oz

**Question:** What lesson do we learn from Dorothy and her friends about how to handle anxiety in the face of the unknown?

a. Trust the unknown, embrace the experience.

b. Don't ever trust anyone except yourself.

c. Resist the urge to feed fear of the unknown. Manage your perceptions and hold onto your power.

d. Remember that both parties are equally anxious.

## Part 2: Reasons for the Fear

It's human nature to want to make a positive impression on other people. Billions of dollars are spent each year to create just the right image so that others perceive us in a certain way. For example, consider your wardrobe, jewelry, personal hygiene (haircuts, makeup, waxing), vehicles, houses—the list is endless. We deliberately spend money to create the image we want to convey to others.

Speaking in public often accentuates concern about our image, in proportion to the size of the audience. The prospect of making less than a great impression can leave you feeling vulnerable. Uncertainty erupts, fanning flames of anxiety. This anxiety that many experience is common indeed. Numerous research instruments and studies spanning decades reveal that a majority of people report experiencing anxiety when faced with speaking in front of a group of people (Bodie, 2010; McCrosky, 1970; Stein, Walker & Ford, 1996).

In relative terms, do you know how much anxiety you experience? Is it high, medium, or low? Let's find out! In 1970, McCroskey developed the first scale to measure communication apprehension as it relates to public speaking anxiety. This scale is highly reliable. Take the Personal Report of Public Speaking Anxiety (PRPSA) test to determine your anxiety level.

> 66 If I went back to college again, I'd concentrate on two areas: learning to write and to speak before an audience. Nothing in life is more important than the ability to communicate effectively. 99
>
> – *Gerald R. Ford*

### Interaction 1.2: How Much Public Speaking Anxiety Do You Experience?

**Instructions:** Personal Report of Public Speaking Anxiety

This instrument is composed of thirty-four statements concerning feelings about communicating with other people. Indicate the degree to which the statements apply to you by marking whether you (1) strongly agree, (2) agree, (3) are undecided, (4) disagree, or (5) strongly disagree with each statement. Work quickly; record your first impression.

1. While preparing to give a speech, I feel tense and nervous.
2. I feel tense when I see the words "speech" and "public speech" on a course outline when studying.
3. My thoughts become confused and jumbled when I am giving a speech.
4. Right after giving a speech I feel that I have had a pleasant experience.
5. I get anxious when I think about a speech coming up.
6. I have no fear of giving a speech.
7. Although I am nervous just before starting a speech, I soon settle down after starting and feel calm and comfortable.
8. I look forward to giving a speech.
9. When the instructor announces a speaking assignment in class, I can feel myself getting tense.
10. My hands tremble when I am giving a speech.
11. I feel relaxed when I am giving a speech.

12. I enjoy preparing for a speech.

13. I am in constant fear of forgetting what I prepared to say.

14. I get anxious if someone asks me something about my topic that I do not know.

15. I face the prospect of giving a speech with confidence.

16. I feel that I am in complete possession of myself while giving a speech.

17. My mind is clear when giving a speech.

18. I do not dread giving a speech.

19. I perspire just before starting a speech.

20. My heart beats very fast just as I start a speech.

21. I experience considerable anxiety while sitting in the room just before my speech starts.

22. Certain parts of my body feel very tense and rigid while giving a speech.

23. Realizing that only a little time remains in a speech makes me very tense and anxious.

24. While giving a speech, I know I can control my feelings of tension and stress.

25. I breathe faster just before starting a speech.

26. I feel comfortable and relaxed in the hour or so just before giving a speech.

27. I do poorer on speeches because I am anxious.

28. I feel anxious when the teacher announces the date of a speaking assignment.

29. When I make a mistake while giving a speech, I find it hard to concentrate on the parts that follow.

30. During an important speech I experience a feeling of helplessness building up inside me.

31. I have trouble falling asleep the night before a speech.

32. My heart beats very fast while I present a speech.

33. I feel anxious while waiting to give my speech.

34. While giving a speech, I get so nervous I forget facts I really know.

**Scoring:** To determine your score on the PRPSA, complete the following steps:

**Step 1.** Add scores for items 1, 2, 3, 5, 9, 10, 13, 14, 19, 20, 21, 22, 23, 25, 27, 28, 29, 30, 31, 32, 33, and 34

**Step 2.** Add the scores for items 4, 6, 7, 8, 11, 12, 15, 16, 17, 18, 24, and 26

**Step 3.** Complete the following formula:

PRPSA = 72 - Total from Step 2 + Total from Step 1. Your score should be between 34 and 170. If your score is below 34 or above 170, you have made a mistake in computing the score.

Why do you think people fear public speaking? Stein, Walker and Forde (1996) asked participants a similar question and found people were afraid of: doing or saying something embarrassing (64%), their mind going blank (74%), being unable to continue talking (63%), saying foolish things or not making sense (59%), and trembling, shaking, or showing other signs of anxiety (80%). When I asked this question, a variety of answers emerge from the audience. The following list, The Top Ten Reasons People Fear Public Speaking, is based on a survey I conducted based on over 2000 student reports (Steele J.R., 2016).

**Table 1.1: Top Ten Reasons People Fear Public Speaking (lowest to highest)**

| #10 | Fear of the audience. | The number of people is intimidating. |
|---|---|---|
| #9 | Fear of rejection. | The audience will shut you down and not want to listen. You don't think your thoughts are worth it! |
| #8 | Fear of the unknown. | You are not used to the experience. You feel insecure trying something new. There is a general paranoia of "But what if…!" |
| #7 | Fear of harsh criticism. | Criticism can be very difficult to handle. Feedback of any type can leave you feeling vulnerable as you open yourself to hear another's thoughts about you! |
| #6 | Fear of being unprepared. | Concerned about *not* being able to answer questions or that other people might know more than you do. |
| #5 | Fear of looking stupid. | Lack the confidence to stand in front of an audience. You don't want to have to be held accountable for your words. |
| #4 | Fear of failing or not doing something right. | "Oh, my, what if I don't represent myself well?" or "How can I express this idea better?" |

**Table 1.1: Top Ten Reasons People Fear Public Speaking (lowest to highest)**

| | | |
|---|---|---|
| **#3** | **Fear of making a mistake.** | You don't want others to witness your imperfections. You want others to see you as perfect! "What if I fail?" or "What if I forget all my words and blank out?" |
| **#2** | **Fear of being judged by people.** | Knowing that eyes are evaluating you and sizing you up! |
| **#1** | **Fear of attention.** | Being looked at or singled out in front of peers. It seems most people don't wish to be the center of attention. |

Does this list accurately display your reasons for the fear? Undoubtedly, speaking in public is a real fear that most people experience to some degree. A student of mine named Elvis, a veteran of the first Iraq war, was years older than typical freshmen when he returned to college. He told me, "I have faced real combat situations with bullets flying and missiles exploding and never experienced the stress of being in that little space in front of these desks. You have no idea what that space does to a man."

## Part 3: Fear Exposed

### What We Feel: Psychological

Public speaking evokes a wide range of emotions within presenters that range from mild to severe, from stress to fear, even to phobia. People talk about their fear, comedians joke about the fear. For example, Jerry Seinfeld said, "According to most studies, people's number one fear is public speaking. Number two is death. Death is number two? Does that seem right? To the average person that means that if they have to go to a funeral, they'd be better off in the casket than giving the eulogy." While Seinfeld may be taking a few liberties with the research, public speaking evokes a strong response in most people. Some have exposed themselves to the stage enough that they have come to enjoy the experience—it can be a rush, almost intoxicating, as anxiety turns into euphoria when the audience response is positive.

This section is specifically valuable for those who have not conquered this anxiety and do not understand these emotions. Stein, Walker, and Forde (1996) interviewed 499 respondents. One third reported that they had excessive anxiety when they spoke to a large audience. McCrosky (1970) reports that 70% of college students express a fear of public speaking. Let's take a moment to distinguish between three key words: fear, phobia, and anxiety.

 The only thing we have to fear is fear itself.

– *Franklin D. Roosevelt*

## Interaction 3: Who's Afraid of Public Speaking?

Identify which of the following famous people expressed a deep fear of public speaking.

| | | | |
|---|---|---|---|
| | Adele Aristotle | Rowan Atkinson | Warren Buffett |
| Winston Churchill | Leonardo DiCaprio | Harrison Ford | Sigmund Freud |
| Mahatma Gandhi | Rebecca Gibney | Hugh Grant | Samuel L. Jackson |
| Thomas Jefferson | Steve Jobs | Nicole Kidman | King George VI |
| Abraham Lincoln | Sir Isaac Newton | Joel Olstean | Anthony Quinn |
| Julia Roberts | Margaret Sanger | Jimmy Stewart | Barbara Streisand |
| Bruce Willis | Oprah Winfrey | Reese Witherspoon | Tiger Woods |

*Answer: All of the above had a deep fear of public speaking*

### Fear

Many words have been written about fear throughout the ages. In his inaugural address, Franklin D. Roosevelt, the 32nd President of the United States declared (1933), "The only thing we have to fear is fear itself." I once heard a speaker report that "FEAR" stands for False Evidence Appearing Real. No matter if it is real or imagined, fear is a big industry. Fear is instinctual; it is a primitive emotion aroused by a perceived threat to our personal safety or interests. Some fears are objective, such as a car hydroplaning on the highway, while others are psychological, as in a fear of a person or situation that seems to threaten status or prestige. Sometimes we are conscious of our fears, while other times we are completely unaware. Whatever the case, fear can wreak havoc on our soul. Experience conditions us to respond with fear or not. Our ideas about fear differ greatly.

A hint of fear can add intensity to an experience. Some may be attracted to fear, maybe most. But not all seek it out. Plenty of us refuse to read Steven King, ride roller coasters stand on the edge of cliffs or climb the high diving board. Consider cultural traditions such as Day of the Dead observed in many Latin cultures which honors deceased loved ones by creating altars, masks and visiting the dead graves with gifts. Another holiday which originated in Eastern Europe features Krumpus, a horned folklore figure that is half-goat, half demon, who during the Christmas season, punishes children who have misbehaved. Throughout the world, scary costumes are donned and décor displayed to celebrate Halloween. Each year millions of people flock to Haunted Houses to be scared. What started as Fright Nights back in 1991 quickly became Halloween Horror Nights as Universal Studios realized that people's desire to be scared was big business. Today, Universal Studio's theme parks in Orlando, Japan, Singapore, and Hollywood annually scare hundreds of thousands of park goers who subject themselves by happily paying over $100 to be terrified! The emotion evoked from this the anticipation of being frightened adds excitement. Capitalizing on fear can be a big business—too many profit over others' plight.

**You always have two choices: your commitment versus your fear.**

*–Sammy Davis, Jr.*

### Dread

What is dread and how does it differ from fear? We usually think of dread as a state of apprehension that persists over a longer period. When is the last time you have really dreaded an event or required confrontation? It can be a horrific feeling, impacting our outlook. It's that feeling that many speakers get when they realize they have a future speaking engagement. Research shows that the highest level of anxiety is experienced immediately after a speech is assigned (Behnke & Sawyer, 2001). When we talk of fear of public speaking this is different than dread. The fear of public speaking tends to occur closer to the speaking engagement, usually just before a performance. Dread, however, is the anxious wait contemplating an unknown outcome.

### Social Phobia

The Encyclopedia of Phobias, Fears and Anxieties defines social phobia as "extreme fear of being evaluated, criticized, censured, embarrassed and humiliated, or in some way, punished in a social setting by the reactions of others" (Doctor, 2008 or Hamner & Arana, 2007). They go on to explain, "The essential feature of a social phobia is a persistent distinct fear of social or performance situations in which embarrassment may occur." Remember the top reasons people fear public speaking? Notice the direct correlation with this definition. Each concern listed in the definition is amplified by standing in front of an audience.

**Table 1.2: Fear Exposed**

## FEAR EXPOSED

| What we feel | How we react & respond |
| --- | --- |
| **Dread** = terror or apprehension of future event | **Stress** = pressure exerted on one thing by another |
| **Fear** = primitive (DNA) emotion to a perceived threat | **Anxiety** = distress or unease marked by physiologically, verbal & nonverbal signs |
| **Phobia** = persistent irrational fear (most extreme) | **Fight, Flight or Freeze** |

A specific phobia has been coined to address this phenomenon: "glossophobia," coming from the Greek word 'glosso,' meaning tongue, and 'phobos,' meaning fear or dread. Glossophobia is characterized as intense anxiety brought on by having to speak in public (Doctor, 2008). About 7% of all people self-identify as having a social phobia (these numbers vary between different regions and cultures Pollard, et al., 1989). While that number amounts to several million people, this is not the majority of the population. Glossophobia does not discriminate; it affects people of all backgrounds, cultures, experiences, and ages. In the Social Psychiatry and Psychiatric Epidemeology (Furmark, et al., 1999), public speaking was cited as the most common social fear. Of those who identify as having a phobia, 89.4%

include public speaking (Faravelli et al., 2000). Of those that have a social phobia, Pollard, et al. (1989) found only about 8% seek help.

Those who do not seek help experience:
- 10% lower graduation levels,
- 15% reduction in ability to move into a managerial position,
- 10% reduction in wages.

 Courage is resistance to fear, mastery of fear, not absence of fear.

–Mark Twain

These statistics do not begin to capture the impact these phobias can have on our relationships. If the thought of communicating to a group causes you to avoid the situation, drop classes, or quit, or if this anxiety disrupts your everyday life, you are experiencing a phobia. Seek professional help! A licensed therapist in conjunction with a public speaking coach would be a great combination.

The good news is that the success rate is high for those who get help. David Barlow, director of Boston University's Center for Anxiety and Related Disorders says 90% of people can be cured (Travis, 2004). New research is exploring ways to scientifically eliminate anxiety. Techniques range from inoculation therapy (Compton, Thornton & Dimmock, 2017) aimed at helping presenters interpret their speech-related anxiety more positively to honing public speaking skills in front of nonjudgmental "audience dogs" (Fandos, 2016). Unbelievably, students at American University are encouraged to practice their speeches to an audience of canines! Here's a quote from their program, "Addressing a friendly and nonjudgmental canine can lower blood pressure, decrease stress and elevate mood—perfect for practicing your speech or team presentation." So help is on the way and in many forms!

### Interaction 1.4: How Does Your Body React When You Stand in Front of an Audience to Speak?

Circle all that apply.

| Physiological | Dry mouth | Enhanced sweat production |
|---|---|---|
| | Increased heart rate | Nausea |
| | Increased blood pressure | Stiffening of muscles |
| Non Verbal | Nervous shaking | Redundant behavior such as rocking back and forth, pacing, touching a part of the body repetitively, etc. |
| | Avoiding looking at the audience | |
| | Twisting legs | Blinking or *not* blinking (deer in the headlight look—eyes wide open) |
| Verbal | Stuttering | Using filler words including "like," "um," and "so," etc. |
| | Speaking too quickly | |
| | Speaking too softly | Inability to speak at all—freezing up |

## Interaction 1.5: Is Your Life Limited by Fear, Dread or Phobia Associated with Speaking?

Does your unease regarding public speaking limit your life? If so, how?

If you could overcome or manage your fear, how would your life be different?

### How We React & Respond: Physiological

Unfortunately, the mental anguish public speaking causes is not the end of this anxious saga, our physical response and individual reactions can be agonizing, even debilitating. Reports from people who have examined their fear and anxiety about public speaking consistently support the conclusion that symptom severity is directly correlated with degree of stress experienced and the anxiety created. Although the terms "stress" and "anxiety" are often interchanged, there is a difference, let's distinguish between them.

### Stress

Whenever pressure is applied from one thing to another, stress occurs. As it pertains to public speaking, when we agree to speak at an event, pressure about the speaking engagement is applied to the speaker. The Merriam-Webster Dictionary (2017) defines stress as, "a state of mental or emotional strain or tension resulting from adverse or very demanding circumstances." Our reaction to the stress creates anxiety. Simply put, "stress is the response we have to a threat and anxiety is a reaction to the stress" (ADAA, 2017). Adrenaline is a hormone released in stressful situations. When it flows, it triggers specific organ responses similar to symptoms of shock. These responses may include increased heart rate, trembling, sweaty palms, gastrointestinal illness including nausea, knots and butterflies and a lump in the throat. Any of these may result from the stress created by speaking in public. (Chambers, et al. 1984; Clements and Turpin, 1996 and Behnke, Beatty, & Kitchens 1978). While there are many tips to manage stress from relaxation techniques to avoiding caffeine and alcohol, the Anxiety and Depression Association of America (2017) reminds us that physical activity is a proven way to reduce stress.

### Anxiety

Anxiety is a manifestation of stress created by the pressure applied from the"dread", "fears" and or "phobias." It is among the many adverse effects of stress. The medical definition of anxiety by the Merriam-Webster Dictionary (2017) is, "an abnormal and overwhelming sense of apprehension and fear often marked by physical signs (such as tension, sweating, and increased pulse rate), by doubt concerning the reality and nature of the threat, and by self-doubt about one's capacity to cope with it." Therefore, the degree of anxiety you experience physically is in direct proportion to the amount of fear you perceive. In cases where anxiety persists over a six month period of time, it can be considered a legitimate mental disorder, stress on the other hand is not (Groberman, 2017).

### Fight, Flight or Freeze

Typically, there are three responses to severe stress: fight, flight, or freeze. In 1915,

Cannon first identified that fear is often accompanied by a physiological reaction controlled by the autonomic nervous system. Adrenaline flows, causing a variety of reactions: pulse rate increases, sweat glands activate, mouth dries, limbs tremble, face pales (Caxton Encyclopedia, 1977). Historically this has been referred to as the "fight or flight" syndrome, and even Darwin explained this evolutionary phenomenon (Workman, 1977). Scientists recently added another response to the list, "freeze," giving us three responses to stress: fight, flight, or freeze.

Let's explore how these reactions manifest themselves in different ways as it relates to public speaking. My experience as a "coach" has allowed me to witness each of these reactions. The "fight" response often manifests itself as friction between the speaker, the instructor, the speech, the event coordinator and sometimes even audience members. Come presentation day, the excuses that pour in can literally drown the class. I have had situations where out of fifteen speeches scheduled for a particular day there were three deaths from family members, four hospital emergencies, and five car breakdowns which tragically rendered the presenters unable to deliver their speech. Perhaps the most memorable excuse I have heard from a presenter who was practicing her speech on her balcony when a bird flew overhead and pooped on the ground where she was causing her to step on it, slip and fall over a chair and table finally landing on the concrete patio. In the process she pulled out her back completely and lay for hours unable to move in the scorching hot sun on her balcony until her roommate returned. Her description was so vivid, I allowed her another presentation opportunity just for the laugh she provided. Her back, miraculously healed by the next class. "Flee" amounts to finding excuses to avoid the event, maybe even running out before the speech or even mid speech. "Freeze" is when you find yourself facing the audience and you are unable to move or speak.

What is your instinctual reaction to a threat? Do you fight, run or freeze? Who wants to endure the torture of any of these responses? When it comes to public speaking, people often seek to escape from the experience or avoid it altogether. In 2017, 1511 adults responded to the Chapman University Survey on American Fears. Results disclosed that 25.9% were afraid or very afraid of public speaking, coming in second place just below reptiles. To see a full list of fears from the Chapman study visit this link : https://blogs.chapman.edu/wilkinson/2016/10/11/americas-top-fears-2016/

Reactions vary drastically. On one side of the pendulum lies a serious social phobia and on the other a manageable, mild anxiety.

## Avoid Using Filler Words

Our reaction can cause us to speak utter nonsense! This verbal reaction is so prevalent it needs to be addressed. How can you avoid filling pauses with filler words? A filler word or discourse marker is an apparently meaningless word, phrase, or sound that marks a pause or hesitation in speech (Safir, 1925). Also known as a pause filler or hesitation form. Some of the common filler words in English are um, uh, er, ah, like, okay, right, and you know. While these words often pepper general conversation, studies show that anxiety or stress trigger a significant increase in the number and variety. For some, stuttering or "disruptions in the production of speech sounds, also called 'disfluencies' actually occurs" (ASHA, 2017). The American Speech-Language and Hearing Association (ASHA), explains that "these disfluencies can impede communication when a person produces too many of them." So like, um, this topic is you know, like really, really important folks. Ah, I mean, we kinda, like, all use these, um, phrases and, or, ah, words to kinda, um, get our message across. And... ah, sometimes we can kind of like elongate our aaaannnnddds ooorrrrr other conjunctions. OK? Does that make sense?

### Interaction 1.6: Filler Word Trivia

**Filler Word Trivia: circle your favorite filler words.**

| | | | | |
|---|---|---|---|---|
| Like | Right | Ah | I mean | Okay |
| Er | You know | So | Totally | Um |

**Who uses the most filler words? Check all that apply:**

- ☐ Women
- ☐ Men
- ☐ Younger
- ☐ Older
- ☐ Disorganized Person
- ☐ Conscientious Person

**Why do we insert filler words? Check all that apply:**

- ☐ Stall for time
- ☐ Strengthen a statement
- ☐ Reduce harshness of statement
- ☐ Include listener
- ☐ Show you are thinking
- ☐ All of the above

*Answer: Women, Younger, Conscientious Person (Laserna, Seih & Pennebaker, 2014)*

When filler words are used, they impair the communication process for two reasons. First, they dilute the message. How would you feel if you asked for a drink and received one diluted with water or too much ice? What would your reaction be? If you don't want your audience to have the same response, work on developing awareness of using these words and practice pausing to think before you speak. Secondly, Brennan & Williams (1995), found that audiences interpret pauses filled with meaningless phrases to mean that speakers do not know what they are talking about. This decreases the speaker's credibility.

The beginning of the speech is generally the most stressful. This causes many speakers to begin with a barrage of irrelevant words, phrases and thoughts. Careful attention and preparation can help you avoid this trap.

### Interaction 1.7: Reduce Filler Words

**Step 1:** Choose one of these topics: aliens, Academy Awards, sports, self-driving cars, pets, Sunday afternoons, habits, rainy days, theater, college, stock market, politics, or travel.

**Step 2:** Speak spontaneously for two minutes, delivering an impromptu speech using the word prompt you selected *without* using any filler words. Make every attempt to include the elements of a speech—an introduction, body and conclusion. Time yourself. Be sure you speak *without* using any filler words. The first time you use one, you are forgiven, the second time, your time is up! How long can you speak without using a filler word?

Record yourself speaking and listen for the patterns you use to "fill the space..." This is a great activity to do with friends, even at a party; you can also do it alone by recording your speech. Repeat this activity as often as you like until you can reach the goal and control your use of filler words.

### Positive Benefits of Stress and Anxiety

Is stress and anxiety inherently a bad thing for us to experience? No. Stess and anxiety can help or harm us. Stress related to an upcoming event can propel you to work harder on preparation and be ready to give a great speech! On the other hand, if fear overtakes and debilitates you, rendering you unable to focus and perform, it harms you.

### Yerkes-Dodson Law

Most speakers and performers exhibit some type of anxiety before they take to the stage. A certain amount of anxiety when performing complex tasks, such as speaking in front of an audience, can be a good thing when it spurs the speaker to optimal performance. Research (Yerkes-Dodson, 1908) has shown a relationship between arousal and performance. A heightened sense of physiological arousal may lead to enhanced performance, but only to a certain point after which performance decreases. This graph shows the relationship.

**Figure 1.1: Yerkes-Dodson Law**

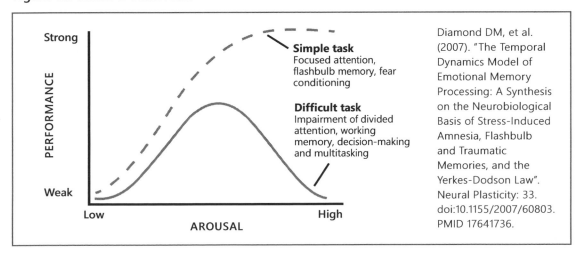

Diamond DM, et al. (2007). "The Temporal Dynamics Model of Emotional Memory Processing: A Synthesis on the Neurobiological Basis of Stress-Induced Amnesia, Flashbulb and Traumatic Memories, and the Yerkes-Dodson Law". Neural Plasticity: 33. doi:10.1155/2007/60803. PMID 17641736.

The key concept to understand here is that everyone gets a bit nervous when speaking in public. If you can keep your anxiety in "the zone" then you can perform at your peak. Conversely, if you don't overcome your anxiety when speaking, then your performance may suffer.

**Reducing Anxiety**

An array of situations can serve to heighten or decrease the amount of anxiety you experience. Some may feel anxious about a particular event at a particular time (state anxiety); others feel anxious about the event because of the circumstances (trait anxiety) (Behnke & Sawyer, 2001). Other typical factors include the number of people in the audience, who the people are, how critical they will be, how their opinions can impact you, whether or not you are prepared, the layout of the room, your expertise in the field, and the significance of your presentation.

As you develop your public speaking skills, do everything you can to reduce the anxiety you feel. John Travis (2004) in his article, Fear Not, shows we can conquer fear. "It's not a simple matter of erasing scary memories. Instead, it seems that people can learn to suppress a fright reaction by repeatedly confronting, in a safe manner, the fear-triggering memory or stimulus."

What are ways that we can "repeatedly and safely confront the stimulus"? A variety of strategies can help. It makes sense that being well prepared would reduce your anxiety. One of the first studies in 1989 by Daly, Vangelisti, Neel, & Cavanaugh revealed that familiarity with the audience and environment helped to reduce anxiety. O'Hair et al, (2001) found that practice could instill individuals with confidence and positive attitudes toward speech performances. Smith and Frymier (2007) found that practicing before an audience is key—the larger the audience, the better! The bad news is that people who experience the most anxiety prefer focusing on slides and cards rather than facing an audience (Verderber & Verderber, 2002).

**Table 1.3: Research Says You Can Reduce Your Anxiety**

| Research Says You *Can* Reduce Your Anxiety | |
| --- | --- |
| 1. **Know your audience** (Daly et. al, 1989). | 5. **Deliver speeches to audiences** (Smith & Frymeir, 2007). |
| 2. **Know your room** (Daly et. al, 1989). | 6. **Share a personal story** (Widrich, Year & Hsu, 2008 & Stephens, Silbert & Hasson, 2010). |
| 3. **Practice in front of people** (Smith & Frymeir, 2007). | 7. **Engage audience** (Steele, 2016). |
| 4. **Practice** (Travis, 2004 & O'Hair et. al, 2001). | 8. **Clear purpose & points** (Steele, 2014 & Llopis, 2015). |

In my experience, the quality of the content makes a big difference. When the message is personally meaningful and speakers have found ways to connect with the audience, they experience less anxiety. They are often filled with enthusiasm or excitement about giving the speech. Just like research shows that you will improve by practicing in front of an audience

(Smith & Frymier, 2007), as you deliver more speeches to live audiences, familiarity with the experience will increase your comfort with speaking. The more times you speak in public, the less anxiety you will encounter, particularly if these times are closer together rather than years apart. A large array of anxiety-reducing techniques are available to help you manage the stress! You are not alone. Most people are highly affected by the experience of speaking in public. Just remember Mark Twain's quote from the beginning of the chapter. All speakers feel nervous and anxious; however, most can harness that anxiety to empower their message.

People everywhere, from successful business people such as Bill Gates and Steve Jobs, to politicians such as Margaret Thatcher, Winston Churchill, Abraham Lincoln, and political activist, Margaret Sanger, are reported to have experienced extreme anxiety at the idea of speaking in public (Ashby, 1995; Clark, 2011). For decades, debilitating fear kept Barbara Streisand from perform on stage for decades as a result of her debilitating fear. And early in their careers, Leonardo DiCaprio and Reese Witherspoon hoped that they would not win an award to avoid delivering an acceptance speech! Even great leaders like Mahatma Gandhi had to summon the courage to speak their truth to the public—and sometimes failed. In one instance, Gandhi actually stopped speaking and handed the speech to someone else to read. He explained, "My vision became blurred and I trembled, though the speech hardly covered a sheet of foolscap," he recalled (Clark, 2011).

Numerous extremely successful people like business magnate, investor and philanthropist Warren Buffet (2017), President Gerald Ford and astronaut Story Musgrave (2015) unequivocally proclaim that the most important class they ever took was Public Speaking (2015). They **state that** they would never have experienced the success they did attain without confronting their fear and learning to express their ideas and opinions in a way that others would heed (Kunheart & Oaks, 2017).

In the movie Becoming Buffett (2017), Buffett describes the debilitating shyness he faced, terrified to even state his name. Today, he is one of the richest people, with a net worth of billions. He knows this never would have been possible if he had not summoned the courage to enroll in a public speaking development course. Still today, his college diplomas do not hang above his desk, but his certificate from his Dale Carnegie Speaking Course does. When it comes to investments, Buffett believes developing your public speaking skills is the best investment you can make in your life. Dale Carnegie eloquently insists, "There are four ways, and only four ways, in which we have contact with the world. We are evaluated and classified by these four contacts: what we do, how we look, what we say, and how we say it."

## Why We React: A Theory That Helps Explain the Turmoil Caused by Speaking Publically

### Facework

The most helpful theory I have found in the field of communications to explain why we react to speaking in public is the concept of Facework first defined by Erving Goffman (1956). The concept of face refers to the "dignity or prestige" we seek from others… a sense of worth that comes from knowing one's status. Goffman defined the concept of face (1956), as "the positive social value a person effectively claims for himself by the line others assume he has taken during a particular contact" (p. 268). Goffman believed that all people have a face and it was their goal to put forth the most positive images of themselves in public (Cupach & Metts, 2008, p. 203-206). Goffman wanted to answer two primary questions: (1) why and how people construct their public images and (2) what strategies people use to maintain or restore their own or others' images if those images are lost or threatened (Cupach & Metts, 2008, pp. 203-204).

Think back to the last time you were alone—totally alone and out of sight. What did you do? How did you behave? Did you scratch a private spot, pick your nose, or expel some gas? What did you wear or not wear?

Now let's recreate the scene. Suppose your boss was there with you. How might your behavior change? Would you dress differently? Would you sit the same way? Would you monitor your body language or physical movements? Most likely, the answer is yes.

One amazing part of our relationship with pets is that we don't have to manage our "face" when they are around—they are thrilled to see us no matter how our hair looks or what clothes we're wearing. They couldn't care less if we are dripping with sweat or dressed to impress.

When it comes to people, no matter how close to us they are, some self-monitoring occurs. Think about the clothes you last wore in public. What did this outfit say about you? Why did you choose this outfit? Think about clothes you've noticed on people you've recently seen. Pay attention to wardrobe choices of random strangers you see in a public place. Notice the color, the style, and the size. Subtle characteristics like style, condition, fit, color, and other elements send messages about who we are. Some people spend more time managing their image than others, and even the amount of time spent speaks volumes about who we are.

Let's move beyond our clothing to further explore "face." Have you ever heard the saying "to save face"? We emotionally invest in our "face." We can "lose face," "maintain face," or "gain face"; we must constantly attend to our "face" during an interaction. Usually, people cooperate, but why? Both parties are vulnerable. When people don't cooperate, we're upset! Consider the 2009 MTV Video Music Awards Ceremony where Taylor Swift, a young woman awestruck by the realization that she had won an award, faced a large audience. As she began to share words of thanks, rambunctious rapper Kanye West sauntered on stage. He snatched the microphone from Swift's hand and said, "I'm sorry, but Beyoncé had one of the best videos of all time." He then made an obscene gesture to the audience.

Consider how these celebrities managed their "face" in this scenario. What was the outcome? Three people were involved: Kanye West, Taylor Swift, and Beyoncé Knowles. Who lost face, who gained face, and who was the victim?

Kanye West undoubtedly lost face, but who knows? With his bad boy image, perhaps his fans thought it "cool." In their eyes, perhaps he gained face, but by the rest of the world's standards, he was disgraced so much that he apologized. Most everyone felt sorry for Taylor Swift. She didn't do anything to agitate the situation, but his obnoxious behavior ruined her moment. (Remember, she had the power when she held the microphone! Startled by Kanye's appearance, she turned it loose, thus becoming a victim.) Beyoncé handled the situation with grace and dignity, bringing Taylor back on stage when she won another award and sacrificed her "moment" by allowing Taylor the opportunity to recapture hers. This singular moment revealed Beyoncé's character. As a result, she came out better for the incident, having gained more respect and more prestige.

During personal relationships, we deal with managing our face all the time. Most of the time it is not threatened, but occasionally it is! When situations cause us to feel threatened, they cause us to retreat, defend, defuse, or surrender. While we may manage these challenges in daily life, being challenged in front of a group is disconcerting. Someone might ask us a question we don't know. What if an audience member knows more than we do? What if we mess up by falling or forgetting our words? The "what ifs" of managing our "face" publicly can understandably cause our heart to beat a bit faster, our hands to sweat, and for us to dread the event entirely.

While other communicaiton theories can be used to explain speech anxiety, we will stop here. Hopefully this information gives you better understanding of your fear and its source. Perhaps you see the truth behind the Great Fear, just like Dorothy, Toto, and her friends experienced when Toto pulled back the curtain revealing the "Great Oz" as a mere mortal. Their fears were not justified—they were scared of nothing more than smoke and lights. Your audience is filled not with ogres, but with people just like you and me. Now that you have taken the first step to know why public speaking freaks you out, you are ready to move to the next step and face your fear.

 You gain strength, courage and confidence by every experience in which you really stop to look fear in the face. You are able to say to yourself, 'I have lived through this horror. I can take the next thing that comes along.' You must do the thing you think you cannot do.

– *Eleanor Roosevelt*

## Chapter 1 Review Questions

1. Describe the similarities between Dorothy and her friends facing the Great Oz and a person facing an audience.

2. Why do you believe people experience speech anxiety?

3. Describe some of the physical responses to speech anxiety. Do you exhibit any of these? Which ones?

4. What is the name of the phobia associated with the "fear of public speaking"?

5. How does the Yerkes-Dodson law apply to public speaking?

6. Describe a communication theory which explains why the fear/anxiety exists.

7. According to Stein, Walker and Forde, what is the least reason people fear public speaking and what is the main reaon? What is the difference between the two?

8. What are three typical responses to stress?

9. How does dread differ from fear?

10. Describe the difference between Stress and Anxiety.

11. What are three ways you can reduce anxiety?

12. How do we emotionally invest in our face?

13. Which quote from this chapter resonates with you the most?

**Practice Speech Exercise**

Use the Practice Speech Exercise to implement the strategies discussed in this chapter. Each Practice Speech Exercise has a designated level.

### Level 1: Awareness

You have a desire to develop your public speaking skills. You have a common knowledge or an understanding of basic techniques and concepts but have strong emotions about the experience. Anxiety level, high.

### Level 2: Novice

You have delivered a few speeches and want to improve. You need direction to speak confidently and effectively. You are anxious to employ new tips, techniques, formulas, and strategies to wow your audience. Anxiety level, high to medium.

### Level 3: Intermediate

You know the basics of delivery and design. Expert help may be required from time to time, but you can usually prepare a speech on your own. You know that there are an array of opportunities in both your design and delivery technique and seek support to improve. Anxiety level, medium.

### Level 4: Advanced

You can perform the actions associated with this skill without assistance. You are able to recognize strengths and weaknesses in yourself and others. You realize that you can always improve and you desire to do so. Anxiety level, medium to low.

### Level 5: Expert

You are known as someone who can speak comfortably to an audience. You can even provide guidance, troubleshoot, and answer questions if asked. You can critique others competently. You are hungry and yearn to deliver your best speech ever! Anxiety level, low.

Following the instructions for the Practice Speech Exercise is a Sample Speech. You have the option of using the sample speech or creating your own speech following the instructions. Each Practice Speech Exercise is designed to develop your skill as a speaker. Practice deliberately. Enjoy the confidence and competence you will experience as a result of your focus, effort, and commitment.

*Note: Record yourself delivering these speeches. It is the best way to grow and develop.*

## Practice Speech: Story Time

**Time Limit:** 60-90 seconds or length of book.

**Target Audience:** Volunteer at the local library for a story hour with a group of twenty children, four to six years old. Assume that the reading area is located within a larger room, though separated somehow. You will need to speak loudly to keep the tykes' attention and everyone can hear you.

**Instructions:** Read a short, engaging child's book or story. Practice it a few times. Be sure that you rehearse enough to maintain eye contact 75% of the time. Speak with a relaxed throat and voice for natural projection. Use inflections to create excitement and enthusiasm. Use facial expressions to portray the story's emotions. Energize the story in every way you can, with vocal sounds and props if available.

**Delivery Options**

Option 1: Read the story to an imaginary audience in the largest room you can find. Use pillows or stuffed animals to substitute for the young tykes described in your target audience.

Option 2: Read the story to an imaginary audience in an outdoor open space like your backyard or a public park. Allow the plants and trees to substitute for the young tykes described in your target audience.

Option 3: Find some children who would enjoy listening to your story.

Option 4: Go to the library or local bookstore and actually read to a group of children.

**Purpose:** Ease yourself into the delivery process by providing a non-threatening venue. Focus on the variety of vocal inflections you use. Project your voice as much as you can. Create excitement by the energy you put into your voice.

**Skills to practice:** Breathe deeply. Explore your voice: your projection, your vocal inflection. Relax; get comfortable speaking in a non-threatening environment.

**Resources:** If you need a story, you may find a suitable one on this online list: http://www. magickeys.com/books/.

http://www.storylineonline.net is a website with an array of stories read by various authors. You can listen to the emphasis they put on words, the pace, and the emotion they add. If you worry about sounding monotone or boring, listen to the reader read one page, turn down the volume, and follow their example of emphasis as you read the page.

## Sample Speech: The Boy Who Cried Wolf!

**Author:** Aesop's Fables

**Note:** You can read the entire background or just introduce and share the author.

**Background:** Aesop was reportedly a slave and storyteller who lived in Ancient Greece between 620 and 564 BC. Aristotle, Herodotus, and Plutarch all referenced Aesop and his fables, but no written stories penned by him have been found. At least six Greek and Latin authors captured the stories on paper, but their writings were lost over time. Even so, over the past 2,500 years, his words have not only survived, but also travelled around the globe. They have been modified and repeatedly shared in many forms, from sermons to children's stories. Due to constant revision and interpretation, today's body of fables attributed to Aesop bears little relation to those he originally told. The first English version of Aesop's Fables was printed in 1484 by William Caxton (Keller, J. E., & Keating, L. C. (1993), and even those have evolved.

### The Boy Who Cried Wolf

There once was a shepherd boy who was bored as he sat on the hillside watching the village sheep. To amuse himself he took a great breath and sang out, "Wolf! Wolf! The Wolf is chasing the sheep!"

The villagers came running up the hill to help the boy drive the wolf away. But when they arrived at the top of the hill, they found no wolf. The boy laughed at the sight of their angry faces.

"Don't cry 'wolf', shepherd boy," said the villagers, "when there's no wolf!" They went grumbling back down the hill.

Later, the boy sang out again, "Wolf! Wolf! The wolf is chasing the sheep!" To his naughty delight, he watched the villagers run up the hill to help him drive the wolf away.

When the villagers saw no wolf, they sternly said, "Save your frightened song for when there is really something wrong! Don't cry 'wolf' when there is *no* wolf!"

But the boy just grinned and watched them go grumbling down the hill once more.

Later, he saw a **real** wolf prowling about his flock. Alarmed, he leapt to his feet and sang out as loudly as he could, "Wolf! Wolf!"

But the villagers thought he was trying to fool them again, and so they didn't come.

At sunset, everyone wondered why the shepherd boy hadn't returned to the village with their sheep. They went up the hill to find the boy. They found him weeping.

"There really was a wolf here! The flock has scattered! I cried out, "Wolf!" Why didn't you come?"

An old man tried to comfort the boy as they walked back to the village.

"We'll help you look for the lost sheep in the morning," he said, putting his arm around the youth, "Nobody believes a liar . . . even when he is telling the truth!"

## Practice Speech: Poem Out Loud

**Time Limit:** 60 seconds

**Target Audience:** Envision reading an inspiring poem to a group of 75 guests honoring a mentor or a positive influence in your life (a parent, teacher, or boss) for their service to a non-profit organization like Kids in Distress or the American Cancer Society. You have the opportunity to convey your feelings about your mentor by reading this poem.

**Instructions:** Read a short poem that you find meaningful. Be sure that you rehearse enough to maintain eye contact 75% of the time. Decide on the type of feeling you want to convey to your audience. Is this a happy poem to make people smile? Or is this a poem to be taken more seriously? Each type of poem demands a different tone of voice and pace of words. If available, listen to an online reading of the poem and incorporate vocal inflection in your own reading. Then practice conveying the concepts, theme, and feeling of the poem through your voice.

**Delivery Options**

Option 1: Read the poem to an imaginary audience in your living room. Stand tall in front of the pillows on your couch for they will act as your audience.

Option 2: When you see a group of people on TV, pause the scene and practice giving your speech to them. Stand tall. Look them in the eye when giving your speech.

Option 3: Read your poem aloud to someone you trust. It can just be one person. Stand tall and establish eye contact. Be sure to create the tone you want.

**Purpose:** Get comfortable projecting your voice with different emotions and vocal inflections. Notice how your body, facial expressions, hand gestures physically react to the emotion and emphasis you add to the various lines.

**Skills to practice:** Project your voice; add emotion, inflection, and energy. Relax and deliver a reading in a non-threatening environment.

**Resources:**

Here is a website of 500 famous poems. You can select one that speaks to you!
https://allpoetry.com/classics/famous_poems

Both of these resource have many poems to choose from, but they also provide resources to listen to poetry and tips on reciting. Listen to the inflection in the reader's voice and try to mimic strategies you hear. This will help you learn to use more inflection in your voice.
http://www.poetryoutloud.org/poems-and-performance/find-poems
https://www.poetryfoundation.org/poems-and-poets/poems

## Sample Poem: The Road Not Taken by Robert Frost

**Context:** Robert Frost was one of the most popular American poets. He was born 1874 and died in 1963. Like "The Road Not Taken," published in 1916, Frost's poems often feature the New England countryside. This poem may be his most frequently cited work.

Two roads diverged in a yellow wood,
And sorry I could not travel both
And be one traveler, long I stood
And looked down one as far as I could
To where it bent in the undergrowth;

Then took the other, as just as fair,
And having perhaps the better claim,
Because it was grassy and wanted wear;
Though as for that the passing there
Had worn them really about the same,

And both that morning equally lay
In leaves no step had trodden black.
Oh, I kept the first for another day!
Yet knowing how way leads on to way,
I doubted if I should ever come back.

I shall be telling this with a sigh
Somewhere ages and ages hence:
Two roads diverged in a wood, and I —
I took the one less traveled by,
And that has made all the difference.

*Note: After you have read it with meaning, it might be fun to listen to actual professional readings of the poem located on YouTube.*

# References

Alex, Groberman Fri, January 13, 2017. (n.d.). Difference Between Stress and Anxiety. Retrieved July 19, 2017, from http://www.psyweb.com/articles/anxiety/difference-between-stress-and-anxiety

Anxiety [Def.2 Medical]. (2017) In Merriam Webster Online, Retrieved March 1, 2017 from https://www.merriam-webster.com/dictionary/anxiety

Berger, C. R. (1988). "Uncertainty and information exchange in developing relationships. In S. Duck, ed., Handbook of Personal Relationships. New York, Wiley.

Berger, C. R. and R.J. Calabrease. (1975). Some exploration in initial interaction and beyond: Toward a developmental theory of interpersonal communication. Human Communication Research, 1. 99-112.

Bodie G.D. (2010) A racing heart, rattling knees, and ruminative thoughts: Defining, explaining, and treating public speaking anxiety. Communication Education, 59: 1, 70—105.

Brennan S. E., Williams M. (1995). The feeling of another's knowing: Prosody and filled pauses as cues to listeners about the metacognitive states of speakers. Journal of Memory and Language, 34, 383-398

Cannon, W.B. (1915) Bodily changes in pain, hunger, fear and rage: an account of recent researches into the function of emotional excitement. New York: D. Appleton.

Clark, T. (2011). Nerve: poise under pressure, serenity under stress, and the brave new science of fear and cool. New York: Little, Brown.

Clear, J. (2014). The science of positive thinking: How positive thoughts build your skills, boost your health, and improve your work | Huffington Post. Retrieved from http://www. huffingtonpost. com/james-clear/positive-thinking_b_3512202.html

Diamond DM, et al. (2007). "The Temporal Dynamics Model of Emotional Memory Processing: A Synthesis on the Neurobiological Basis of Stress-Induced Amnesia, Flashbulb and Traumatic Memories, and the Yerkes-Dodson Law." Neural Plasticity: 33. doi:10.1155/2007/60803. PMID 17641736.

Doctor, R. M., Khan, A. P., Adamec, C. (2008). Glossophobia. In The encyclopedia of phobias, fears and anxieties. (Third Edition, pp. 253). New York: Facts on File, Inc.

E. K. Acton, "On gender differences in the distribution of um and uh," University of Pennsylvania Working Papers in Linguistics, vol. 17, no. 2, p. 2, 2011.

Faravelli, C., Zucchi, T., Vivani, B. et al, (2000). Epidemiology of social phobia: A clinical approach. Eur Psychiatry, 15:17—24.

Frost, R. (1916). The road not taken. Retrieved April 11, 2017, from https://www.poetryfoundation. org/resources/learning/core-poems/detail/44272

Furmark T. (2002) Social phobia: Overview of community surveys. Acta Psychiatr Scand 105: 84—93. PMID

Furmark, T., Tillfors, M., Everz, PO. et al. (1999) Social phobia in the general population: prevalence and sociodemographic profile. Soc Psychiatry Psychiatry Epidemiology (1999) 34: 416.

Galvin, K. M. (2011). Making connections: readings in relational communication. New York: Oxford University Press.

Gerald R. Ford. (n.d.). AZQuotes.com. Retrieved March 14, 2017, from AZQuotes.com Web site: http://www.azquotes.com/quote/1056562

Keller, J. E., Keating, L. C. (1993). Aesop's fables, with a life of Aesop. Lexington: University of Kentucky Press. English translation of the first Spanish edition of Aesop from 1489, La vida del Ysopet con sus fabulas historiadas including original woodcut illustrations; the Life of Aesop is a version from Planudes.

Kunhardt, P. W., & Oakes, B. (Directors). (2017, January 30). Becoming Buffett [Video file]. Retrieved February 16, 2017, from http://www.imdb.com/title/tt6438096/

Laserna, C., Seih, Y, and Pennebaker, J. (2014) Um . . . who like says you know: Filler word use as a function of age, gender, and personality," Journal of Language and Social Psychology, vol. 33, no. 3, pp. 328—338, 2014.

Littlejohn, S. and Foss, K. (2009). Uncertainty reduction theory. In the Encyclopedia of Communication Theory. (Vol. 2, pp. 976). Thousand Oaks: Sage Publications, Inc.

Mark Twain. (n.d.). AZQuotes.com. Retrieved March 14, 2017, from AZQuotes.com web site: http://www.azquotes.com/quote/661749

M.B. Hamner, G.W. Arana, in Encyclopedia of Stress (Second Edition), 2007.

McCroskey, J. C. (1970) . Measures of communication-bound anxiety. Speech Monographs, 37, 269-277.

Musgrave, S. (2015) "Lessons for life," The STEAM Journal: Vol. 2: Iss. 1, Article 24. DOI: 10.5642/steam.20150201.24

O'Toole, G. (2012) Eleanor Roosevelt quote, No one can make feel inferior without your consent. Retrieved April 06, 2017, from http://quoteinvestigator.com/2012/04/30/no-one-inferior/

Pollard, A., Henderson,J., Frank, M. & Margolis, R. (1989).Help-seeking patterns of anxiety-disordered individuals in the general population, Journal of Anxiety Disorders, Volume 3, Issue 3, 1989, Pages 131-138, ISSN 0887-6185

Roosevelt, F. D. (1933). The Joint Congressional Committee on Inaugural Ceremonies. Retrieved April 06, 2017, from https://www.inaugural.senate.gov/about/past-inaugural-ceremonies/37th-inaugural-ceremonies/

Sapir, E. (1927) "Speech as a personality trait," American Journal of Sociology, pp. 892—905, 1927.

Stein M, Walker J, & Forde D. (1996) Public-speaking fears in a community sample: Prevalence, impact on functioning, and diagnostic classification. Arch Gen Psychiatry 53: 169—174. PMID

Stress. (2017). Retrieved July 19, 2017, from https://www.adaa.org/understanding-anxiety/related-illnesses/stress

Stuttering. (n.d.). Retrieved April 06, 2017, from http://www.asha.org/public/speech/disorders/stuttering.htm

Travis, J. (2004) Fear not. Science News Volume 165, No. 3, January 17, 2004, p. 42. Available at Science News.

"The Wizard Of Oz (1939)." Greatest Films - The Best Movies in Cinematic History. N.p., n.d. Web. 6 Apr. 2017.

Workman, B. (1977). "Fear" In The New Caxton Encyclopedia London, England: The Caxton Publishing Company Limited. The International Learning Systems Corporation. 8: 2359.

Yerkes R.M., Dodson, J.D. (1908). "The relation of strength of stimulus to rapidity of habit-formation." Journal of Comparative Neurology and Psychology. 18: 459—482. doi:10.1002/cne.920180503.

# Chapter 2:
# Conquer Your Fear

## Objectives

By the end of this chapter you should be able to:

1.  Explain why popular myths about public speaking can harm one's delivery.

2.  Identify anxiety-reducing tips.

3.  Establish a deliberate practice that incorporates the 5 Speech Delivery Tactics.

4.  Discover the secret to overcoming your fear of public speaking.

5.  Believe you can transform your ability to communicate.

**Part 1: 12 Public Speaking Myths**

**Part 2: 5 Tips to Reduce Your Fear**

**Part 3: Practice Matters**

**Part 4: The Ultimate Secret**

**Part 5: Believe You Can**

**Practice Speech:** Amaze and astound your favorite pet or plant.

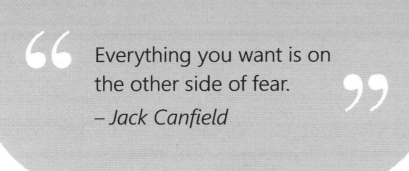

> Everything you want is on the other side of fear.
> – Jack Canfield

FEAR

## Chapter 2
# Conquer Your Fear

It astounds me how much misinformation circulates about public speaking. Due to the emotionally charged experience public speaking provokes, when people I meet learn about my passion for all things public speaking, they are intrigued and excited to share their experience with me! Typically, they begin by talking about what happened in their public speaking course or the specifics of a particularly challenging speech they delivered. Their experience tends to lie on one end of the spectrum or the other. Either they delivered an amazing speech that shocked them and their audience, or they were traumatized by the event, considering it one of the more horrific experiences of their lives.

The conversation is rarely complete without hearing their favorite anecdote to triumph over fear, assured that this too is in my repertoire of tricks. Unfortunately, the majority of the tips and suggestions they offer, do not help at all! In some cases, they can actually hinder a presentation. If you want to enjoy the many benefits mastering public speaking can offer, you must use the right tools. Let's begin by debunking some common myths.

## Part 1: 12 Public Speaking Myths Debunked

Given the psychological and physical anxiety public speaking can cause, it is no wonder people grasp at age old remedies and suggestions that have virtually become urban legends. Often these "simple" suggestions can actually thwart your ability to connect with your audience and even interfere with the speech. Let's review some common ideas about improving your performance and see if you can distinguish fact from fiction!

## Interaction 2.1: Myth or Fact

Mark each box: 'M' for **Myth** if you think the myth has merit, and 'F' for **Fact** if you think it doesn't.

☐  1.  Imagine the audience naked or in their underwear.

☐  2.  Avoid eye contact—focus at a point above the audiences heads.

☐  3.  Begin with a joke.

☐  4.  Too much rehearsal is bad for me—I'm better just speaking off the cuff.

☐  5.  Just go straight for the Q & A.

☐  6.  You are born with the talent of public speaking—you cannot learn it.

☐  7.  Memorize your speech.

☐  8.  Shut off the lights to show an electronic presentation.

☐  9.  Being a good public speaker involves eliminating nervousness.

☐  10. A mistake will destroy the speech.

☐  11. Hide behind the lectern.

☐  12. My experience trumps credible sources.

**Myth #1: Imagine the audience naked or in their underwear.**

If you actually follow through with this, be wary. It can go one of two ways: there are some people we just don't want to imagine this way and others we do! Either way the images will undoubtedly distract you from your message—how can you be caring about the audience "getting" your message while thinking such thoughts? Besides, it is rude, and disrespectful. Your unsuspecting audience came to hear your speech, not to be undressed. Don't be a pervert!

**Myth #2: Avoid eye contact—focus at a point above the audience's heads.**

This is some of the worst advice I have ever heard. If you want your message to connect with the audience—look at your audience. If you look over their heads, they'll know it. You are not going to "get one over" on them. Could you imagine going on a date where your date continually looked over your head, avoiding your eyes for the entire evening? How would you feel? An audience, especially between 10-100 people can tell. Eye contact is a crucial point of connection with your audience. Capitalize on it—don't abandon it! Furthermore, if you really care about the audience getting your message, you want to be able to "see" that happening. Besides, when you make eye contact with a person, you are talking one-on-one, which will lower your anxiety. Just be sure to move from one person to another: don't give your entire speech to just one person.

As a speech coach, some clients actually focus their eye contact only on me, perhaps because they see me as their evaluator. That's awkward and uncomfortable for me. Eventually, I refuse to look up because I begin to feel stalked. The other audience members feel abandoned and ignored too. If you have a person in the audience who is evaluating you, a boss or an instructor, don't stalk him or her—appreciate each audience member equally.

### Myth #3: Begin with a joke.

Careful, careful, careful! When it comes to an audience, or even interpersonally, jokes can be a loaded gun. Fire them with extreme caution—and when it comes to speaking publicly, it just might be safer to keep them under lock and key. Humor is a very personal thing and differs from person to person. Successful business executives often begin a speech with the joke of the day, which is has no bearing on the purpose of their speech. Their audience will probably laugh, even when they don't find it funny. More likely, they will laugh because he's the boss. Social guidelines dictate that one should laugh to help the boss save face! Many jokes commonly used by managers and bosses around the world serve to disenfranchise workers, not empower them, something you want to avoid. Never include jokes that don't connect to your message and purpose. Poking fun at yourself can sometimes be okay, but leave the "jokes-for-joke's sake" out!

### Myth #4: Too much rehearsal is bad for me—I'm better just speaking off the cuff.

Practice. Practice. Practice. In all my years of teaching, I have never seen an instance where too much rehearsal ruined a speech. I have seen people try to "wing" it, arguing that if they actually plan and practice the entire speech, "they" disintegrate. This statement simply doesn't make sense. Imagine a builder stating, "If I use architectural drawings, the building will implode. I know it works for other builders, but me?— I'm better off just swinging the hammer and seeing where it takes me!" This idea is just laziness, pure and simple.

There are people who turn the speech into a performance—there is a difference! Memorization can lead to a performance-based speech. When and if they forget a word or think they forgot a word, those speakers are rattled and lose momentum. It can be difficult to get back on track.

During a speech, the speaker should be engaged in a conversation with the audience, rather than conducting a performance for the audience. A speech is more personal than a performance. And guess what? A mistake is ok. Cue cards with key words provide momentary direction if necessary. But most importantly, in a speech, the impact your words have on a particular audience matters most.

Make no mistake, whether a well-prepared speaker or an unprepared one—the audience sees you at face value and will discern the difference. When you invite an audience to your "word party," prepare to serve them consciously combined, selected words that deliver a strong message.

> Optimism is the faith that leads to achievement. Nothing can be done without hope and confidence. 
>
> –Helen Keller

### Myth #5: Just go straight for the Questions and Answers.

While not every scenario allows for this mindset, some subject matter experts feel like they should just open themselves to the audience and allow questions to flow. They will just respond "off the cuff" to questions posed and ..."Voila"...a speech is born. While many speaking situations warrant a question and answer session following your remarks, it is best to meet the expectations of the people who offered you the opportunity to address this group and the audience members themselves. Once the audience hears your points, they can direct their questions to the purpose at hand.

### Myth #6: You are born with the talent of public speaking—you cannot learn it.

It is remarkable how many people really believe that speakers are born with a special talent. Many honestly believe that people who convey their ideas with ease do not, or have not, felt the angst that the rest of us do. This is a limiting thought—release it! I'll never forget one of my first speeches. I got up with hands shaking and papers fluttering. Somehow, I made it through, but I desperately battled to keep the papers still—I clutched them with one hand only to hear the papers rattling in the air. When I desperately grasped the other side of the papers to silence them, both hands bumped around like I was driving down a pothole-ravaged dirt road. After I completed my speech and sat down, my speech coach, Broadway Joe, stated, "Good job! We could have even danced to the rhythm of your knees knocking!" With practice and effort, I learned to channel my energy to connect with my audience. While some do experience greater degrees of anxiety than others, the skill of public speaking is developed with focus and effort—it is up to you to invest that effort. Think about it: if Helen Keller, a woman who, despite losing her ability to see and hear, was able to overcome insurmountable obstacles and actually deliver dynamic speeches that resonated with audiences, so can you! Let her words inspire you! "Optimism is the faith that leads to achievement. Nothing can be done without hope and confidence."

### Myth #7: Memorize your speech.

When you focus on visual memories, you look up and to the right (Gompel, et. al., 2007). The resulting loss of eye contact connected with delivering a memorized speech can impair connection with the audience. Experienced speakers delivering memorized speeches may seem too rehearsed, too perfect. The speech turns into a performance. Less experienced ones may look a bit crazy, as if they were listening to the voices in their head. In either situation, the speaker loses connection with the audience, especially when they lose eye contact as they try to "remember." You may seem to be showing off..."Look at me, see how much I remember!" That has nothing to do with communicating your message to your audience.

**Myth #8: Shut off the lights to display slides.**

If you turn the lights off in a room to display slides, what happens to the audience's attention? It focuses on the bright image. What happens if you turn the lights half off to make the slides brighter? The energy of the room decreases and the audience's attention goes to the slides. As a speaker who has an important message to deliver to an audience, where do you want their attention? On you!

Visual presentations, such as a PowerPoint, are there to support you, not take center stage! Too often people dim the lights as a prerequisite for presenting their slides. Think about the impact it has upon the audience. Sometimes the lights are automatically dimmed "to help the audience see" but some speakers like the lights off so that they don't have to see the audience —they can hide in the dark!

A speech is not a game of hide-and-go seek. Don't allow yourself to hide in the darkness; you will lose way too much of your ability to connect with the audience. Dimming the lights significantly dulls energy in the room. Don't surrender your ability to connect with your audience to technology. If you must turn the lights off to show an image, turn them back on as soon as possible and reclaim the stage. That doesn't mean you should avoid slides. They can be a great help to a speech. To ensure your audience can see them with the lights on, choose a light background and dark text. Most projectors today are strong enough that the audience can usually see such screen content with the lights on.

The Occupational Safety and Health Administration, (OSHA) regulation CFR 1915.18 and 1926.56 outline the workplace standards for lighting. Lighting has a huge impact on individuals and productivity in the workplace. Your presentation should adapt the minimum standards a productive workspace requires, which means leave the lights on when you are speaking to an audience!

**Myth #9: Being a good public speaker involves eliminating nervousness.**

There are psychological and physiological reasons our bodies react to public speaking by producing adrenaline. These evolutionary functions are not going to disappear just because you deliver a few speeches. We can harness this energy and use it to our benefit. The night before I begin a new class, speak to a new audience, or have the opportunity to share my ideas to a group, I always sleep restlessly. This is evidence of the fact that I care and that performance energy surges through my body. Why would I want to eliminate or lose that enthusiasm? Don't expect it to evaporate.

Your nervousness is a source of tremendous power. Later in this book, you will learn how to channel your anxiety to enhance connection with your audience, thus empowering you as a speaker. Use it; don't lose it!

**Myth #10: A mistake will destroy the speech.**

Don't dwell on your mistakes. Fix it, if necessary, and then move on. Mistakes happen— we're human. Your mistake will only make you seem more so, and the audience may even better relate to you. Consider this, if you walk down the street, stumble and trip, do you go back and re-walk the block? No! Just keep walking, in a few steps you will find your equilibrium. If you falter momentarily in a speech, don't stress…just keep going.

Should you apologize to your audience if you make a mistake? Only if you need to! In my estimation, more than three quarters of the time it is unnecessary. What does the word "apology" mean? "A regretful acknowledgment of an offense or failure," Merriam-Webster (2017) states. Does stumbling over a word require an apology? Is retracting a statement or adding an example after you started a sentence really "an offense or failure"? If a situation causes confusion, for example, distributing the wrong handout, or mixing up your slides, perhaps a small apology is warranted. Just remember that an apology shines a glaring light on the mistake! Too often speakers apologize when most of the audience never even realized anything had gone wrong. That's like me telling you, "Guess what? This morning when I woke up, I had a huge zit on my chin." What is the first thing you'd do? Look for the zit! Most apologies in speeches amount to the same thing—they draw attention to a flaw that might have gone unnoticed. Repeated apologies scream of a lack of confidence. Secure confident people only apologize when necessary.

### Myth #11: Hide behind the lectern.

This is one of my pet peeves. Why, when you are trying to connect with an audience, would you hide behind a lectern? Whenever possible, step out from behind the lecture, roll up your sleeves, and get real with the audience. Your body language speaks volumes! Use it to express yourself. Rather than staying in one place, move around from one side of the audience to the other. Use your movements to make your message more interesting.

In some scenarios, etiquette does call for a more formal presentation behind a lectern, but dynamic speakers do not use the lectern as a crutch.

### Myth #12: My experience trumps credible sources.

Good, credible research reflects positively upon you, no matter how much of an expert you are in the field. Providing support for your ideas and claims adds credibility to your message. Good quotes from famous people add value. Listen to the speeches of well-respected individuals; they are not afraid to drop a name or a quote or good evidence.

Speakers who lack credibility tend to overvalue their ideas and skip the work necessary to support their ideas. Quality research takes time and effort. Your audience deserves to have a presentation filled with current, relevant, accurate information.

When you include a citation, always provide context explaining who the person or organization is and why their input matters. There is a tremendous amount of available information on the Internet, and quality varies, so validate accuracy before you present material to an audience.

# Part 2: Five Tips to Reduce Your Fear

Remember, the anxiety associated with public speaking is natural—and can be a boon. You want to plug into the excess energy that develops from your innate self-consciousness and fear. Essentially, turn lemons into lemonade. This energy, these excess "nerves,", breathe life into your delivery.

Why should a speaker harness this energy as a source of power for their words? Consider why people spend exorbitant sums of money to see a musician live in concert, purchase season tickets to see a sports team compete, attend a theatrical performance, or stand outside in the freezing cold for hours to see a President inaugurated. It's because it is real, live, and full of energy! It is different than seeing it through the lens of a camera. A speech is also real, live, and vibrating with energy.

How can you use this energy positively? It begins by reining it in and learning how to control it. That takes practice! Putting yourself on stage. It's a lot like entering a gym after not working out for ages. For me, those first few times were nerve-wracking. Everybody seemed to know what they were doing and how each machine worked. I carefully observed others, trying not to look like a novice. I would eyeball people across from me and watch how they handled equipment, then follow their example. For the next few days, my muscles were so sore! But with diligence, focus, and practice, newbies now stare at me, for I now look experienced.

When was the last time you entered a speech gymnasium? Completed a workout designed to improve your communication skills? If you are like most individuals, probably not recently! No wonder it seems foreign, scary, and maybe bizarre to stand before an audience. Just like the gym scenario, with practice, hard work, and dedication, you can improve, and soon look like a pro! Stick to a routine, push yourself to try the different tools available, and you will stretch muscles you didn't even know you had. You will develop a presenter's form and shape worthy of admiration.

" **The expert in anything was once a beginner.**
–Helen Hayes "

Perhaps you are still cringing at the thought of standing before an audience. Here are five tips that are sure to reduce your anxiety.

### Tip 1: Visualize: Imagine Yourself Nailing the Speech!

You can improve your performance by improving your visualization skills. Visualize yourself confidently delivering the speech, the audience applauding—really create the experience in your imagination. This technique was first used by athletes in the 1960s. Scientific research begun in 1984 by the Russians during the Olympics (Ayers, 1988 & 2009), verified that it helps athletes reach peak performance. If it can work for athletes do you think this can help you improve as a speaker? This technique goes beyond simple visualizing, it involves anticipating the smell, the sounds, and the energy pulsing through your veins—experiencing the speech as fully as possible while you practice. Christopher Clarey from the NY Times explains how "Olympians Use Imagery as Mental Training." It turns out that this technique is not only good for athletes. Ayres and Hoft (2009) found it works to reduce speech anxiety too.

### Tip 2: Use Your Breath to Control Your Nerves

It is critical to breathe. Breathe deeply. Breathe consciously. When you control your breath, you can better control your nervous energy. If you control your nervous energy you can control the pace of your speech, add emphasis, and project your voice. If you can control your voice, you can control your body language, hand gestures, and eye contact. If you can control your breath, voice, and body, you control your delivery. Harvard Health recently published a report entitled, "Relaxation Techniques: Breath Control Helps Quell Errant Stress Response" (2015). The report is readily available on the Internet and provides a guide to invoke the relaxation response when nerves surface. If you are one who experiences high levels of anxiety, the article teaches the basics of deep breathing which you can use to manage the stress and anxiety you feel delivering a speech.

All speakers can benefit from taking three deep breaths (long in, long out) when they feel tense or nervous. Notice how your shoulders come up and your muscles relax. Take three deep breaths just before you start your speech and maybe again when you finish.

### Tip 3: Think Positively

Believe that your content matters! Rather than feeding negative thoughts, focus on the positive. Look at yourself and say, "I'm going to do a great job on this speech!" or "My audience really appreciated my message" or "I stood before the audience confidently, clearly projected my words with excellent emphasis and used my body to convey my emotions." Think positively—it sure beats the negative mantra. Joe Ayres (2009) conducted two studies, each found that speech anxiety correlates to negative thoughts and that students who used positive thoughts and visualized their success decreased their anxiety and improved their attitude about the experience. Isn't that a better alternative to a negative implosion of self-doubt culminating in crippling anxiety? Get in the habit of squashing negative thoughts like cockroaches. Current research supports the notion that our thoughts really matter. James Clear (2013) provides a general overview outlining its significance as related to various research studies in his article, "The Science of Positive Thinking: How Positive Thoughts Build Your Skills, Boost Your Health, and Improve Your Work." Industrialist Henry Ford got it right when he said, "Whether you think you can, or you think you can't—you're right."

### Tip 4: Practice Power Poses

Amy Cuddy's (2012) research on body language (How body language shapes who you are) and her suggestions to use power poses to increase your confidence has hit the list of the Top 10 TED videos of all time. If you haven't seen it yet, it's fascinating. Her research shows that practicing power poses for just two minutes a day can make you more confident and help you perform better on a given task. Practice standing in a power pose before you deliver a speech. Watch the difference in your confidence as you deliver! Internationally known CEO Coach and Consultant, Somers White states "90% of how a talk will go is determined before the speaker steps on the platform." How you hold yourself, the image you project, matters to both you and your audience.

### Tip 5: Dress Professionally

As a speaker, you are the leader—look like a leader! Remember the significance of first impressions. Make the right first impression! Your appearance adds credibility to your message. When you decide what to wear, consider the event itself. The dress code at a wedding is a bit different from a funeral and much different than addressing a group of business colleagues. For business, always follow the rules of professional business attire—what you would wear for an interview. Sometimes people, especially young ones, put on what they wear to go out on the town. There is a time and place for most everything, but avoid the "sex pot" look in front of an audience. Dress conservatively, even if it is painful for you and not your style. You don't want to distract from your message.

One memorable student delivered a speech by Franklin D. Roosevelt, "A Date Which Will Live in Infamy!" He delivered it with flair, wearing a t-shirt that displayed a picture of a dachshund dog with a kippah on its head and text that read, "My wiener is kosher." Now what do you think the audience was thinking as he eloquently delivered his speech?

A young woman in one class provides an example of the perils of party garb. When she stood up, I could literally see her underwear! That childhood chant, "I see London, I see France…" looped through my head, although I can't speak for the rest of the audience. During a speech you want the focus to be on the message, **not** your clothing, or what is or isn't, underneath!

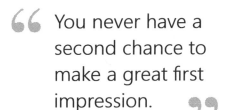

> You never have a second chance to make a great first impression.
>
> — *Will Rogers*

**Table 2.1: Professional Attire Guidelines**

| Women | Men |
|---|---|
| **Business Suit** Dark solid or pinstripe, preferably navy, dark brown, gray or charcoal. (Skirts should touch your knee! Avoid deep slits or short skirts.) | **Business Suit** Dark solid or pinstripe, preferably navy, dark brown, gray or charcoal. No wrinkles and *clean* of course! |
| **Shirt** Solid white or soft pastel. Avoid the urge to reveal some cleavage—keep those sisters covered! No sheer material or gaping at the button holes! | **Shirt** Solid white or pale blue/cotton. Avoid two-tone shirts that have a different color collar than the rest of the shirt. |
| **Hose** Rule of thumb is to wear natural-colored sheer pantyhose, especially if you are wearing a skirt. With slacks, solid or sheer natural both work. | **Ties** Conservative, medium width. Avoid extra-wide ties, or thin, narrow ties or holiday or novelty ties. |
| **Shoes** Low or medium pumps, closed toe and heel. Solid color or a soft-grained pattern that match suit. | **Shoes** Loafer or lace up, conservative, well shined. |
| **Accessories** All jewelry should be conservative, understated and match the suit. Earring/necklace/pendant no larger than a dime. Stick with stud earrings, not dangling ones. Simple, small necklace, but avoid messages (i.e. "LOVE"). | **Socks** Solid color matches suit, half calf. |
| **Grooming** Shower, hair should be well groomed and neat. Makeup should compliment your complexion *not* create a new one! Avoid the night out-on-the-town look. Less is more. Remove piercings. | **Grooming** Your appearance should be as important as your clothes. Shave, shower, remove piercings, and control your hair. |

Dressing professionally not only has an impact on what others think of you but also how you view yourself (O'Callaghan, J. (2014). Your clothes matter, they contribute to your credibility and confidence. Karen Pine (2014) found that "clothing has a significant effect on self-esteem and confidence." We not only are what we wear, but we also become what we wear. "Clothing affects our mental processes and perceptions, which can change our minds and the way we think," she continues (Pine, 2014). If you want to be a confident public speaker, look confident!

In today's society, many people balk at professional dress code standards and resist putting on a suit. Let's face it, when you are unaccustomed to dressing professionally, it takes effort to do so, and you feel like a fish out of water in unfamiliar attire. Pine (2014) found that the majority of people put on a suit to gain confidence rather than to be attractive. Your effort shows the audience that you care—it reveals the same to yourself. This builds your confidence, and in return, your audience will feel that perceptive edge and incline their ear to your message.

Each of these techniques are great things to do—implement them into your practice and see which ones work best for you.

### Interaction 2.2: Which of These Five Tips Will Be Most Beneficial to You?

Number these five techniques from most beneficial to least.

_____ Imagine Yourself Nailing the Speech!

_____ Use Your Breath to Control Your Nerves

_____ Think Positively

_____ Practice Power Poses

_____ Dress Professionally

## Part 3: Practice Matters

Practicing really does matter (Daly et. al. 1989; Menzel & Carrell, 1994 & O'Hair et al, 2001). How should you practice? A good practice strategy can make a big difference. These two components need to be addressed as you design your best practice: 1. Incorporate the steps for deliberate practice, and 2. Apply five Practice Tactics to deliver your best speech

### Deliberate Practice

Have you ever considered what your practice habits are? I recently had the opportunity to hear Angela Duckworth speak. As the director of the Character Lab, Duckworth studies the science of success. Her book *Grit: The Power of Passion and Perseverance* (2016) instantly became a New York Times best seller. It seems that people are vitally interested in learning "the secret to outstanding achievement is not talent but a special blend of passion and persistence called 'grit'."

One of the things that stood out to me the most in her speech was her research on practice. She explained that there are different types of practice. Deliberate practice is by far the most beneficial. This structured way of practicing with the intent to improve was first explored by Ericsson, Krampe & Tesch-Romer in 1993. They proposed that a long period of deliberate practice contributes more to success rather than innate ability, or "talent." Ayers & Holf (2009) later found that "it is not the amount of preparation but rather the type of preparation that makes a difference." How people practice in any field and at any level varies, but it always involves negotiating motivational and external constraints. It makes sense that "practicing more intensively than others" leads to personal triumph. If you have committed to conquering your fear, why not make the most of your practice? Practice with intent and follow what Duckworth (2011) refers to as the "cycle of genius" by implementing these four steps.

### How to Establish a Deliberate Practice

1. Set an intentional "stretch" goal. Which means, to target a specific area in which you want to improve. Identify measurable improvement points along the way. Each time you practice, "stretch" yourself to reach that next point. Be sure that your practice supports your efforts to improve to that point. Evaluate your progress.
2. Focus 100%! Eliminate any distractions. It is necessary to hit a deep level of focus. This is a huge challenge in today's society with the constant interruptions of our cell phones and social media.
3. Get feedback! The feedback should be immediate and of high quality. Top athletes or performers get feedback that occurs on the spot. The feedback needs to be from qualified experts.
4. Reflect and refine. Duckworth explains that this step is the hardest. You must have the courage to receive feedback without being defensive.

### Interaction 2.3: Quality Practice

Researchers studied each of the items listed below to identify which could predict the best speech performance. Check each one that you think proved to work.

| | |
|---|---|
| _____ cue cards | _____ visual aids |
| _____ state anxiety | _____ silent rehearsal |
| _____ total preparation time | _____ oral rehearsal |
| _____ other research | _____ grade point average |
| _____ number of rehearsals for an audience | |

*Answer: Any of these attributes can predict success. Total preparation time, number of rehearsals for an audience, grade point average, and state anxiety predicted the quality of a speech performance. Menzel and Carrell (1994).*

Practice isn't the thing you do once you're good. It's the thing you do that makes you good.

— *Malcolm Gladwell*

**Five Steps to Practice a Speech**

**Step 1. Familiarize yourself with the words of the speech.**

Read the speech aloud 5-10 times to get familiar with the words. This is one of the most productive strategies you can use. Imagine that you take a short cut every day by walking through the grass. How long does it take a footpath to form? Do the same thing to your brain—form a groove so that when you stand in front of the audience your mouth will naturally utter the words you have practiced.

**Step 2. Choose the right inflection and emotion.**

Try this exercise: take the words, "Are you ready." These three words can be said an infinite number of ways. Say this phrase using the following emotions: angry, resentful, terrified, forgiving, sad, excited, free, suspicious, and sexy. For each emotion, imagine how your favorite actor would deliver the phrase and what would change for each emotion. No doubt, the volume, the pace, the body language, and even the breath would vary for each different emotion. Try to act each emotion with these three words! When you practice a speech, be aware that there is an entire range of emotions you can use, each containing fluctuations and pauses that convey different meanings. Identify three ways you could say your first sentence—record yourself on your phone and/or ask for an opinion from someone else in order to identify which works best. By doing this, you choose how you will deliver your words rather than the delivery just happening to you. Apply this technique to different sections of the speech, especially the most important ones.

**Step 3. Identify key words you will emphasize.**

Review your speech; underline the words that need to "pop". Always emphasize four types of words: numbers, conjunctions, pronouns, and adjectives. Each time I see a number, conjunction, pronoun, or adjective, I let my vocal inflection vary—the pitch will melodically go up and down, speed up and slow down like a little roller coaster ride.

**Step 4. Focus on the beginning of your speech.**

Know your first line flawlessly! Your first line should not be too long or contain complex words that are difficult to pronounce. Make the words matter. Never begin with a "Hi, my name is." Or "How's everyone doing today?" And especially not "Today I'm here to talk with you about. . ." Begin with an Attention Grabber and complete control of your voice, words and body as you deliver those first words.

**Step 5. Practice in front of an audience.**

Numerous research studies have shown that delivering your speech to a practice audience improves the delivery of your speech with the real audience (Smith & Frymier, 2007; Verderber & Verderber, 2002). The practice delivery removes much of the system shocking elements of delivering a speech.

As you build your confidence and conquer your fear of speaking, begin with simple, small speeches that are fun and non-threatening. Put yourself into it. Planning cool things to do with the audience like using an interesting prop or including an activity that creatively involves them can add excitement to your speech and inspire you to actually anticipate the delivery. Eventually, with the right preparation and focus (discussed below) this anxiety will transform into energy that empowers your words! Secretary of State, Hillary Clinton said, "If you're not comfortable with public speaking—and nobody starts out comfortable; you have to learn how to be comfortable—practice. I cannot overstate the importance of practicing. Get some close friends or family members to help evaluate you, or somebody at work that you trust."

## Part 4: The Ultimate Secret

### Get Over Yourself!

By now, if you have followed the tips, techniques and strategies outlined in this chapter, you should feel confident that you have acquired useful information to support your efforts to conquer your fear, reduce anxiety, and develop a deliberate practice to quickly improve.

However, there is one last thing you must do that makes all the difference. I refer to this as the Ultimate Secret to overcoming your fear and anxiety. Are you ready? Before you deliver a speech, what is the conversation you must have with yourself? Does it go something like this? "I'm so nervous! I am so nervous! I am so nervous! What will they think of me? I'm so nervous! I am so nervous! I am so nervous! What if I make a mistake? I am so nervous! I am so nervous! I am so nervous! Can't I please escape?"

If this is familiar, my advice to you is get over yourself! Focus more on the audience than you do your own nerves. Easier said than done, you may think. But consider this question, if your mind is focusing on you and your nerves . . . who is thinking about the audience? No one! They are abandoned and ignored.

Isn't the whole purpose of the speech to share an important idea with the attendees? If you myopically focus on your stress, it becomes a slippery slope. The more you obsess, the more you obsess. Unfortunately, the audience is left to suffer and witness a bundle of nerves rather than hearing poignant points from a competent speaker. The good news is you can overcome anxiety; your focus must change from yourself to the audience, inward to outward. This is what I refer to as the ultimate secret to overcoming your fear and anxiety!

Here is the pre-speech self-talk for someone who has applied the secret. "I am nervous . . . but this information is really going to benefit my audience. (Envision audience.) I wonder who is going to attend? Who will benefit the most from point three? Geez, after all my practice, I

**Figure 2.1: Model of Communication**

speaker (sender)          message          audience (recipient)

can't wait to see that role-play work. I've got to remember to call on one person who looks really interested and another who is a bit shyer."

Can you see by the emphasis shifting from self to the audience? The energy completely shifts, leaving room for you to manage your anxiety and focus on your message.

Examine the diagram in Figure 2.1 representing a very basic model of communication: the speaker, the message, the audience. When you give a speech, how much of the focus do you believe should be focused on each of these variables? The speaker? The message? The audience?

While there isn't a scientific answer supporting exact values for each, common sense dictates that the focus should be on the audience rather than the speaker. Too often, this is not the case—the speech is an egocentric obsession rather than audience-centered presentation. Make no mistake: you cannot take the speaker out of the formula. The speaker is a vital part of the speech but never forget it is all for and about the audience. Care more about the audience receiving your message than about your own nerves. It is that simple.

When a parent who typically faints at the sight of blood runs to save his or her injured child, they don't faint! Especially if there is no one else around. In that moment, the parent cares more for the child's safety than their own phobias. Care about your audience. Care more about your audience receiving the message than your fear of delivering it to them! By caring, you will get over your nerves and deliver a message that connects with your audience. Stop focusing on what they think about you; just think about them. Dale Carnegie's quote substantiates this idea, he says, "You can close more business in two months by becoming interested in other people than you can in two years by trying to get people interested in you."

 Humility is not thinking less of yourself. It's thinking of yourself less. 

— *C.S. Lewis*

## Part 5: Believe You Can!

You may be thinking, is it worth the effort? Absolutely! The benefits are far reaching! As you build this skill set, you may also develop in other areas. When I first began coaching public speaking, I was unaware of the wide-spread effects that would occur. I soon saw the personal growth individuals experienced as they faced their own anxiety and found their voices. With effort and focus, improvement was clearly evident; they stood taller and walked with more confidence.

Before long, numerous clients received raises at work and unsolicited compliments on their communication skills—leaders emerged. James Humes said, "The art of communication is the language of leadership." Did you know that many people promoted to a leadership position are advised to take a public speaking course? Public speaking is arguably the most challenging form of communication. If you can master the art of communicating to a group of 20 people effectively, you can better deal with two people or even yourself.

Believe that you can do it! Cartoonist and creator of Dilbert, Scott Adams, addressed the insecurity beginning speakers feel. He said, "We don't always have an accurate view of our own potential. I think most people who are frightened of public speaking can't imagine training could help them feel different. Don't assume you know how much potential you have. Sometimes the only way to know what you can do is to test yourself." Remember Anais Lin's words, "Life shrinks or expands in proportion to your courage." Summon the courage to conquer your fear. Examine your presentational strengths and weaknesses and employ the various tips and strategies outlined in this chapter to manage these for personal benefit. As a result, you will become a better communicator, which will accentuate your life in many positive ways. Being "speech-actualized" can transform your life! It is well worth the effort.

When people take that first step and commit to the process, personal growth is soon evident. Angela Duckworth explains that talent plus effort equals skill. Skill plus effort equals achievement. Effort counts twice! Push past your comfort zone because as author Neale Donald Walsch explains, "Life begins at the end of your comfort zone."

 The most difficult thing is the decision to act, the rest is merely tenacity. The fears are paper tigers. You can do anything you decide to do.

— *Amelia Earhart*

# Chapter 2 Review Questions

1. Prior to reading the chapter, did you believe any of the myths? Which one? Explain why it is a myth.

2. Identify a new tip you offer to a developing speaker.

3. Practice one of the paractice speeches being sure to follow the Five Steps to Practice a Speech, write a one paragraph analysis of the experience.

4. Have you ever followed Duckworth's guidelines to establish a deliberate practice? Explain. Identify a time in your life when you practiced poorly. What did you do differently? How did it impact your performance? Is it better to practice with intent?

5. What is the "ultimate secret" to overcoming your fear of public speaking?

6. What are some tips for reducing anxiety?

7. List the steps for establishing a deliberate practice.

8. What are the five steps to practicing a speech?

9. Identify atleast three public speaking tactics or myths that have been debunked. Explain why these are no longer the case.

10. Why is it critical to breathe properly during a speech?

11. Why is dressing professionally for a speech important? Provide one example for male and female of what's considered appropriate.

12. What does the concept of being "speech actualized" mean?

13. In the model of communication presented what are the three components featured? Which should be the most important during a speech?

14. Which quote from this chapter resonates with you the most?

## Practice Speech: Amaze and Astound Your Favorite Animal

**Time Limit:** 60 seconds

**Target Audience:** Deliver these heart warming quotes about animals to an animal; either a cat, dog, bird or fish—you can even choose an animal at the zoo should you be inspired.

**Instructions:** Select your favorite five quotes from the great animal quotes listed after these instructions. Implement your best practice techniques. Establish a deliberate practice using Duckworth's steps.

1. Determine your stretch goal. For each quote, apply one suggestion from each list.

| Delivery Tips & Techniques | Anxiety Reducing Strategies |
|---|---|
| Familiarize yourself with the words of the speech | Imagine yourself nailing the speech |
| Choose the right inflection and emotion | Use your breath to control your nerves. |
| Identify key words you will emphasize | Think positively |
| Focus on the beginning of your speech | Practice power poses |
| Practice in front of an audience. | Dress professionally |

2. Focus 100%—no outside interruptions!

3. Use feedback! Were you aware of attention from your audience? Record yourself and ask for feedback from someone you trust.

4. Reflect and refine!

**Purpose:** Establish a deliberate practice. Implement anxiety-reducing strategies with a non-threatening audience. Explore the array of available options to make your words interesting and compelling. Get comfortable standing in front of an audience who you know won't judge you! As you approach this speech, be aware of your nerves and fear, then remember that your audience is an animal. This should relieve your fear and help you deliver your speech boldly, with emotion, incorporating the strategies above. Always consider your audience.

**Skills to practice:** Establish a deliberate practice. Project your voice, add emotion, inflection and energy. Relax… deliver a reading in a non-threatening environment.

## Sample Animal Quotes

"Animals are such agreeable friends—they ask no questions, they pass no criticisms."
—George Eliot

"Until one has loved an animal, a part of one's soul remains un-awakened." — Anatole France

"If having a soul means being able to feel love and loyalty and gratitude, then animals are better off than a lot of humans."— James Herriot

"The animals of the world exist for their own reasons. They were not made for humans any more than black people were made for white, or women created for men." — Alice Walker

"Happiness is a warm puppy." — Charles M. Schulz

"The greatness of a nation and its moral progress can be judged by the way its animals are treated." — Mahatma Gandhi

"An animal's eyes have the power to speak a great language." — Martin Buber

"Man is the cruelest animal." — Friedrich Nietzsche

"Meow" means "woof" in cat." — George Carlin

"If you pick up a starving dog and make him prosperous he will not bite you. This is the principal difference between a dog and man." — Mark Twain

"How it is that animals understand things I do not know, but it is certain that they do understand. Perhaps there is a language which is not made of words and everything in the world understands it. Perhaps there is a soul hidden in everything and it can always speak, without even making a sound, to another soul." — Frances Hodgson Burnett

"Clearly, animals know more than we think, and think a great deal more than we know."
— Irene M. Pepperberg

"A dog is the only thing on earth that loves you more than he loves himself." — Josh Billings

"If a dog will not come to you after having looked you in the face, you should go home and examine your conscience." — Woodrow Wilson

"Animals are born who they are, accept it, and that is that. They live with greater peace than people do." — Gregory Maguire

"I am fond of pigs. Dogs look up to us. Cats look down on us. Pigs treat us as equals."
— Winston S. Churchill

"Heaven goes by favor. If it went by merit, you would stay out and your dog would go in."
— Mark Twain

# References

Anais Nin. (n.d.). AZQuotes.com. Retrieved March 14, 2017, from AZQuotes.com Web site: http://www.azquotes.com/quote/214868

Apology. (n.d.). Retrieved April 13, 2017, from http://www.dictionary.com/browse/apologies

Ayres, J. (2009). Coping with public speaking anxiety: The power of positive thinking. Communication Education, 37: 4, 289-296.

Ayres, J. & Hopf, T.S. (2009). Visualization: A means of reducing speech anxiety. Communication Education, 34: 4, 318-323.

Benson, H. (2006) Stress Control: Techniques for preventing and easing stress, Harvard Health Publications.

Cuddy, A. (2012, June) Amy Cuddy: Your Body Language Shapes Who You Are [Video le]. Retrieved from https://www.ted.com/talks/amy_cuddy_your_body_language_shapes_who_you_are

Duckworth, Angela. Grit: The power of passion and perseverance. Simon and Schuster, 2016.

Duckworth A. L., Peterson C., Matthews M. D., Kelly D. R. (2007). Grit: Perseverance and passion for long-term goals. Journal of Personality and Social Psychology, 92, 1087—1101

Duckworth, A. L., Kirby, T. A., Tsukayama, E., Berstein, H., & Ericsson, K. A. (2011). Deliberate practice spells success why grittier competitors triumph at the national spelling bee. Social psychological and personality science, 2(2), 174—181.

Ericsson, K. A., Krampe, R. T., & Tesch-Römer, C. (1993). The role of deliberate practice in the acquisition of expert performance. Psychological review, 100(3), 363.

Ericsson K. A. (2009). Enhancing the development of professional performance: Implications from the study of deliberate practice. In Ericsson K. A. (Ed.), The development of professional expertise: Toward measurement of expert performance and design of optimal learning environments (pp 405—431). Cambridge, UK: Cambridge University Press.

Hillary Clinton. (n.d.) BrainyQuotes.com. Retrieved March 13, 2017. Web site https://www.brainyquote.com/search_results.html?q=Hillary+Clinton+public+speaking

James C Humes. (n.d.). AZQuotes.com. Retrieved March 14, 2017, from AZQuotes.com Web site: http://www.azquotes.com/quote/1496850

Lady Bird Johnson. (n.d.). AZQuotes.com. Retrieved March 14, 2017, from AZQuotes.com Web site: http://www.azquotes.com/quote/521347

Menzel, K. E. and Carrell, L. J. 1994. The relationship between preparation and performance in public speaking. Communication Education, 43: 17—26.

O'Callaghan, J. (2014, May 30). You are what you DRESS: Clothing has a significant effect on self-esteem and confidence, claims expert. Retrieved April 14, 2017, from http://www.dailymail.co.uk/sciencetech/article-2644076/You-DRESS-Clothing-significant-effect-self-esteem-confidence-claims-expert.html

O'Hair, D., Stewart, R. and Rubenstein, H. 2001. A speaker's guidebook, Boston, MA: Bedford/St. Martin's.

Pine, K. J. (2014). Mind What You Wear: The Psychology of Fashion.doi:B00KBTB3NS

Scott Adams. (n.d.) BrainyQuotes.com. Retrieved March 13, 2017. Web site https://www.brainyquote.com/search_results.html?q=scott+adams+public+speaking

Smith, T. E. & Frymier, A. B. (2007). Get 'Real': Does Practicing Speeches Before an Audience Improve Performance? Published online: 03 Feb 2007 Journal Communication Quarterly, Vol. 54, 2006, 1

Van Gompel, R., Fischer, M. Murray, W. & Hill, R. (2007). Eye movements: a window on mind and brain. Elsevier, New York, NY.

Verderber, R. F. and Verderber, K. S. 2002. Communicate!, 10th ed., Belmont, CA: Wadsworth.

# Chapter 3:
# Transform Your Delivery

## Objectives

**By the end of this chapter you should be able to:**

1. Recall key terminology necessary to critique a speech.

2. Detect behaviors speakers use to create interest and evoke an audience.

3. Spot speaker behaviors which cause audience members to typically disengage or respond negatively.

4. Discover the Ten Delivery Principles.

5. Examine which delivery principles you will find to be most challenging.

6. Master Delivery Principle 1-6 using the Practice Speeches.

**Part 1: Key Words Every Public Speaker Must Know (Vocabulary)**

**Part 2: 10 Delivery Principles Every Speaker Should Use**

1. Set the Stage
2. Control the Energy
3. Speak Up!
4. Sweeten It!
5. Power of the Pause
6. Engage, Engage, Engage
7. Use Your Space Wisely
8. Respect the Time
9. Dance with Your Audience
10. Have Fun!

**Practice Speech:** Famous

**Practice Speech:** Movie

**Practice Speech:** Introduction

> ❝ When you have confidence, you can have a lot of fun. And when you have fun, you can do amazing things. ❞
>
> – *Joe Namath*

DELIVERY SKILLS

## *Chapter 3:*
# Transform Your Delivery

Speakers with terrific delivery technique are confident, and they create a meaningful connection with their audience. How do they do it? Although they sound like separate threads, confidence and connection are two sides of a coin. The more rapport you establish, the more confident you become. Confidence inspires creative approaches to developing powerful connections. The great news is that building confidence is a learnable skill. Master it and you will leave audiences spellbound.

What do you think you can do to develop your confidence and find a way to actually connect with them? Consider a speech, presentation, speaker, or teacher who has really connected with you. What did they do to create that rapport?

*Note: If you are having a difficult time thinking of one, why not take the time to watch some of the most viewed talks on TED Talks?*

### Interaction 3.1: Behaviors of Great Speakers

Put a checkmark next to each behavior great speakers exhibit and an 'X' next to behaviors great speakers never do.

_____ Great pace, not too slow, not too fast

_____ Aware of audience verbal or nonverbal cues

_____ Responded to audience verbal or nonverbal cues

_____ Spoke fast, difficult to grasp information or spoke slow, frustrating to follow

_____ Unaware of audience verbal or nonverbal cues

| | |
|---|---|
| _____ Considered perspective of individual audience members | _____ Did not respond to audience verbal or nonverbal cues |
| _____ Accurately anticipated audience response to the message | _____ Made blanket generalization about groups and/or sub groups |
| _____ Balanced information with explanation | _____ Poorly anticipated audience response to the message |
| _____ Told stories | _____ All information without explanation |
| _____ Got you to think about your stories | _____ No personal stories told, stuck to the facts. |
| _____ Creatively involved audience | |
| _____ Used visuals or props that helped information take form and meaning | _____ Did not ask audience members questions |
| | _____ Spoke to the audience but failed to involve them |
| _____ Creatively incorporated visuals and/or props by engaging audience | _____ Visuals or props distracted from information |
| _____ Carefully considered what to do and how to do it | _____ Poorly incorporated visuals or props |
| _____ Rewarded audience members for response | _____ Shared the content without evidence of careful thought or consideration |
| | _____ Sat down and received applause |
| _____ Expressed gratitude for audience's undivided attention | |

_Answer: left column is checkmarks, right column is 'X's._

Which list of options did you check off? _Hopefully you were able to recognize that the left-handed column presented characteristics of great speakers._

Chances are, the best speakers didn't hurry! Chances are, they had time to listen and respond to your verbal or nonverbal cues. Chances are, they considered your perspective and how you responded to the message. Chances are they considered various options for inflection on specific key words, emphasis and implemented pauses to create affect. Chances are, they didn't fill the entire presentation with information, but shared personal stories and asked questions to prompt you to recall experiences related to the topic. Ultimately, these individuals thought carefully about what to do and how to do it for maximum results with the audience.

But, how did they do it?

This chapter includes scripted strategies to help you become the best speaker you can be. The first step is building a workable vocabulary that allows you to accurately express a speaker's strengths, weaknesses, opportunities, and threats.

# Part 1: Key Words Every Public Speaker Should Know

Every speaker should know the key vocabulary terms in the list below. Familiarize yourself with them. Reminder cards can help cement any unfamiliar words or ideas in your brain. Mastering this terminology will help you accurately evaluate your performance and others. The core definitions were adapted from Merriam Webster Online Dictionary.

*Note: The score is so you can rate yourself and others in the activities described after the vocabulary words. 1 is the lowest, 5 is the highest.*

**Interaction 3.2: Use the Right Word to Rate the Speaker**

**Step 1:** Familiarize yourself with these words.

**Step 2:** Listen to a TED Talk at www.TED.com

**Step 3:** Score the speaker on a scale of 1-5 on how well they illustrated each of these words in their speech. Mark the number on the left space of the Score on the Vocabulary Words.

**Step 4: Self Analysis.** Consider your capacity as a speaker. Using the scoring provided on a scale of 1-5, how would you rate your ability to do each of these well in a speech. Redeliver one of the speeches you have delivered for the first two chapters or evaluate your use of the vocabulary words when you complete the practice speeches at the end of this chapter. Score yourself on the right slot next to each word. On a scale of 1-5, rate your ability to fully realize the opportunity each word offers to enhance your speaking ability. Periodically reevaluate yourself and assess your progress.

**Table 3.1: Vocabulary of Speech**

| Verbal Elements | Definition | Score 1-5 | |
|---|---|---|---|
| | | self | speaker |
| Articulation | Speak clearly, distinctly | | |
| Cadence | Rhythmic sequence or flow of sounds in language | | |
| Emphasis | Intensity, significance or stress that gives impressiveness or importance to something | | |
| Enunciation | Pronounce all syllables clearly | | |
| Language | Specific word choice used. | | |
| Inflection | Change in pitch or loudness of voice; the change of form that words undergo to mark such distinctions as those of case, gender, number, tense, person, mood, or voice. | | |

| Verbal Elements | Definition | Score 1-5 | |
|---|---|---|---|
| Pace | Rate of performance or delivery: Tempo | | |
| Pitch | Difference in the relative vibration frequency of the human voice that contributes to the total meaning of speech | | |
| Projection | Control of the volume, clarity, and distinctness of a voice to gain greater audibility | | |
| Pronunciation | Articulating a sound or word. | | |
| Volume | Degree of loudness or intensity of a sound | | |
| Wording | Act or manner of expressing with words; selected to express a thought. | | |

| Nonverbal Elements | Definition | Score 1-5 | |
|---|---|---|---|
| | | self | speaker |
| Audience connection | Degree to which you cause your audience to focus on your message; created by a combination of mannerisms, poise, leadership, enthusiasm, food, visuals, voice, projection, etc. | | |
| Aura | Distinctive atmosphere surrounding a given source. | | |
| Body Language | Bodily mannerisms, postures, & facial expressions that can be interpreted as unconsciously communicating a person's feelings or psychological state. | | |
| Commitment | Loyalty, devotion, or dedication. | | |
| Confidence | Feeling or consciousness of one's powers or of reliance on one's circumstance; faith or belief that one will act in a right, proper, or effective way. | | |
| Contextual Background | Parts of a written or spoken statement that precede or follow a specific word or passage, usually influencing its meaning or effect, set of circumstances or facts that surround a particular event. The social, historical, and other antecedents or causes of an event or condition. | | |

| | | | |
|---|---|---|---|
| Dress | Choice of clothing. | | |
| Dynamic | Relating to energy; marked by usually continuous and productive activity or change. | | |
| Energy | Vigor, liveliness, and forcefulness. The capacity of a body or system to do work. | | |
| Eye Contact | Act of looking directly into the eyes of another person. | | |
| Facial Expression | Communicates information about emotions. | | |
| Gestures | Form of nonverbal communication in which visible bodily actions are used to communicate particular messages, either in place of speech or together and in parallel with spoken words. | | |
| Manage your "Face" (Face work) | If challenged by your audience, avoid engaging in a tit-for-tat exchange save face by recognizing the challenger and redirecting the focus of the speech in the direction you want. When challenged by one's audience, always handle your response politely & never give away your power as the speaker. (You exemplify leadership for the audience.) | | |
| Pause | Brief suspension of the voice to indicate the limits and relations of sentences and their part; a reason or cause for pausing (as to reconsider). | | |
| Poise | A well-balanced state; easy self-possessed assurance of manner; gracious tact in coping or handling. | | |
| Posture | Way in which someone carries his or her body; body position or bearing. | | |
| Practice | Activities involved in preparing for a presentation, considering not just words but additional elements such as handouts, visuals and other elements. Ready and able to deal with something. | | |
| Proxemics | Space dynamics. Study of how we perceive and use intimate, personal, social, and public space in various settings including awareness and dictates of cultural paradigms. | | |

| Set the Stage | Before you speak a word, command audience attention nonverbally by projecting the significance of your words, through your energy and intensity. | | |
|---|---|---|---|
| Sweeten It | Extend or cause to extend. | | |
| Tone | Used to set the mood; any sound considered with reference to its quality, pitch, strength, source, etc.; quality or character of sound; a particular style or manner, as of writing or speech. | | |
| WIIFM | An acronym standing for, "What's In It For Me?" WIIFM is the stuff that shows how or why what you have to sell or say matters to those who you are trying to sell or say it to. | | |

Simply reading a list of vocabulary words or completing an activity is not enough to develop your public speaking ability. Comprehension and mastery aren' t that easy. Whenever you have the opportunity to hear a speech, think about the words and principles. Flip the channels on the TV or watch videos of speakers on YouTube or other websites. Explore how well or poorly the speakers illustrate the vocabulary words.

## Part 2: 10 Delivery Principles Every Speaker Should Use

How does a poor speaker improve? These 10 Delivery Principles have proven successful in improving the skills of speakers at any level. Review the list of Delivery Principles and their definitions. The Delivery Principles are in a particular order. As you attempt to master each, begin by challenging yourself with the first three Delivery Principles and evaluate your progress. As you master each, move to the next principle. The sample speeches at the end of each chapter are designed to help you develop these principles.

Table 3.2: 10 Delivery Principles

| Delivery Principle | Definition |
|---|---|
| DP1 **Set the Stage** | Start smart. Your speech begins well before your opening words. First impressions matter. Explore each step that leads to the first impression:<br>**Step 1:** Before the speech,<br>**Step 2:** Taking the stage,<br>**Step 3:** Establishing initial audience connection, and<br>**Step 4:** Speaking your first words. Plan accordingly. |

| Delivery Principle | Definition |
|---|---|
| **DP2**<br>**Control the Energy** | Be alert to competing energies unique to each speaking environment. Speaker's energy, audience energy, and room commingle to create a complex dynamic. Anticipate and respond appropriately to create a conducive, receptive environment. |
| **DP3**<br>**Speak Up!** | Engage your diaphragm to speak up. Speaking from your diaphragm ensures that words are fueled by your breath and resonate from deep within you. Over time, speaking from your throat rather than your diaphragm can damage your vocal cords. There is a direct correlation between controlling nervous energy and speaking up. The more you confidently speak, the more confident you feel. |
| **DP4**<br>**Sweeten It!** | Make the speech all that it can be by taking advantage of every opportunity your speech allows. Each speech contains specific opportunities to consciously engage the audience and make the content come alive. Plan ways to capitalize on every opportunity. Look for ways to activate each of the five senses. Implement each delivery principle as well as you can. Most people have few opportunities to stand before an audience and create change…make the most of the opportunity. Guess what? When you plan cool things, you will get excited to share them with your audience. |
| **DP5**<br>**Power of the Pause** | Use the power of silence to solicit a specific response from the audience. Four types of pauses are transitional, dramatic, impact, unplanned. Although they may arise spontaneously, for best effect, plan pauses in advance. |
| **DP6**<br>**Engage, Engage, Engage** | Plan thoughtful ways to keep your audience involved in your presentation prior to taking the stage. The 4 Ps for an engaging speech include personal stories, probing questions, physical activities, and props. |

| Delivery Principle | Definition |
|---|---|
| **DP7**<br>**Use Your Space Wisely** | Study how to take best advantage of different space configurations to solicit the best audience response. Cultural influences create a powerful response to space dynamics within each of us. Breaking cultural norms can be a very powerful way to gain the audience's attention. Your space includes staging various different elements including use of stage, interaction with podium/lectern, movement into the audience, and the placement of the speaker's body in respect to audience. |
| **DP8**<br>**Respect** | Speaking engagements fit into events in a very specific way both in purpose and the time allotted. First and foremost, seek and respect guidelines on time and have an awareness of where the presentation fits into the event. Depending upon the location and cultural nuances at play, you as the speaker should adapt to the specific event context. |
| **DP9**<br>**Dance with Your Audience** | Develop an acute awareness of how each audience member responds to each word, pause and gesture you convey during your speech. Read, respond and react appropriately to fulfill the ultimate purpose for the speech. |
| **DP10**<br>**Have Fun!** | Once you have mastered the other Delivery Principles, have fun. Relax and be "in the moment," able to enjoy and have fun with the experience. The more you remain in the moment, the less anxiety you'll feel, and the more easily you'll be able to actually look forward to your audience appreciating your efforts. |

**DELIVERY PRINCIPLE 1: Set the Stage**

When exactly does a speech begin? Does it begin when you stand up? When you begin speaking? When you walk onto the stage? When you agree to speak to the audience? No doubt, there are various answers to this question, but it is my belief that the speech begins well before you speak your first word. I believe the speech begins when you agree to present to an audience. The audience feels everything that goes into putting the speech together. A quote by Somers White supports this idea, "90% of how well the talk will go is determined before the speaker steps on the platform." Keep this in mind while we discuss this point.

**Before the Speech**

Whenever you enter a room where you will be presenting to an audience, consider the fact that the impression your audience formulates of you begins long before you start speaking. Have you ever seen presenters enter the room with their shoulders slightly slumped, looking a bit disoriented and fumbling through materials while moving toward the front? After taking the stage, they look down at a stack of cards, breathing in, and starting to speak to the cards? How good is this speech going to be? Great? Probably not. How did you know? Nonverbal cues! Herodotus, a Greek historian who has coined many clever quotes, said, "Men trust their ears less than their eyes."

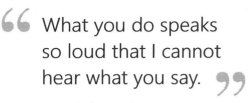

> ❝ What you do speaks so loud that I cannot hear what you say. ❞
>
> *– Ralph Waldo Emerson*

In contrast, have you observed a speaker who is completely prepared as you enter the room? Handouts, props displayed, they greet you with a smile and a nod or "Hi, welcome." As they take the stage, they stand poised, their shoulders back, their eyes looking directly into audience members. When they take that breathe in to begin, they keep that rapport and confidently deliver their first line. How do you think this speech will rate? Excellent? I agree. They showed me before they ever got started.

Nonverbal communication accounts for more of any given situation than the words themselves. So always be careful of what your nonverbal behaviors are saying—especially during meetings or job interviews. First impressions endure, even if you manage to overcome them later. Nonverbal signals important for speakers include factors such as:

1. **Posture:** Does your posture emit confidence or your insecurities? Be mindful of nervous behaviors, such as nail biting or tapping a hand or foot.

2. **Clothing:** Dress professionally as a sign of respect to your audience (unless there is a legitimate reason not to do so—some events require other attire). Clothing is a form of respect. Dressing well and looking your best for a presentation adds credibility and increases your self-confidence. Wear comfortable clothes. This doesn't mean jeans are okay, but don't wear a shirt or slacks that are tight, making you uncomfortable. Wardrobes should always have a "go-to" professional outfit. Hats can interfere with eye contact, and historically have been considered rude for men to wear them inside. Body piercings can distract attention from your intended message.

3. **Hygiene:** In today's society, smelling like cigarettes can definitely distract from your message. Use scents sparingly to avoid irritating those who have allergies or dislike them. Be particularly careful of this during interviews.

4. **Organization:** If you seem frazzled and disorganized, you send the message that you are unprepared and out of control. This is not a strong way to begin your presentation. You will have to work extra hard to change an unfavorable first impression.

5. **Time Management:** Arrive at least an hour before your presentation, even if you cannot enter the room; if you are driving and traffic can be a factor, err on the side of caution. Test any electronics. Arrange props and any associated materials. Never have your audience watch you "get ready." That communicates that you are not prepared and is a sign of disrespect.

6. **Expressions:** Your facial expressions matter. They have a direct impact upon the impression you make with your audience. Monitor them throughout the entire event. Beware of revealing anxiety and stress in your expressions. Smile . . . smiling is huge (provided the tone of the speech permits)! Smiles help the audience feel comfortable and emit a sensitive, caring, and friendly affinity. It is natural and easy to focus on your next words or even your stress—don't let these thoughts control your facial expressions. Breathe, remember to let your face relax and respond appropriately to your audience members.

7. **Eye Contact:** Provide good, clear eye contact. Don't look away from people or stare at the floor or a wall. You want to make eye contact and manage your message. The eyes are windows to a person's soul, so use your eyes to communicate the intangible message of your speech. Let your enthusiasm for your message put a sparkle in your eyes!

8. **Disruptions & Interference:** Be careful that you do not allow any interruptions or interference with the audience's ability to view your beautiful face and eyes. Beware, it happens all the time. For instance someone gets a cute haircut, the cut is designed to reveal a lovely angle. The only problem is it falls across the face, which is fantastic for everyday activities but interferes with the audience's ability to see your facial expressions. Always secure hair out of your face and eyes. Recently, I was delivering a workshop. Each person in the workshop actually delivered a short speech. One of the seasoned speakers had just gotten a darling new haircut, it was quite becoming. When she sat down, I shared this advice. After several other speakers delivered their speeches, another woman with a similar cut delivered her speech, the same thing happened—the hair intruded in the message. Immediately the previous speaker sought me out and said she, "Got it". Speakers with long hair that is not tied back face the same issue. Get your hair out of your face and eyes, give the audience full access.

   If you wear glasses, be sure that they are clean and that they did not slide down on your nose obstructing your audience's ability to look into your eyes. Having worn glasses since elementary school, I know only too well how, amid the fear and anxiety of presenting often our glasses become an after thought, just a natural extremity. It is easy to forget to take stock of how they impact our appearance. Often when I coach speakers who wear glasses, it is difficult to see into their eyes as their spectacles have slid down. In that position, rather than serving as an amplified mirror to a person's soul, it appears to be a line crossing out their eyes. Some glasses are designed to be smaller and stylish with a predominant line right across the top of the brow. Only problem is if they slide down at all, the glasses interfere with a clear view of their eyes. Personally if I can avoid wearing my glasses and opt for contact lenses, I do.

### Taking the Stage

Once you walk into your delivery space (your platform), take charge and own it. You must exhibit leadership skills here so the audience will trust you not to waste their time. Public speaking is the language of leadership; lead your audience. Have the confidence to accept the responsibility you've accepted by addressing the audience directly.

A confident beginning will be easier if you have taken the time earlier to get comfortable with this space. Take the advice in Point 5. Arrive early and get set up so that when it is time for you to address the audience you can fully focus on connecting with the audience. Preparation prevents fidgeting, wrestling through papers and belongings trying to locate cards or thumb drives. Allow plenty of time to set up and test equipment of any sort. Expect that something will go wrong and give yourself time to trouble shoot. The last thing you want after the effort you have put forth for this presentation is to look unprepared and stressed because you didn't get there 15 minutes earlier. If you are incorporating slides, displayed on a projector, never depend upon the internet or local intranet to work—always have your content on a USB drive. Connect the drive to your keys so it doesn't get lost! Finally, print your presentation, be sure to have hand-outs in case the projector fails.

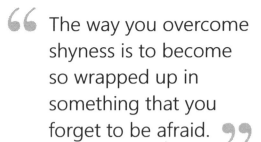

> The way you overcome shyness is to become so wrapped up in something that you forget to be afraid.
>
> – *Lady Bird Johnson*

### Beginning the Speech

Most speakers begin speaking before the audience is ready to listen. Hold on! Wait for them to turn their attention to you. Once you take the space, hold your head up confidently, plant your feet comfortably, and ground yourself. Breathe. Smile. Warmly look into your audience's eyes. Wait for them quietly, without words. When I set the stage, I like to silently ask them if I can "have this dance," meaning when I speak, I plan to lead the audience in a tango with my words. Give them time to stop doing what they are doing and direct their attention to you. Demand their undivided attention. They will give it to you if you wait. We teach people how we expect to be treated. If you move on without everyone's focus, you give the audience permission to not pay attention.

This Set the Stage principle goes beyond the "stage." Every time you address an audience or even a friend, there is internal and external noise that competes with virtually every word you say.

- **External Noise:** External noise would be a cell phone ringing or a lawn mower moving past the window.

- **Internal Noise:** Internal noise is pervasive; people think about all types of things all the time like, "Why does my head hurt? Why did she say that to me? Will I get that check on time to pay my rent? Why did Joe look at me that way? What present should I get for... I wonder if we will... tonight? His or her smile this morning was so..."

  Make no mistake; every time you interact with others, their minds are all over the place, and you are competing for their attention. Tell the audience nonverbally that you spent time and energy to make this worth their while. Multitasking has become a societal norm; holding people's attention increasingly becomes more of a battle—a tug of war. Convey your request for their full attention in every aspect of your body language and request their full attention. They will give it to you. Wait for it... give a pregnant pause and the audience will literally lean forward in anticipation.

### First Spoken Words

Your first words are always the most important words of the speech. They need to convey excitement and evoke curiosity so people will want to keep listening. Many people carelessly begin their speech with meaningless filler words like: " Um... So... Well..." Or they begin without impact, nothing to grab the audience's attention. "Hello, how are you today?" or "Good afternoon" or my personal favorite worst opener, "Today, I'm here to speak with you about XYZ." Put more effort and thought into your first impression (we will discuss some dynamic ways to grab the audience's attention when we discuss the Formula). Deliver your first words with intent. Looking the audience right in the eyes and speaking meaningful words loudly. Memorize your first few lines. Rehearse them well so you can consciously engage the audience by looking them directly in the eyes, speaking loudly, emphasizing key words with a compelling inflection while maintaining body language that is confident, approachable, and open.

When you project your voice, plug in your loudspeakers, and use your diaphragm. Make your vocal inflection interesting. Try saying your first words different ways, using various approaches to your intonation, pacing, and emphasis. Choose which delivery strategy works best. You can even record yourself on your cell phone so you can hear which actually sounds best.

A big mistake that people make is to look down at their cards when they reach the front rather than establishing and maintaining eye contact right away. Know your first line—have it memorized and practiced. Your first words should be strongly projected, filled with energy, designed to solicit their full, undivided attention. The pitch should go up then down. Speak slowly. Your first words are the most important. Once you have spoken, use that dynamic energy to "swing them on the dance floor" with the words you so carefully designed! Enjoy!

If your audience is focused on responding to a text or otherwise occupied, they will miss key information from the introduction you worked so hard to develop. Imagine your speech as a plane taking off. The plane can't leave the boarding gate until everyone is buckled into their seats. Your audience should be buckled in when your speech begins! You don't want them disoriented and trying to catch up as you progress through your introduction and body. If you nail your opening, the rest of your speech is set up for success.

Consider how this parable relates to your approach to your speech.

---

### TWO WOLVES

*An old Cherokee told his grandson:* "There's a battle between two wolves inside us all. One is **evil**. It's anger, jealousy, greed, resentment, inferiority, lies and ego. The other is **good**. It's joy, peace, love, hope, humility, kindness, and truth."

*The boy thought about it and asked,* "Grandfather, which wolf wins?"

*The old man quietly replied,* "The one you feed."

---

This parable highlights why Setting the Stage makes all the difference. When you begin your speech with confidence and control, standing poised, establishing direct eye contact with your audience members, speaking clearly with pauses and vocal variation you "feed" the positive emotion for a "good delivery". As a result, your confidence will grow. If you begin your speech driven by fear, allowing anxiety to sabotage delivery by causing slumping, looking down, speaking too fast, rocking from side-to-side, or not waiting for your audience—you will "feed" that intent throughout the rest of the speech. Setting the stage correctly allows you to feed the good wolf!

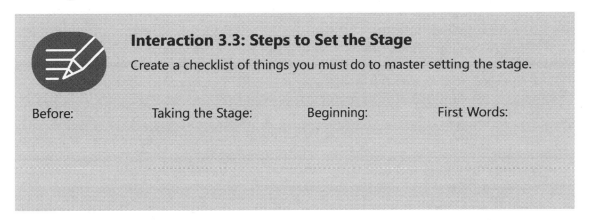

**Interaction 3.3: Steps to Set the Stage**

Create a checklist of things you must do to master setting the stage.

Before:                Taking the Stage:              Beginning:              First Words:

### DELIVERY PRINCIPLE 2: Control the Energy!

Energy management is crucial to the speech process, and controlling the energy within the room while giving a speech is one of your chief responsibilities as a speaker. You must assess and manage the variables you observe. Your energy is the vigor, liveliness, and forcefulness that drives your message. The audience also has energy, and you must be able to monitor the energy level of your audience while simultaneously managing your own. Perhaps this sounds complicated, but you do it all the time. Essentially, energy is life, and without it, you are dead! Any time we're around other people we react to each other's energy.

Think back to a time in childhood when you came home and walked into the house. Can you recall having an overwhelming sense that something was terribly wrong? Instead of assessing the situation and naturally greeting whoever was usually there, you quietly tiptoed to your bedroom. Perhaps you offered to help prepare dinner instead of just asking, "What's for dinner?" Instinctively, you knew...something was wrong! You just hoped that it was nothing you did! You also knew better than to antagonize your guardians or give them an opportunity to turn that negative energy in your direction.

Sometimes the opposite happens. Have you ever gone to meet a friend and without even looking at their face, you knew they were ecstatic and something fantastic had happened? You assessed the situation and responded accordingly. But how exactly can we make these predictions? Body language and nonverbal cues obviously play a part, but your friend's energy permeated the room—you felt excitement and enthusiasm without speaking a word. A person cannot exist without their energy. Our energy vibrations protrude around our bodies—indeed, others feel them.

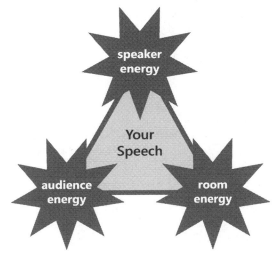

In any given speech, several different types of energy need to be harnessed.

### Room Energy

The dynamics of the room also impact the energy of the presentation. If you have anything to say about it, do everything that you can to find the perfect space for your presentation, a space that would satisfy Goldilocks.

- **Size:** A space that is too large for the group makes it difficult for you to fill the energy of the room without overwhelming the audience. It also makes the event feel unattended and unsuccessful. A crowded room is uncomfortable for everyone.
- **Temperature:** Find out who controls the temperature of the room in case you need to alter the temperature. If a room is hot, stuffy, or cold, it is harder to hold your audience's attention. If you know a room will be cold or hot and have no control, warn the audience members.
- **Lighting:** As you learned in the last chapter, lighting influences the energy of the room. Low lighting reduces the energy; bright lights increase it. Keep the light as bright as you can, even if you use slides to support your presentation. You are the presenter. You should be the focal point of the presentation. Be sure to use a light background and dark text on slides and a projector with enough lumens to be visible by the audience. If you show a short video clip, turn the lights off and focus completely on the clip, then turn them back on right away.
- **Beware:** Lowering or turning the lights off during your presentation invites people to sleep or daydream without being caught.
- **Set Up:** Consider the arrangement of the furniture in the space. Which design is best suited for this presentation? Speaking at a round table in a conference room rather than facing rows of seats from the front of the roomwill influence your presentation style. In this scenario, you probably have less movement, but you are closer—part of the group. Adapt your presentation style to the room arrangements and use each to your advantage.

Always find out as much as you can in advance about variables that influence the presentation. Request a description of the room from your contact for the speech and discuss any special arrangements that may be possible and desirable. Accommodate your audience whenever possible. Few things can disrupt the energy of your presentation more than an uncomfortable environment.

### Speaker Energy

This is the energy you, the speaker, emit to the audience. What can influence your energy?

- **Your energy related to the presentation:** Your excitement, enthusiasm or belief you have in the topic or the audience receiving the message. Your confidence level in presenting the content. The degree of anxiety you feel.

- **Your energy related to other factors:** Personal situations like your health or well being that day can affect your energy during a presentation. A family or work crisis can be draining. Perhaps you ran into traffic and arrived later than planned.

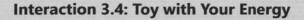

### Interaction 3.4: Toy with Your Energy

Stand up with your feet shoulder width apart. Hold your arms out with your palms facing each other. Take a deep breath. Slowly let it out. Close your eyes and slowly, very slowly, bring your palms together. As you move your hands toward each other, concentrate on what you feel. Do you feel a slight resistance? Are the inside of your palms growing slightly warm? How about a little tingly feeling? As your palms move closer, the resistance might increase. Play with it; see if you can mold it into an energy ball. Continue to push your palms together and actually push the energy into yourself.

What you've just experienced is your personal energy; the energy surging through your body that keeps all of us alive. This energy is your life force. Your body has an energy field some refer to as your aura. Scientists know that the aura exists because it can be measured with advanced technology called bio-electrography (Jacka, 2011).

### Audience Energy

- **Collective Energy:** Each audience has a collective energy, a personality that develops by the sum of its parts. As a speaker, it is your responsibility to be aware of the energy of the group—you will have to interact with your group's personality. As soon as you enter a room, begin your assessment. Put little feelers out. Do people seem stressed, bored, excited, engaged, or disengaged? Notice the dynamics, the norms, the common or shared objects—a nametag, uniform or the way, group members introduce themselves.

  *Note: An audience member who begins rummaging around, texting, avoiding eye contact with the speaker, and obviously paying little attention, distracts other audience members and harms your ability to deliver your best speech. When you are in the audience yourself, pay attention, be respectful and support the speaker by being receptive to the message. A negative attitude from one audience member can change the dynamic of the entire group and the outcome of the presentation.*

- **Individual Energy:** Each person in the audience is unique. Sometimes you find real gems. These people help advance your message, while at times others may seem compelled to impede it. Obstructive people are often seeking recognition. Give it to them! As you observe the group, take note of the extroverts or those individuals who stand out—there is a good chance they will make themselves noticed during your presentation, that engagement will either help or hurt your presentation. If you have the chance ahead of time, introduce yourself, ask them a question, and look for ways to include them by acknowledging them at an appropriate point during your message. This is a great way to get them on your side using their energy to support and enhance your message rather than distract.

  Questions come from individuals. If you open yourself up to questions, take time to think before responding. Repeat the question to yourself, be sure you don't jump to conclusions too soon, or too emphatically. So many times as an instructor or workshop facilitator, someone asked a question and I responded reflexively... and incorrectly! I made an assumption based on what I thought they meant, and I was just wrong. Stress can cause your mind to reach false conclusions about the purpose of the question. This tends to happen more often with groups of people you know. If this happens, don't be afraid to own your error, take responsibility and say, "I'm sorry, I totally misunderstood the question!" To prevent misunderstanding, reflect a question back to the person who asked it. "What did you think it meant?" or "Could you repeat the question? I want to be sure I understand." Then smile.

**Merging the Energy**

Remember Charles Humes' statement "Every time you have to speak, you are auditioning for leadership." Your responsibility as the speaker is to lead the group. How can you get the collective energy of the room to support your direction?

First gauge your own energy level. Next, gauge the energy level of the audience and the room. Your energy level must be higher than that of the group, but not too high. Each time you face an audience, you have to know where their energy is and gauge the level of energy you project to them accordingly. Ideally, you want the audience to increase their energy level until it reaches yours. Have you ever been in an audience where the speaker's energy was lower than the audience's? The audience probably was zoning out! As a result, they derived little benefit from the presentation. When the speaker's energy sinks below the audience, you've lost them for the balance of the speech. Always control the energy of the room.

**Does Your Anxiety Interfere with your Ability to Control the Energy?**

If your anxiety level seems to control you, precluding you from controlling your own energy or the energy of any audience member, try this.

1. **Focus on Audience:** Practice the "Secret" for overcoming anxiety: get over yourself. Think about your audience receiving your message than your own nerves.

2. **Test each tip to reduce your anxiety level.** (These tips are located on page 41 in Chapter 2.)

3. **Deliver a few speeches.** How? Where? Attend one of our workshops either virtually or in person. Our workshops run periodically, check our website for the latest offerings: www. yourbestspeechever.com. If you complete the certification series, you will have delivered five speeches! I guarantee that your anxiety level will decrease simply as a result of your body becoming familiar with the experience of being in front of an audience. Take a public speaking class or join an organization like Toastmasters that is there to help you develop your public speaking skills.

4. **Master the Set the Stage Principle!** The Delivery Principle of Set the Stage requires that you control your energy before you begin your speech. If you work through the steps of Set the Stage, your ability to control your energy will increase … I promise!

**How to Control Shaking**

If you suffer extreme anxiety, you may be thinking but what if I'm shaking? How can I control my energy? The answer is to **go bigger** with your movements! Consider this, if your leg is moving… walk to the other side of the audience with intent. If you do, your leg will no longer be shaking. You went bigger than the nervousness, and took control of your energy. The same works for your hands. If you notice your hands shaking, make larger hand gestures and then you will be in control of them movements. If the speech does not allow for movement, direct the excess energy into your voice. Lead actor Michael J. Fox from the legendary movie,

*Back to the Future*, suffers from Parkinson's disease. With his organization he is dedicated to finding a cure from Parkinson's disease through aggressively funded research. He starred in the hit series *Spin City* despite his disease. He would shake, but if you observed him, his movements were large and exaggerated. He jumped over a couch or circled a desk with his hands stretching back and forth in front of him. In this way, he was able to control the tremors or perhaps override the tremors with a larger movement, thus gaining a sense of control.

Gauging your energy level effectively during your delivery is vital. If you let the energy fall too low, you risk losing the audience to boredom, internal noise or even sleep; if it is too high, you risk losing them because they refuse to take the leap up to where you are—they may even think you're a bit nuts. The more I teach energy level, the more I realize how it directly connects with the next principle, Speak Up.

### DELIVERY PRINCIPLE 3: Speak Up!

Where is your message coming from? Allow it to resonate from deep within you. The deeper it resonates from within you, the more it becomes your own. I find that as a coach, if I ask the speaker to speak up, their energy level automatically increases, and their presence fills the room more fully. Speak your message and plug in your body's loudspeaker: your diaphragm. If you speak with shallow breaths, it sounds shallow—there isn't enough breath to project the words so the throat muscles are used. Practice breathing deeply from your diaphragm, is your message resonating deep within you or at a surface level?

> Speak clearly, if you speak at all; carve every word before you let it fall.
>
> – *Oliver Wendell Holmes, Sr.*

Having coached thousands of developing speakers, I'm amazed at how this one simple tip helps individuals push through their fear. Speaking up increases your energy, and amazingly,

**Figure 3.1: Speaking from the Diaphragm**

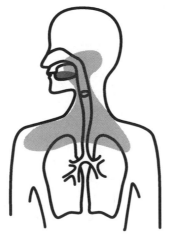 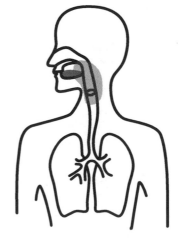

**Speaking from the diaphragm**
sound areas: upper chest, vocal chords, and back of mouth

**Speaking from the throat**
sound areas: throat and upper neck

fear subsides! Nervousness washes away and you are able to channel your anxiety to work for you. It empowers you! Expand…go big!

When you speak up, you open your diaphragm. As a result, your whole body expands, and your posture is more confident. Conversely, shrinking, retracting, and mumbling typically result from fear and anxiety. By concentrating on opening your mouth, breathing deeply, and speaking up, you will move into the confidence zone.

Pay attention to your diction as you speak! Take care to enunciate and pronounce each word distinctly. Pronunciation involves saying the word correctly with the appropriate stress and intonation. Enunciation involves stating something clearly—think of it as expressing something one syllable at a time.

### Interaction 3.5: Are You Speaking from Fear or Confidence?

**Try this physical experiment.**

*Version 1:* Adopt a posture that projects fear. What happens to your body? Do your shoulders slouch and head move forward and down? In this position, say, "This will be my best speech ever."

*Version 2:* Now adopt a posture that projects pride and confidence. Remember Amy Cuddy's Power Poses we discussed in Chapter 1? Stand like Wonder Woman or Superman! Can you feel your shoulders move back, head up? Now say, "This will be my best speech ever."

**Question:**
1. Which version had you Speaking Up more?
2. Which version had you believing more in your pronouncement?

Isn't it amazing how a change in our posture can cause us to project a completely different emotion? Besides adopting "power poses," how do you project your voice? Increasing your volume requires exerting more energy. Focus on this relationship between your volume level and the energy you exert to speak. Raise your energy level and your projection naturally follows (unless you are intentionally trying to whisper). Connecting with your diaphragm and breathing deeply gives you more breath to empower your words.

One trick to determine if you are using your diaphragm is to punch yourself in the stomach—if you keel over, your diaphragm is not engaged. This may sound extreme, but when I speak to an audience, you can haul out and punch me in the gut and my voice will not even shake. When I'm "Speaking Up," my diaphragm is engaged and the muscles are able to withstand the assault. During workshops, if I hear someone speaking from their throat without engaging their diaphragm, I demonstrate this technique and punch them in the gut—it works!

Some suggest imagining an orange in your throat, so your throat widens allowing more sound and air to flow through it. I have found that if you reach forward and hold your heels (preferably while sitting in a chair) you force the air out of your stomach and you can feel it pass through your throat from your diaphragm. This can help you become aware of where your breath should originate. Many vocal therapists suggest an activity that involves lying on your back with your knees up, placing your hands underneath your belly button and breathing deeply. The point here is to engage your diaphragm to experience "belly breathing."

Focusing on breathing correctly can also calm your nerves—just don't hyperventilate! When you are breathing more deeply, your posture improves and your words are stronger as they're coming from deep inside you—amazingly, your confidence increases.

Another trick that tends to immediately connect you with your diaphragm is to envision someone you love standing inthe middle of the street; your voice is the only thing that can make them aware of the oncoming bus about to hit them. What do you say? "WATCH OUT!!!" In that moment, where did that message originate? Hopefully, from deep within you! Find that place and practice speaking from there.

You can easily conduct a search on the internet to find countless more techniques to speak from your diaphragm. There are numerous resources available online to help you work on your ability to project. Projecting well is a prerequisite for speakers, actors, and singers. Search the Internet for 'Using Your Diaphragm Exercises' and/or 'Articulation and Diction Exercises'.

**Resources to Develop Your Vocal Ability**

**Delivery Principle: Speak Up!** https://www.youtube.com/watch?v=9JvYqs9KL90&spfreload=10 Video Link:

- https://www.youtube.com/watch?v=9JvYqs9KL90&spfreload=10

**Using Your Diaphragm Exercises:**
- http://messagemasters.squarespace.com/articles/speak-from-the-diaphragm.html
- http://www.wikihow.com/Sing-Using-Your-Diaphragm
- http://www.trainingzone.co.uk/topic/soft-skills/can-you-hear-me-back-practical-tips-projecting-your-voice
- http://www.wikihow.com/Talk-With-a-Deeper-Voice
- http://choirly.com/how-to-breathe-with-your-diaphragm/

**Articulation and Diction Exercises:**
- http://www.quickanddirtytips.com/business-career/public-speaking/diction
- http://procw.hubpages.com/hub/voice-warmups
- http://www.weheartdrama.com/63/vocal-exercises-tongue-twisters/

*Note: At the time of this printing, these links were live. Should any become inactive, search with key words like "project your voice", "diaphragm exercises", "articulation and diction" to find additional information.*

Respect the power of words. Treat them with care. I like to envision that my words are like "balls", my mouth like a pitcher propelling the words to the back wall, over the heads of my audience members. Never project words into the ground or into notecards or a paper. Words have energy, and they need to carry across the room and reach the back wall so the entire audience can experience the energy from them.

## DELIVERY PRINCIPLE 4: Sweeten It!

Have you ever heard the saying, "Sweeten the Deal"? Essentially that means, "Make a bargain or a business transaction more appealing by adding value to the transaction." This principle also speeches. Make your speech more appealing by packing it full of value for your audience. Allow me to explain.

### Interaction 3.6: Name that Tune!

Name a song you think everyone, from 9-99 years old, knows and likes.

Remember the simple children's song, *Row, Row, Row Your Boat*? Over the years, I have asked thousands of people, from all different places, that same question. Most have heard the song.

Interestingly enough, when I go around the room and ask individuals what their favorite song is, and then ask the other audience members if they have heard the suggested song, few have any idea of what the song is. So, what makes this song so widely known by diverse audiences representing various cultures, age groups, and backgrounds? Undoubtedly, there are many reasons, but it is a children's song! There are many children's songs, but few are as easily recognizable by such diverse audiences as this one. It is repetitive, true, but many repetitive songs are easily forgotten. It must be something more! I think it stands the test of time because they sweetened it! They made the song all it could be.

Sing this song and notice the monotony of the first line. "Row, row, row your boat gently down the stream."

**Figure 3.2: Song Row, Row, Row Your Boat**

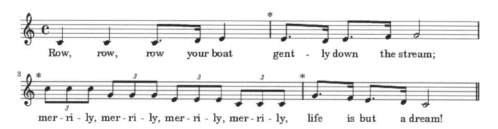

Just when you are about to tune out—"BAM!"—The entire tempo changes; it speeds up, and gets downright exciting! "Merrily, merrily, merrily, merrily, life is but a dream!" If this song only had the "row, row" part, I venture to say it would be forgotten and never heard of again. Equally so, if the song had only the "merrily, merrily" part, it too would be forgotten. The two together combine perfectly to make the song all the song that it can be!

Each speech has an array of constraints and opportunities dictated by the specific event. Constraints might include the time allowed, the availability of technical devices (slides), the nature of the event, tone, time, topic, and, of course, the audience.

**Applause:** Some speeches call for applause, lots of it. Coming from the United States, one situation that stands out to me is the State of the Union address, which purposefully tries to evokes applause from all sides of the aisle: Democrats, Republicans and Independents, although that can be harder in these partisan days.

**Timing:** Some topics and goals can be covered and achieved in a five-minute speech, while others require more time. Timing is also important and the length of the speech determines what you can do and how much you can do within it. Culture can also affect perceptions of time. Some cultures operate faster, some slower. Consider audience culture to determine how you do what you do. You should never try to fit more into a speech than time allows. This causes unnecessary stress to everyone: you, your audience and the event coordinator.

> 66 All you need is something to say, and a burning desire to say it… it doesn't matter where your hands are. 99
>
> *—Lou Holtz*

**Tone:** Some topics or situations are susceptible to some techniques (e.g. humor and levity) while others are not. For instance, consider Lincoln's famous Gettysburg Address. He delivered this speech to memorialize the brave men whose blood was shed in the goriest battle on U.S. soil. Given its purpose, a serious tone was warranted. This speech will never warrant applause; it is solemn. Remarks at a funeral will differ from those at a wedding; a different tone is set.

**Locations:** Some locations will limit what you can and cannot do. Often times a toast at a wedding occurs in the middle of the dance floor, with no podium or lectern or projection system. In this scenario, you can't display baby pictures of the bride. If you have access to technology, it can add another dimension to your presentation. If not, you must contend with what you have and make accommodations, but sometimes what might seem like a limitation, can actually turn into an opportunity.

Your job as a speaker is to make the most of each situation that arises. This is what I refer to as, "Sweeten It." Let the speech be all that it can be!

Your tone, inflection, rate, and emphasis all speak volumes to your audience. Author and Coach Raju Mandhyan once said, "If the eyes are the windows to your soul, then your voice is the music that bursts from your soul." Constantly work at improving vocalization and adding rhythm and timing to the way you speak.

A speech of introduction can vary dramatically, depending on circumstances of the introduction and the nature of the person being introduced. The options available to you will differ depending upon the purpose of the speech. During an introduction in a casual or informal setting, you may be able to include a picture of the person in their youth, maybe even doing something slightly embarrassing. A more formal introduction would depend more upon the words than visual tools, maybe even a video (keep it short) highlighting their life's accomplishments.

When it comes to "Sweeten It", consider all of the possibilities. Body language is huge! Move your arms, move your legs. For instance, if you are demonstrating raising your hand, raise your hand—high, not half way. Amplify movements: reach high, reach low! Don't be afraid to incorporate the floor. In one workshop, to emphasize a point I literally got down on my knees, bowed down and kissed the ground. Doing something unexpected like that stirs audience energy, intensifying attention. Surprise tactics like that emphasize important points, making them memorable.

People sometimes ask about hand gestures. American football player and coach Lou Holtz stated, "All you need is something to say, and a burning desire to say it…it doesn't matter where your hands are." When you are truly committed to your message and audience, the message springs naturally from your body. Hand gestures instinctively follow as passion flows.

To really *sweeten it*, try considering how to incorporate other multiple senses—here are a few ideas.

---

### Ways to "Sweeten It"—Use Your Senses

**Touch:**  Tactile involvement adds another dimension to your speech. Challenge yourself to find a way to have audience members touch something during the presentation. The method can cover the gamut from interacting with a prop, to physical interaction like having audience members shake hands, to role-play with each other, to collecting a reward or gimmick for participation. Reward participants with an object, perhaps promotional. Money works like magic for gaining an audience's attention.

**Smell:**  Provide food, like fresh baked cookies or other foods that smell great. It may work to spray scents on paper and pass them around—(ask audience members about possible allergies). Visualization is another way to incorporate smell. For example, prompt the audience to think of a smell that represents a point of nostalgia for them. Simply mentioning the smell of something as you speak triggers olfactory involvement.

**Taste:**  How can you incorporate taste into your presentation? Using a treat to reward the audience for participation or retention works well. Did you know that just the thought of a treat motivates many audience members to pay much more attention? Never forget the power of the palette—our taste buds! If you can offer a tasty treat to participants, audience members appreciate the gesture. It can make an adequate speaker more memorable!

**Sight:**  What can you do to show the audience intriguing sights? Is there an image or cartoon that illustrates a point, adding impact and maybe a laugh? Can you use an interesting prop or even a short clip from a movie to serve as an attention grabber or to highlight a point, or serve as an example?

**Sound:**  You may be able to play non-disruptive background music before the program starts, or play a short music clip at some point to add drama. Audio clips with a short saying can emphasize a point. One of my favorite ways to incorporate sound is to plant a sound (ringing phone, cartoon character's tag line, or short music clip) by using a buddy who blends in with the audience. This technique serves to merge sound and your use of space, which we will discuss shortly.

---

Imagine what a speech could be if all the senses were incorporated. Research supports that such effort not only makes the content more interesting but more memorable as well. Cuban (2001) found:

**1%** of what is learned is from the sense of **taste**

**1.5%** of what is learned is from the sense of **touch**

**3.5%** of what is learned is from the logic of **smell**

**11%** of what is educated is from the logic of **hearing** and

**83%** of what is learned is from the sense of **sight**.

It stands to reason that putting forth the effort and incorporating these senses is a bonus for your audience.

### Interaction 3.7: Sweeten It

1. Think of the speeches you have heard. What is the best example of one where the speaker creatively, made the speech all that it could be?
2. What did they do to "sweeten it"?

Imagine you are delivering the following speeches. What could you do to sweeten the speech and incorporate several senses?
   a. Introduction speech for Willy Wonka.
   b. Speech about why marriages fail.
   c. Speech about how to paddle board.
   d. Safety speech about how to respond in a crisis to a hurricane.

Perhaps you thought of ideas like these:
   a. Sound & Sight: Song Pure Imagination from Movie, Taste & touch: Willy Wonka candy with a golden ticket.
   b. Touch/Sound/Sight Role Play: Two participants act out marriage vows, while wedding music plays. Taste & smell wedding cake.
   c. Sound/Song Surfin' Safari, Touch/sight: paddle board, life vest, paddle. Taste/smell tropical juice drink or pineapple.
   d. Sound: Emergency broadcast system. Touch/Smell/Sight 72 hour survival kit (include treats) flash light, radio.

### DELIVERY PRINCIPLE 5: Power of the Pause

Sir Ralph Richardson, who ruled the British stage in the mid-20th century, stated, "The most precious things in speech are the pauses." Agreed. When used correctly, pausing may be the most effective strategy you can use to capture audience attention. In a sense, it's a form of teasing or "finessing" the audience. When eloquently executed, the audience literally anticipates your next words. But far too often, speakers rush to fill the silence with nonsensical noise, "like, um, er, huh!" Robert Byrd, a long serving Senator from West Virginia, known for his orations, discussed the use of pauses or lack thereof, on the Senate floor, (Saffire, 1991). Byrd said to his colleagues, "I think there can be an art in the use of a pause. And I find nothing wrong with a pause. It does not have to be filled with "you know." This pestiferous phrase betrays a mind whose thoughts are often so disorganized as to be unutterable—a mind in neutral gear coupled to a tongue stuck in overdrive." Wow! Eloquently stated. Practice pausing on and off the stage; prefer to pause rather than spout nonsense.

**Figure 3.3: Types of Pauses**

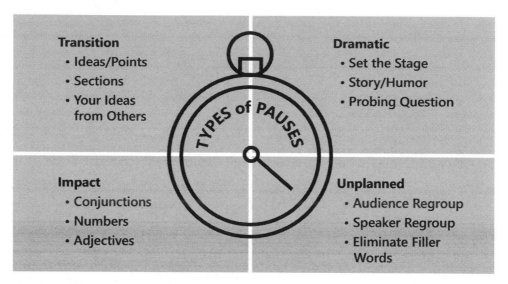

Pauses also emphasize what you just said by giving the idea an extra second to sink in. Your facial expressions, especially raising your eyebrow devilishly, can help the audience process your words. Pauses convey emotion and energy. Effectively used, they communicate authority or status, enhancing your leadership role. Ultimately, your ability to mindfully pause, intentionally adding emphasis to your words, turns your speech into a form of dance with the audience.

Overdramatic pausing is an abuse of your power. Mark Twain (1903) emphasized the significance of pauses in his essay, *How to Tell a Story*, "The pause is an exceedingly important feature in any kind of story, and a frequently recurring feature, too. It is a dainty thing, and delicate, and also uncertain and treacherous; for it must be exactly the right length—no more and no less—or it fails of its purpose and makes trouble." So how long should you pause? That depends upon your purpose; we pause for different reasons for different times.

### 1. Transitional Pause

Transitional pauses are shorter. They are used between thoughts to allow the audience to process and absorb the information. Pause...then change the inflection of your voice slightly as you begin your next thought. Use pauses of varying lengths between sentences, points, and even words. It is crucial to let your audience know you have finished with one thought, idea, and point and are now progressing to the next. Use them even with transitional phrases to emphasize the shift.

> ❝ The right word may be effective, but no word was ever as effective as a rightly timed pause. ❞
>
> —*Mark Twain*

### 2. Dramatic Pause

Dramatic pauses, also referred to as pregnant pauses, are intentionally used to add impact. Although the pregnant pause, which is "full of meaning," is often used to "accentuate a comedic event" or to give the impression that "it will be followed by something meaningful." When you are speaking, there are many scenarios where a bit of drama will add impact. Your next point must reward the audience with something worth their attention. This type of pause can take two to six seconds, depending on what you expect from your audience.

> **Well-timed silence hath more eloquence than speech.**
>
> *– Martin Fraquhar Tupper*

- **Set the Stage:** Always use an exaggerated, dramatic pause as you Set the Stage. Continue the pause after you have established eye contact, while you silently request complete audience attention. Hold that moment while they wait for your words. Cherish it—you will literally see your audience lean forward in anticipation. Then begin speaking.

- **Humor:** Use a pause when there is a secondary meaning that will take the audience a moment to get. Smile, wait, and raise your eyebrows.

- **Probing Questions:** This type of pause prompts the audience to think after you ask questions and is a great way to involve them. Their stories are often more interesting than yours. Get them to connect their stuff with your thoughts. Touching your chin (like The Thinker) at this point opens space for them to process their thoughts.

*Note: Be sure that when you employ the long pause, what you have to say is worth the wait.*

### 3. Impact Pause

Often, I use the impact pause to emphasize specific words in a speech. I generally seize the opportunity to add emphasis using my voice and that exaggeration typically includes a pause or at least the word being elongated for instance, "aand" between conjunctions, numbers, adjectives, and pronouns. A vocal variation typically accompanies the pause. I think of my voice as riding a roller coaster. Combining pauses with vocal variety prevents a monotone delivery. Be aware whenever a conjunction, number or adjective leaves your mouth pause and vary your voice! For example, using one of the most memorable lines from Winston Churchill's 1940 *Blood, Toil, Tears, and Sweat* speech, you would pause and vary your voice at each of the conjunctions, numbers, adjectives, and pronouns. Read this statement emphasizing and pausing on the appropriate words.

"You ask, what is our policy? I can say: It is to wage war, by sea, land and air, with all our might and with all the strength that God can give us; to wage war against a monstrous tyranny, never surpassed in the dark, lamentable catalogue of human crime. That is our policy."

These pauses are short—they take between half a second and a second.

### 4. Unplanned Pause

This type of pause can be used in an array of scenarios and serve different purposes. These pauses can take between two to six seconds.

- **Audience Regroup:** Occasionally, if you feel energy of the audience waning. Feign that you forgot a word, and are searching to find the right one. In most situations, the audience will come to your aid and supply the word you were fighting to remember, thus providing a vibrant feeling to your speech.

- **Speaker Regroup:** You can also use this if you become flustered or have confused thoughts. Sometimes just stop. *Pause.* Take a breath. Let your mind catch up to your mouth. You are human. Your audience can often better relate if they see your humanity rather than perfection. Many speakers instinctively try to bluster through. Bad idea! It's usually a swift decline from there. Just stop. *Pause.*

- **Eliminate Filler Words:** Replace the filler word habit with pauses to let yourself grasp the right word. We discussed filler words in the previous chapter. Avoid them. They dilute your message. Learn to pause when stressed rather than speak.

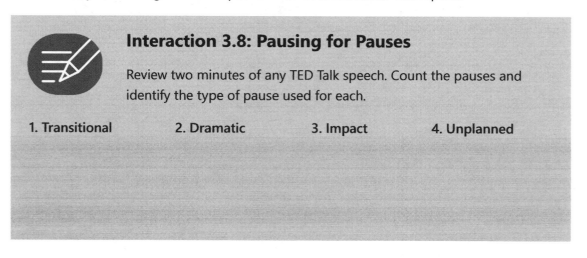

## Interaction 3.8: Pausing for Pauses

Review two minutes of any TED Talk speech. Count the pauses and identify the type of pause used for each.

**1. Transitional**      **2. Dramatic**      **3. Impact**      **4. Unplanned**

### Delivery Principle 6: Engage, Engage, Engage

**Decode the graph**

In this example, the graph speaks volumes of what happened in the speech.

**Figure 3.4: Delivery Graph**

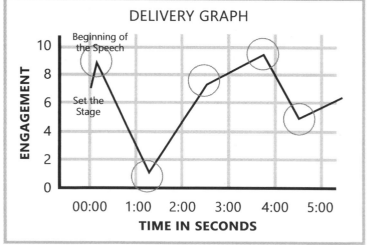

**0:10**   Asked a probing question.

**1:20**   Speaker lost their place, got flustered but regrouped (that's the huge drop).

**2:30**   Prop to illustrate a point.

**3:50**   Told a story.

**4:30**   Got off topic and just started going in circles.

Use a graph to identify the strongest and the weakest moments of a speech. Get clear on why those moments were significant. This information is tremendously helpful in providing relevant feedback to speakers. Carefully analyze what happened to cause the dips and peaks in the graph. In almost every instance, the strongest moments (the peaks) are those where the speaker consciously reached out to connect with the audience. How does this occur?

*Note: You will see the 4 Ps several different times in this book. For instance, here we are laying down a specific principle to engage your audience. In Chapter 4, applying this principle is crucial to making your visuals work for you and finally this principle comes alive when we incorporate it into the Speech Formula in Chapter 7. When you see this content, please don't feel as if I'm being repetitive, rather it is that important. Integrating the 4 Ps is a vital tool in making your speech great.*

### Probe: Ask engaging questions!
- Provide ample time for audiences to think and respond (at least mentally).
- Evoke personal memories that connect them to the subject at hand.

### Personal Story: Tell your story.
- Relating a personal story that " shows a little leg" involves vulnerability and creates connection. Invariably when you open up to the audience, they respond with empathy A self-deprecating joke can often solicit a response.
- Include story specifics: who (names), what, where, when, why, and how.

### Physical Activity: Move two or more people
- Get at least two members of your audience out of their seats. You get a bonus if you get the entire audience to stand and move.
- Calling on specific audience members to respond or asking audience members to engage with the content in some way works well too. Opportunities abound for involving the audience with your content in some creative way.
- Have volunteers hold signs, participate in role-plays, play games, or help in other ways.

### Prop: Object promotes your points
Bring in a tangible object related to your topic and use it as a prop. But think twice before passing it around. Use it to enhance your message rather than distract from it.

The important point here is making the effort to create that rapport and engage your audience. Can you see that in each of these scenarios, the engagement was a "planned" event? Meaning that as a part of the speech development process, the speaker consciously considered how to engage their audience and incorporated these strategies to ensure a dynamic connection. When using the formula to create the speech, you will need to select one of these strategies for each idea you have to keep your audience engaged at every point!

### Interaction 3.9: Which Speech is Better?
Suppose you are delivering a basic speech introducing yourself. This group meets to advance your interest in your hobby—like photography or sailing or even Toastmasters. Do a short speech of introduction about yourself.

Consider which of these two speech versions you would prefer to use.

*Version 1:* A straightforward speech responding to the questions below.

1. State your name.
2. Describe who you are—where you are from, cultural background, current role, or place within an organization.
3. Provide a background—how did you come to be a part of this group? Why?
4. What is the most interesting thing about you? What is your primary interest, goal, or particular passion—specifically as it relates to this group.
5. Is there anything the group should know about you? A great talent, hobby, accomplishment, or pet peeve?
6. What do you hope to gain from the group? Why?

*Version 2:* Engages your audience using each of the 4 Ps.

| Personal Story: | Probe: | Physical: | Prop: |
|---|---|---|---|
|  |  |  |  |

Which Speech would be more effective? Version 1: No Engagement or version 2: Engaged Speech?

## DELIVERY PRINCIPLE 7: Use your Space Wisely (Proxemics)

### Consider Proxemics. Place Yourself in the Right Space.

Have you ever been at an empty movie theater and had someone come sit in the same row? You may have thought, "The whole theater is empty, why sit in my row?" Especially if you live in the United States and even more so if you are from Netherlands! The reason the agitation occurred is due to proxemics or your perceptions of space. For some cultures, the norm would be to fill the row first for it to be complete. Still other cultures find closeness, even with strangers comforting—they don't seek their own space. When it comes to a speech, it is important to consider how to use space to create emphasis and avoid distractions.

Formal speeches, such as a funeral tribute or introducing someone to an audience, demand that you remain behind a lectern. In these instances, the focus should be on the person the words are about, not the speaker. Free use of space indicates ownership. If the words are not yours, or the space is being lent to you, don't act like you own it. For instance, if I am introducing someone, it's their space not mine. If I am repeating someone else's words, I stand still and give the original author the respect of their creation—I don't move about as if the space were mine. When you are the featured speaker, assuming it's appropriate to the setting and occasion, you are free to claim the space and move around. There's a huge difference between a lectern placed at floor level with the audience and a raised platform. Also, with larger audiences microphone cords can limit your movement. However, I encourage you to always consider how you can use space to gain audience attention.

**Figure 3.5: Proxemics**

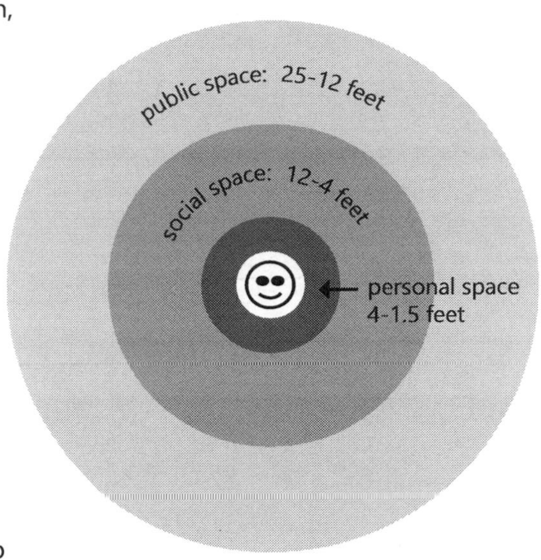

One of the best ways to "grab" the audience's attention is to disrupt the "spatial" norm. If someone is not paying attention and you are able, simply move toward them, then lightly touch them, their chair or their desk. You will immediately get their attention. According to Edward T. Hall (1976), our minds instinctively react to behavior patterns affecting proximity—in other words, we are aware of our territory. Your use of space and proximity to your audience speaks volumes. Our comfort levels and use of space spring from cultural norms. In the U.S., spatial norms are described below:

**Table 3.3: Relative Distance Between People (Hall, 1976, p.41)**

| Public space | 12 to 25 feet range | The distance maintained between an audience and a speaker (in a formal setting). |
|---|---|---|
| Social space | 4 to 12 feet range | Used for communication among business associates, as well as to separate strangers using public areas, such as beaches and bus stops. |
| Personal space | 18 inches to 4 feet | Used among friends and family members. Another example would be between people waiting in lines. |
| Intimate space | out to 18 inches | Involves a high probability of touching. We reserve it for whispering and embracing. |

*Note: These rules differ by culture.*

Imagine a female speaker moving freely around the audience. She begins speaking on the stage some 12 feet from the audience. As she continues speaking, she moves toward the audience, strolling into their space, occasionally taking a seat, peering into an audience member's face, asking a question, entering their personal space. What is the speaker doing in this situation? By engaging with the audience in this way, cultural norms are broken and the audience becomes uncomfortable. As a result, the audience may innately listen more carefully and become concerned when called on. Besides Hall (1984), Hampden-Turner and Trompenaars (1993 & 1997) also include space (proxemics) as one of their dimensions to help decipher cultural codes.

As an audience member myself, the most incredible use of space I have ever witnessed was when I experienced my first Cirque du Soleil show, Mystère.

As you come into the theater, you find your seat. As you wait for the show to start, a clown starts messing with the audience. Show reviewer Aleza Freeman warns potential show-goers "Hold on to your popcorn!" That's the first rule of Mystère—if you don't, it will likely end up everywhere except in your mouth. Second rule: Don't trust the clown. Otherwise, you might end up like the popcorn, anywhere but in your seat. Third and final rule (once you find your assigned seat—with or without the clown's assistance): Sit back, relax, and enjoy the performance of a lifetime.

Having a wicked interest in the theater, I was amazed and shocked at how Cirque de Soleil manipulated proxemics to create an interesting and compelling audience connection resulting in a phenomenal performance. To this day, I'm in awe! The beginning of the show is so simple; a guy in a clown suit eats audience members' popcorn. Sometimes he throws popcorn at audience members, takes the popcorn for real and dumps it over someone's head, or gives it to some hungry-looking bloke! Then the clown moves audience members around as he sees fit.

If the clown thinks that a particular girl would look better with a particular guy, he moves her, taking her by the arm and transporting her to a new seat where he rearranges the existing inhabitants. The audience members are in shock, unsure of how to respond to these broken laws of proxemics. They simply follow the direction of the clown, finding themselves sitting next to some stranger. Rumor has it that since the show began in 1993, the clown's antics have led to five marriages! As an audience member, even though I witnessed incredible feats that defy the human imagination throughout the show, this simple strategy of breaking the rules of proxemics affected my senses the most! Bravo, Cirque de Soleil! Well done.

If the speaking environment limits your physical movements, use your words to go into the audience. Request specific feedback from audience members on the last row. Ask a particular audience member to stand up. If you can include unexpected disrupters that are planted in your audience to creatively add to your presentation, do so. If you have the opportunity to challenge proxemics and enhance your speech, do it!

## Interaction 3.10: Space Dynamics

**Consider the last presentation you heard.**

What might the speaker have done to further engage the audience by considering his or her use of space?

What are the four different stages you need to consider before you begin a speech?
What are the three types of energy to consider?

What does the respect principle refer to exactly?

What must you do prior to attempting DP10: Have Fun?

## DELIVERY PRINCIPLE 8: Respect the Time, Event and Cultural Influences

When someone invites you to speak, always be aware of and respect the time frame, event, and cultural influences. Ignorance is not an excuse. To be effective, ask any questions you need to know about the group and the event. How do you perceive time? How structured is your time? Is your datebook or daily schedule a vital part of your moments? Now consider your reactions to time. If someone is ten minutes late, are you peeved, or do you shrug it off? Whatever your response, time is a powerful communication tool and helps "set the stage" for communication. Time perceptions include punctuality and willingness to wait. We will wait longer for people we respect and will not leave them waiting for us!

The rate of speech and how long people are willing to listen also speaks volumes. Did you know that the timing and frequency of an action, as well as the tempo and rhythm of communication within it, contribute to the interpretation of nonverbal messages? Cultures perceive time very differently. In American and European cultures, we see time as linear; whereas, many other cultures see time as cyclical, thus giving birth to the terminologies monochromic (one time) and polychromic (many times) societies. Edward T. Hall (1976) shed light on much of this area of study by spending years identifying and explaining specific cultural nuances including time and space.

Have you ever heard the phrase "Island time?" A few years ago, I visited the U.S. Virgin Islands for a day and a half. The trip was impromptu and costly, but I seized the moment. I was stressed and anxious, but determined to make the most of my time. That presented a challenge. When I arrived at the resort, it was apparent that there was a huge cultural divide between our perceptions of time. From my perspective, the staff seemed to take as much time as possible to check us in. . .saying "Hi" to everyone, engaging in (what appeared to me to be) meaningless small talk with anyone and everyone who seemed to pass through the lobby.

My body, on the other hand, which had not had a chance to adapt from my crushing workload, was conscious of each tick of the clock on this short vacation. The wait was agonizing, and my anxiety level rose with each tick! It literally took several "lime in the coconuts" (tasty cocktails) to reduce my stress to a normal level and change my internal clock to "island time." The staff at the resort simply thought differently about time. They thought I was crazy for stressing "over nothing." As my waiter told me, "Ya can't change it, mon!"

In case you didn't know, there is actually a word depicting the study of time as it relates to nonverbal communication—chronemics. When it comes to time, never underestimate the importance of timing to an audience. Keep these things in mind as you work on mastering timing.

### Distorted Time

Many people find that time seems exaggerated while standing in front of an audience. A simple second can seem like a minute. Even the best of speakers will misjudge time in front of an audience. This is normal. Try to understand how distorted your perceptions are. Most of the time the more stress or anxiety you experience, the more distorted your perception. As a result, the inexperienced speaker races through his or her speech. What happens when a speaker speaks too quickly? The audience doesn't absorb the message nearly as well. In my opinion, a well-executed speech should have no more than 125-135 words per minute. Less is more! Don't be afraid to cut down your words. Allow the words to have enough time to sink in so the audience can absorb them. Believe it or not, you can convey more information by slowing down than by speeding up. As an added bonus, your audience will remember it more, too!

### Respect

Never exceed the agreed amount of time for your speech. Remember, when you are asked to speak, there is a fixed allotment of time you are expected to adhere to and it is crucial that you respect your segment of time. To not do so is rude and disrespectful to the audience, the event organizers, and any other speakers involved. A lot of planning and organizing is involved in gathering a group of people for an event. The time commitments of the group deserve respect, no matter how important you believe your message to be. It is vital for you believe in the value of your message, but not at the expense of others. If you go over, you put audience members in an awkward position—they start looking at their watch, concerned and stressed about time. If this occurs, they have stopped listening to your message and are focusing on their internal noise.

When you are an invited speaker, you may not realize that the organization has a set schedule. For several years, I was the Program Chair for the Broward Chapter of the National Association of Women Business Owners (NAWBO). This group has been meeting on the first Monday of every month for twenty-seven years. The meetings schedule is set in stone. Speakers asked if they could have more time. No. They could not. Respecting the organization's structure builds more rapport with the group than asking them to vary their set schedule. Less is definitely more. Furthermore, there are times where you may not be given the amount of time you were promised because the schedule was altered. Should that situation arise, you have no alternative but to respectfully accept the change—you are the guest.

The concept of time involves many variables from cultural nuances to perceptions of time, which vary from speaker to the audience, to the organization. At the core is respect for time. Malcolm X stated, "In all our deeds, the proper value and respect for time determines success or failure." When it comes to delivering a speech, value time from the perspective of all stakeholders. Should you be in a group with different cultural norms about time, let's say Island Time, and people stroll in and out at seeming random, roll with the punches. Keep smiling and forge ahead.

### Interaction 3.11: Check Your Time

1. What cultural perspective do you have on time?

2. If you are invited to a party, what time do you arrive?

3. Does the organization where the speech is being given adhere to M (monochromic) or P (polychromic) time?

### DELIVERY PRINCIPLE 9: Dance with Your Audience

Speaking is an exquisite dance with the audience serving as your dance partner! You must feel the rhythm and respond instinctively to their movements. It is your responsibility to lead them, so you must know the routine inside and out! Make the dance fun and interesting with dips and turns. You must keep the pace and modify it with any forgotten footwork along the way. If your toes get stepped on, keep going, with a smile on your face. This is a dance, experienced together—not a jig performed alone. When you respond and the audience responds to the rhythm of your words, it is quite fulfilling.

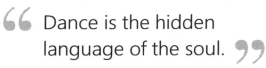

> **Dance is the hidden language of the soul.**
>
> *– Martha Graham*

Dancing with your audience is different than engaging with them. Engagement results from conscious decisions about how and when to involve your audience during your speech. You plan engaging activities or interactions ahead of time. Dancing is spontaneous! How can you "dance" with your audience? If you have worked toward mastery of Delivery Principles 1-8, you are ready to practice this dance.

The dance begins with an acute awareness of how your audience is responding to each pause and each word you say. Notice the order of those two words. The audience reaction to the pauses speaks volumes. Think about the nonverbal response that occurs during a conversation. When someone speaks, you look them in the eye and your nonverbal signals indicate whether you received the message. Perhaps you nod your head to indicate consensus or tilt your head with a perplexed expression on your face signaling that you didn't understand. Your audience will provide you with similar signs. Obviously, the most significant is eye contact. If the audience does not look you in the eye, that typically indicates a problem. No being able to look your audience in the eye is an even bigger problem.

To reach this level of interaction, you must be able to project your voice, control the energy, pause for impact, and engage your audience. If a speaker is fumbling, trying to secure their footing with those basic principles, they can't move to master the intricate footwork many dances require. The key to dancing with your audience is mastering the art of reading your audience. Restate a question if you sense they didn't hear or understand it the first time. Validate consensus before you move on to another point. As the leader, you must choose the right pace for your particular audience.

Pay attention. Use your senses. Relax and let your message soar through your body and enjoy the experience. The dance occurs in the moment—but awareness of the choreography is necessary for it to go smoothly.

### Interaction 3.12: Engage or Dance?

What is the difference between dancing with your audience and engaging them?

Dancing with the Audience: Think of a time when you were in an audience with a speaker who danced with you. How did that feel? How did it work?

Engage, Engage, Engage: What about engagement? Can you describe the difference?

*Answer: Engagement activities are planned ahead of time. Dancing with the audience happens live, during the speech.*

**DELIVERY PRINCIPLE 10: Have FUN!**

It sounds simple enough, but having fun while giving a speech is more difficult than it may seem. Having fun with your words and your audience requires that you master the other delivery principles so you can relax enough to "be in the moment."

To deliver a speech well requires genuine effort on your behalf. Do the work to prepare and become confident, then relax and reap the benefits. Enjoy your time in front of the audience. Look at those faces and savor the moment!

Have fun with your audience, and they will have fun with you. Don't forget to smile when the mood allows. You may not become comfortable enough to relax and enjoy the audience until you've given several speeches. It takes time to become comfortable with yourself, your strengths and your weaknesses. But in time, you will relax and have fun. Be willing to laugh at yourself, appreciate the unexpected things that always arise during a speech. Take the speech seriously—respect your audience by giving them a message worth hearing—but don't take yourself too seriously. Enjoy!

These delivery "Tricks of the Trade" are sure to enhance your performance, in front of an audience. You don't need to buy any high priced "magic potions." As you begin to incorporate these ideas into your performance, you will see immediate results and will transform your ability to deliver a speech. Each time you deliver a speech, review to these strategies to ensure you are implementing them.

> ## We aim above the mark to hit the mark.
>
> – *Ralph Waldo Emerson*

## Chapter 3 Review Questions

1.  Without looking, list as many words as you can that relate to public speaking.

2.  List the 10 Delivery Principles.

3.  Describe speaker behaviors that can cause the audience to disengage and speaker behaviors that cause the audience to engage.

4.  Which delivery principle do you think will be the easiest for you to master? Why? Which will be the most difficult? Why?

5.  Which four words should always have a pause and vocal variety added?

6.  Which quote from this chapter resonates with you the most?

## Practice Speech: Famous

**Time Limit:** 90 seconds

**Target Audience:** Given your desire to develop your public speaking skills, you decide to compete in the Speeches from History competition at the County Fair. The audience ranges from old folks to kids, family to strangers, and the judges. It is set in an outdoor arena where the horses were shown earlier in the day. You do have a microphone, but face competition from noise in other parts of the fair.

**Instructions:** History is filled with moments when someone has formulated and presented a speech worthy of recognition.

- Locate a 45 second excerpt (three to five sentences only) from a fantastic speech in history— words that influenced others. Make sure the topic matters to both you and your audience.
- Provide a context for the speech, explaining why you chose that specific one and why it's relevant to your audience. You can begin with the speech itself or an introduction explaining why you chose it. If you use an introduction, keep it less than half the length of the original text.
- Practice deliberately incorporating the 5 Tactics for Practicing a Speech.
- Record yourself delivering the speech.
- Reflect on your delivery, identifying your strengths and weaknesses. Open yourself to the process of improving your ability to communicate.

**Purpose:**

1. Incorporate the "Ultimate Secret" in overcoming your speech anxiety. Consider your audience needs more than your own.

2. Deliver iconic powerful words that changed lives. Appreciate their worth. Consider the historical significance lying behind those words. Harness this awareness to empower your voice.

3. Establish a Deliberate Practice focusing on the first three Delivery Principles. Make it your stretch goal to master DP1: Set the Stage. Mastery of DP1 involves effectively using DP2: Control Your Energy, and DP3: Speak Up.

4. Record yourself delivering the speech.

5. Reflect on your delivery, identifying your strengths and weaknesses. Open yourself to the process of improving your ability to communicate.

**Skills to Practice:** Ultimate Secret to Overcoming Your Fear. DP1: Set the Stage, DP2: Project Your Voice, DP3: Assess and Cope

**Resources:**
- History Channel: http://www.history.com/speeches
- History Place: http://www.historyplace.com/speeches/previous.htm
- American Rhetoric: http://www.americanrhetoric.com/speechbank.htm
- Gifts of Speech: http://gos.sbc.edu

## Sample Speech: "To Be Fed" originally delivered by Oprah Winfrey

**Interpreted by Alexis Kent**

Context: When Alexis Kent submitted this speech for her Famous Speech assignment, she did the assignment perfectly. She found a speech that spoke to her and proceeded to plug into the needs of her audience. How did she make this happen? She asked a few pertinent questions to get the audience on board—pay attention to the ones she chose for the beginning of the speech. While there are more "iconic" famous speeches, Alexis makes her selection relevant to the audience by providing a meaningful context. Be sure you do likewise. This personifies the Ultimate Secret in overcoming your speech anxiety: thinking more about the audience's needs than your own.

**Introduction:** Think about this, coming into this class for the first time and introducing yourself to everyone sitting in the audience. How many of you were concerned about the first impression you made? What they would think about you? People, by nature, want to feel **accepted** by everyone because, well, how many people really want to be **disliked**? **Oprah Winfrey** delivered this speech after receiving the first **Bob Hope Humanitarian Award** at the **Emmy Awards** on September 22, 2002. I located this speech on Alchin's (2011) database of speeches. This is what Oprah said about the **homeless** people her father brought to family gatherings:

**Speech Excerpt:** And I would often say to my father afterwards, 'Dad, why can't we just have **regular** people at our **Christmas** dinner?' . . . And my father said to me, 'They are regular people. They're just like you. They want the same thing you want.' And I would say, 'What?' And he'd say, **'To be fed.'** And at the time, I just thought he was talking about dinner. But I have since learned how **profound** he really was. . . we all just want to know that **we matter**. We want **validation**. We want the **same things**. We want **safety** and we want to **live** a long life. We want to **find somebody to love**. . . We want to find somebody to **laugh with** and have the **power** and the **place to cry** with when **necessary**.

**Conclusion:** This speech resonates with me because I, just like everyone in this room, want to find that person to **share everything with**. So, just think before you **judge** a book by its **cover**. **"We all just want to be fed."**

**References:** Alchin, L. (2011, February 16). Oprah Winfrey speech: 54th Emmy awards. Retrieved from http://www.famous-speeches-and-speech-topics.info/famous-speeches-by-women/oprah-winfrey-speech.htm

*Note: The bold words were selected by the speaker for emphasis.*

## Practice Speech: Movie

**Time Limit:** 60–90 seconds

**Instructions:** What is your favorite speech from a movie? The golden screen has a way of capturing some incredible speeches that deeply move us. Locate a short excerpt of a monologue or speech from a movie that stands out to you. Loosen up and deliver the speech with the same energy and passion as the speaker from the movie. Relax and have fun!

Target Audience: Adopt the audience from the movie scene you select.

**Purpose:**

1.  Deliver iconic powerful words captured on screen. Appreciate their worth. Use the preselected words to empower your voice.

2.  Focus on the first three Delivery Principles. Make it your goal to master DP1: Set the Stage. Since DPI, DP2 and DP3 are inherently intertwined, mastering DP1 will also satisfy the requirement for mastering DP2: Speak Up, and DP3: Assess and Cope.

3.  Record yourself delivering the speech.

4.  Reflect on your delivery, identifying your strengths and weaknesses. Open yourself to the process of improving your ability to communicate.

**Skills to Practice:** Continue to focus on mastery of DP1: Set the Stage, DP2: Control the Energy, DP3: Speak Up. Use your body to communicate your message—facial expressions, hand gestures and movement.

**Resources:**

American Rhetoric: http://www.americanrhetoric.com/moviespeeches.htm

Film Site offers a database of over 700 of the Best Film Speeches and Monologues. http://www.filmsite.org/bestspeeches.html

## Sample Movie: *Remember the Titans* (2000)

**Coach Herman Boone: Gettysburg Speech**

**Background:** *Remember the Titans* is set during the time of segregation; an all white and all black school are closed down forcing the two schools to become T.C. Williams High School. At the start of football season the head coach, Coach Boone, takes the players on a trip to Gettysburg so they will learn to trust each other and get along. Coach Boone wakes the players and other coaches at 3:00 in the morning and runs the team several miles to the site of Gettysburg. These are the words he speaks to inspire his team.

**Speech Excerpt:** Anybody know what this place is? This is Gettysburg. This is where they fought the Battle of Gettysburg. Fifty thousand men died right here on this field, fightin' the same fight that we're still fightin' amongst ourselves today.

This green field right here was painted red, bubblin' with the blood of young boys, smoke and hot lead pourin' right through their bodies. Listen to their souls, men:

'I killed my brother with malice in my heart. Hatred destroyed my family.'

You listen. And you take a lesson from the dead. If we don't come together, right now, on this hallowed ground, we too will be destroyed—just like they were. I don't care if you like each other or not. But you will respect each other. And maybe—I don't know—maybe we'll learn to play this game like men.

## Practice Speech: Introduction

**Time Limit:** 60 seconds

**Instructions:** Choose a famous person or character and introduce them to your audience. When you introduce someone to an audience, you are typically the conduit. Meaning you have a relationship with the speaker and the audience knows you. Research the person's life and identify the biggest highlights—be sure to include where you found your information. Seek to connect the speaker's highlights, achievements, or insights to the audience's interest or concerns. Not only does this build speaker credibility, but also creates interest for the audience. Begin with an engaging first line and end your speech with a big build such as, "Put your hands together for..." or "Give a warm welcome to..." Keep the audience in suspense, even if they know who the guest is; don't reveal the name of the person until you announce their name at the end, build the excitement for a big crescendo. Whomever you select, be sure to conduct some research about them and share with your audience where you obtained the information.

**Audience:** You serve on a board of your favorite non-profit. This is the big sponsorship gala of the year. The guest speaker is the highlight of the evening and you have the pleasure of introducing the individual to the crowd.

**Purpose:** Make this speech all that it can be. Be creative, incorporate some fun ideas to make the content come alive. Sweeten It—consider every way to make this speech surpass expectations and add Wow Factor".

**Skills to Practice:** DP4: Sweeten It, DP5: Power of the Pause, DP6: Engage, Engage, Engage.

## Sample Speech

Chances are you have welcomed our guest for this evening into your house on many occasions. No doubt, he has delighted your family and friends—he might even have become a regular member of the household as he has mine. Just this morning my five-year-old proclaimed, "What a treat!"

**He** giggled his **way** into the world in **October** of **1965** created by Rudy Perz (Goodsell, 2011). He is a whopping **14 ounces** and a **lengthy 9** inches. Inventors' expert Mary Belvis (2015) reports that he "originates from Minneapolis, where he lives with his wife, **Mrs. Poppie Fresh**, along with their **two** children Popper **and** Bun Bun."

He is a famous **spokesperson**, icon, mascot, **and** trademark for his **company**. He has been seen in over **600** commercials, advertising more than **50** products. He has been **an** opera singer, rapper, rock star, poet, ballet dancer, and **even** a skydiver (Goodsell, 2011).

His website reports (Goodsell, 2011) that he receives over **200** fan letters **per week**, this superstar has been honored with several awards **including**, "Favorite Spokesperson", "Toy of the Year" **and** "Favorite Food Product Character."

He is **not** considered a very smart **cookie**; he often **wastes** much of his **dough** on **half-baked** schemes. Even though he was a **little flaky** at times, he is still considered a **roll** model for millions.

His most famous quote (Belvis, 2015) is... **"Nothin'** says **lovin'** like **bakin'** in the **oven!"** Ladies and gentleman, please give a "Whoo Hoo" for the Pillsbury Doughboy!

*Note: The bold words are selected by the speaker for emphasis.*

*Note: Notice how citations inserted throughout the speech make the speech more credible.*

# References

Cuddy, A. (2012, June) Amy Cuddy: Your Body Language Shapes Who You Are [Video le].
Retrieved from https://www.ted.com/talks/amy_cuddy_your_body_language_shapes_who_you_are

Cuban, L. (2001). Computers in the classroom, Cambridge, M.A. Harvard University Press.
Retrieved from http://www.webpages. uidaho.edu/mbolin/akerele-afolable.htm

Eidenmuller, M. E. (n.d.). Remember the Titans (Gettysburgh Speech). Retrieved April 15, 2017,
from http://www.americanrhetoric.com/MovieSpeeches/moviespeechrememberthetitans.html

Hall, E.T. (1976). Beyond culture, New York: Doubleday.

Hall, E. T. (1984). The dance of life : the other dimension of time. Garden City, N.Y., Anchor Press/
Doubleday.

Hampden-Turner, C., & Trompenaars, A. (1993). The seven cultures of capitalism (Currency
Doubleday, New York).

Herodotus (n.d.) BrainyQuotes.com. Retrieved March 18, 2017, from BrainyQuote.com Web site:
https://www.brainyquote.com/quotes/quotes/h/herodotus379319.html

Humes, J. C. (1993). The Sir Winston method: the five secrets of speaking the language of
leadership. New York: Quill/William Morrow.

Jacka, J. (2010, April 02). The human energy field. Retrieved July 19, 2017, from https://explore.
scimednet.org/index.php/2016/04/02/the-human-energy-field/

Lou Holtz Quotes About Desire. (n.d.). Retrieved April 19, 2017, from http://www.azquotes.com/
author/6852-Lou_Holtz/tag/desire

Lady Bird Johnson Quotes. (n.d.). Retrieved April 19, 2017, from https://www.brainyquote.com/
quotes/quotes/l/ladybirdjo105138.html

Lewis, J. (n.d.). Retrieved April 19, 2017, from http://www.wisdomquotes.com/quote/ralph-waldo-
emerson-84.html

Malcolm X Quotes. (n.d.). Retrieved April 19, 2017, from https://www.brainyquote.com/quotes/
quotes/m/malcolmx385603.html

Mandhyan, R. (2016). The heart of public speaking, 2nd ed. CreateSpace Independent Publishing
Platform.

Martha Graham Quotes. (n.d.). Retrieved April 19, 2017, from https://www.brainyquote.com/
quotes/quotes/m/marthagrah379056.html

Oliver Wendell Holmes, Sr. Quotes. (n.d.). Retrieved April 19, 2017, from https://www.brainyquote.
com/quotes/quotes/o/oliverwend122641.html

Dictionary. (n.d.). Retrieved April 19, 2017, from https://www.merriam-webster.com/dictionary/
dictionary

Ralph Richardson (n.d) Azqutoes.com. Retrieved March 14, 2017 from http://www.azquotes.com/
quote/602438

Safire, W. (1991, June 16). On Language; Impregnating the Pause. Http://www.nytimes.
com/1991/06/16/magazine/on-language-impregnating-the-pause.html. Retrieved March 19,
2017.

Trompenaars, F. and C. Hampden-Turner (1997). Riding the waves of culture : understanding
cultural diversity in business. London, Nicholas Brearley.

Twain, M., & Twain, M. (1903). The writings of Mark Twain. How to tell a story and other essays.
Hartford, CT: American Publ. Co.

United States Department of Labor (n.d.). Retrieved April 19, 2017, from https://www.osha.gov/pls/
oshaweb/owadisp.show_document?p_table=STANDARDS&p_id=10630

# Chapter 4:
# Make Visuals Count

## Objectives

**By the end of this chapter you should be able to:**

1. Compare the value of visuals for presenters vs. the audience.

2. Identify your preferred learning style.

3. List the top mistakes people make creating their slides.

4. Explain why visuals are necessary in presentations.

5. Apply the $C^2$ARES Concept using a content slide.

6. Call on audience members using WPPR (Word, Point, Probe, Review).

**Part 1:** The Value of Visuals

**Part 2:** Learning Styles Differ

**Part 3:** Slides Help You Share Content

**Part 4:** Mistakes People Make

**Practice Speech:** Interacting with Visuals

> ## Everything is important— success is in the details.
> – *Steve Jobs*

## Chapter 4
# Make Visuals Count

When it comes to incorporating visuals in a speech, the sky is the limit! To paraphrase Henry David Thoreau's words, "A speech is but a canvas to the imagination." Visuals are the paint that colors the canvas. Visuals come in many different forms, employing many different dimensions.

### Interaction: Presentation Preference

Question: Which of the following presentations would you prefer to attend?
A. Lecture only
B. Lecture supplemented with slides including images and short video or animation
C. Lecture with demonstration
D. Lecture with audience interaction including props
E. All of the above

In this survey, the respondents overwhelmingly chose B and E—none chose A. It seems like a no-brainer, right? Who wouldn't prefer all that engagement rather than just lecture? If this is the case, why is it that so few presentations actually include all of the strategies listed? A speech is a lot like entertaining. If I have twenty guests, my responsibility, as their host, is to indulge them on every level. All bases must be covered, from hors d'oeuvres, entrees, drinks, entertainment, and even décor. Now that's a party. Each part of a speech requires the same attention to detail. As Steve Jobs said, "Everything is important—success is in the details."

Many people who don't entertain are clueless about the planning and preparation involved in pulling off a good party. It is the same with speeches—they take a lot of planning and preparation, and visuals are part of it.

This chapter is all about **making your visuals work for you rather than against you.**

# Part 1: The Value of Visuals

**Variety of Visuals: So many choices, so little time.**

Slides are definitely the most popular type of visuals used in presentations, but don't ignore other types of visuals that can add and extra Wow factor.

**Interaction: Explore how visuals are used in speeches.**

For each type, answer:

1.  Have you seen this type of visual used in a speech or presentation? Yes/No

2.  Did the visual work effectively within the speech? Yes/No

3.  How often have you seen this type of visuals in a presentation? 1 not very often, 5 commonly used.

4.  Have you every used this type of visual in a presentation? Yes/No

Table 4.1: Variety of Visuals

| Type | Example | Description | Seen | | Worked | | Frequency | Used | |
|---|---|---|---|---|---|---|---|---|---|
| | | | Yes | No | Yes | No | 1 to 5 | Yes | No |
| **1D** | **One Dimensional** | | | | | | | | |
| | **Visualization** | Getting the audience to close their eyes and envision what you tell them to think. | | | | | | | |
| | **Audio** | Frequencies corresponding to sound waves that can be heard by the human ear. | | | | | | | |
| | **Light** | Flashing or blinking lights or lights that change color. | | | | | | | |

| Type | Example | Description | Seen | | Worked | | Frequency | Used | |
|------|---------|-------------|------|------|--------|------|-----------|------|------|
| | | | Yes | No | Yes | No | 1 to 5 | Yes | No |
| **2D** | | Two Dimensional, having length and width, but no depth. | | | | | | | |
| | **Video** | Animations: dynamic visual medium produced from static drawings, models, or objects that are rapidly sequenced together. | | | | | | | |
| | | Clip (cutting): a portion of the whole. | | | | | | | |
| | | Trailer: a short promotional film composed of clips showing highlights of a movie. | | | | | | | |
| | | Talking head: recorded video of one or more people discussing a topic. | | | | | | | |
| | | News: content portrayed from a news organization. | | | | | | | |
| | | Self-Made Video: recording and editing designated for a defined audience. | | | | | | | |
| | **Internet** | a vast computer network linking smaller computer networks worldwide. | | | | | | | |
| | | Websites: pages of content portrayed by a specific sponsor. | | | | | | | |
| | | Internal software designed and written to fulfill a particular purpose of the user. | | | | | | | |
| | **Slides** | Rectangular surface containing content prepared for viewing on a screen. (Static) | | | | | | | |
| | | Too much information (sentences & even paragraphs). | | | | | | | |
| | | Too little information (one word slides). | | | | | | | |

| Type | Example | Description | Seen | | Worked | | Frequency | Used | |
|------|---------|-------------|------|------|--------|------|-----------|------|------|
| | | | Yes | No | Yes | No | 1 to 5 | Yes | No |
| | **Slides (cont.)** | Just the right amount (combination key words brief descriptions, 4 words/4 lines.) | | | | | | | |
| | **Images** | Optical counterpart or appearance of an object. (Static) | | | | | | | |
| | | Printed: produced by applying inked types, plates or the like to paper. | | | | | | | |
| | | Projected: to cause (a figure or image) to appear, as on a background. | | | | | | | |
| | **Charts/ Boards** | Allows for viewing and input. (Dynamic) | | | | | | | |
| | | Flipchart: a set of sheets, such as a cardboard or paper attached on top so they can be flipped to show information. | | | | | | | |
| | | White/Chalk Board: smooth surface that can be written on with colored markers or chalk. | | | | | | | |

| Type | Example | Description | Seen | | Worked | | Frequency | Used | |
|------|---------|-------------|------|------|--------|------|-----------|------|------|
| | | | Yes | No | Yes | No | 1 to 5 | Yes | No |
| **3D** | Three Dimensional, having length, width and depth. | | | | | | | | |
| | **Model** | Representation of a larger item. | | | | | | | |
| | **Objects** | Anything that is visible or tangible and is relatively stable in form. | | | | | | | |
| | | Support: Objects used to represent an idea or concept. | | | | | | | |
| | | Real: Demonstration of original object discussed. | | | | | | | |
| | **People** | Testimonial: Share personal experience. | | | | | | | |

| | | | Seen | | Worked | | Frequency | Used | |
|---|---|---|---|---|---|---|---|---|---|
| Type | Example | Description | Yes | No | Yes | No | 1 to 5 | Yes | No |
| | **People** | Role Play: Act out a scripted scene. | | | | | | | |
| | | Volunteers: Interact with content. | | | | | | | |

| | | | Seen | | Worked | | Frequency | Used | |
|---|---|---|---|---|---|---|---|---|---|
| Type | Example | Description | Yes | No | Yes | No | 1 to 5 | Yes | No |
| **4D** | Four Dimensional | | | | | | | | |
| | **Time** | 3D that changes over time: an action with a 3D object. For example, swinging a bat, throwing a ball. | | | | | | | |

From among the multitude of choices at your disposal, decide which type of visual will work best in your presentation. Your selection will dramatically influence your presentation.

**The Case of Two World Travelers**

I once had the opportunity to hear two different people speak on the same topic in consecutive 15-minute talks. One presenter was a woman and the other, a man. They had not collaborated beforehand and had no idea what the other speaker would present. I was amazed at how different each talk was in both content and audience approach.

The woman made an emotional appeal. She probed the audience, used props, and told an engaging personal story. Her presentation focused on the human element. She engaged the audience by relying on cool props and interesting stories. It was a well-delivered speech. However, she missed the opportunity to design the speech with clear points and a purpose that offered the audience a take-away.

The man used a slide show to assist his speech. He planned and executed his presentation logically, with excellent audience analysis, clear points, and purpose. He started with a big picture overview and then moved on to technical details before showing more of the human element to the story. His slide show had amazing pictures that helped support his words. However, he failed to engage the emotional side of the audience using the various dimensions available.

Both speeches were equally well received by the audience.

Afterwards the speakers had a chance to talk together in private. They both complimented each other, each speaker commenting that the other speaker had made a better presentation.

This story lends me to three observations about how speakers connect differently with audiences:

1. Men and women tend to approach speaking tasks differently (yes, that's a big generalization). Men in general tend to be more organizational and technical while most

women tend to appeal more on an emotional level.

2. Neither speech on its own had all the elements of a great speech. Had they coordinated and combined their speeches they could have had a home run.

3. Good speakers want to connect with their audience. How we do that will differ from person to person. Don't be afraid to step out of your comfort zone and take a risk in order to better connect with your audience.

# Part 2: Learning Styles Differ

**Visuals Can Help You Accommodate Different Types of Learning Styles Represented in Your Audience**

Different types of learners respond to similar stimuli in different ways, thus they need to see and experience content in different ways. Your challenge as a speaker is to accommodate the needs of your audience. Let's explore how an individual's preferred learning style impacts comprehension and retention.

**What's Your Learning Style?**

**Visual**    **Auditory**    **Tactile**

Each audience member has a unique preferred learning style, some visual, some oral and some kinesthetic. Do you know what your preferred learning style is? The list below includes online quizzes designed to determine your preferred learning style. Each approaches the modalities somewhat differently. Try them to see which helps you best understand how you interpret information.

---

**Tests to Determine Preferred Learning Style**

- Educational Planner: http://www.educationplanner.org/students/self-assessments/learning-styles-quiz.shtml

- VARK: http://vark-learn.com/the-vark-questionnaire/

- VARK Description: http://www.gardner-webb.edu/Assets/gardnerwebb/academics/advising/files/vark-learning-styles.pdf

- Learning Styles and Strategies (Felder & Soloman):

- https://www.engr.ncsu.edu/learningstyles/ilsweb.html

- Multiple Intelligences Self-Assessment: https://www.edutopia.org/multiple-intelligences-assessment

---

Beyond your preferred style, how dominant is that style? Like you, each audience member has a specific style and degree of dominance. You have a greater chance of getting through to them, if you consider the array of learning styles represented in any given audience.

Some learners see things sequentially, others globally. You can accommodate various types of learners by incorporating multiple strategies. Tap into a variety of learning styles in each presentation. Using several strategies also reinforces your message to ensure it is clearly received and understood.

> 66 If a child can't learn the way we teach, maybe we should teach the way they learn. 99
>
> – Ignacio Estrada

How do we accommodate different learning styles? To explore this idea, consider this interaction taken from the VARK questionnaire.

**Interaction:**

You have to make an important speech at a conference or special occasion. You would:

| make diagrams or get graphs to help explain things | gather many examples and stories to make the talk real and practical | write out your speech and learn from reading it over several times | write a few key words and practice saying your speech over and over |
|---|---|---|---|
| **Visual** | **Kinesthetic** | **Read/Write** | **Aural** |

Consider each of these options and the associated learning strategy. The selection you chose does not necessarily support those who have learning styles different from yours. The accommodation is not difficult, simply incorporate multiple strategies—think of your audience, not just yourself. Research supports this advice.

A recent study (Shabiralyani, et. al, 2015) concluded, "Using visuals aids as a teaching method stimulates thinking and improves learning environment in a classroom." Audience involvement works wonders for tactile learners. Chinese Confucian Xunzi coined the phrase, "I hear and I forget. I see and I remember. I do and I understand."

## Part 3: Slides Help You Share Content

Slides are a fantastic way to make the information come alive for the audience. Always use a visual to share information that comes from research in a presentation. Slides are a fantastic tool. Why?

**Visuals/Slides are a Win-Win**

| SPEAKER | AUDIENCE |
|---|---|
| 1. They help you, the speaker, break down the content. | 1. They help the audience comprehend the concepts. |
| 2. They serve as a great cue card so you can remember points you want to cover. | 2. The repetition of seeing and hearing help the audience retain the information. |
| 3. They provide another dimension to engage the audience. | 3. They can be entertaining and vary the presentation. |

*Note: **Never** have the same content on your cards. This ensures that you interact with the slide, keeping the audience engaged, as opposed to reading content off of cards.*

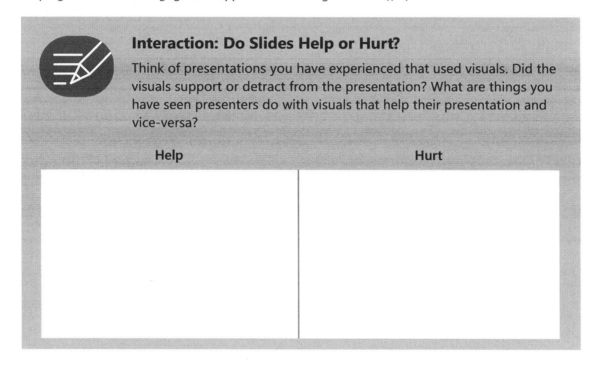

### Interaction: Do Slides Help or Hurt?

Think of presentations you have experienced that used visuals. Did the visuals support or detract from the presentation? What are things you have seen presenters do with visuals that help their presentation and vice-versa?

| Help | Hurt |
|---|---|
|  |  |

**Slide Design**

It takes effort and experience to design a good-looking slide presentation. Don't be afraid to request some input from someone who is experienced using the software. The two biggest mistakes I see people make with slides are

1. Too many words per slides.
2. Content or ideas are not broken down.

A good rule of thumb is to stick to the 4/4 rule. Limit each slide to no more than four lines, with a limit of four words per line. Avoid the temptation to cut and paste entire paragraphs of content. An exception to this is when you have a list of information. Rather than creating individual slides for 10 Myths or 6 Steps, display them on one slide. This allows the audience to capture the big picture and process the 10 Myths or 6 Steps as a single concept. Should you have time you can then go into each by creating individual slides for each myth or step; however if time is limited, displaying one slide allows you to share substantial ideas in a timely manner. Rather than reading each myth or step, rely on the intelligence of the audiece. Remember an audience can always read faster than you can speak. Engage the audience by showing the list of content and then asking them a probing question that requires them to process the content, "Which of these myths stands out to you the most"? or "Which step do you think will be the most difficult?" You can always follow it up by commenting on one or two you feel need to be further explained. In this case, it is always a great idea to provide the audience with a print out of your slides so that they can review any information at a later time. You can print four or six slides to a page so the number of pages are not excessive.

Slide applications typcially allow you to select which format you want to use for each slide.

## Table 4.2: Types of Slides

| Name of Slide | Description | Explanation |
|---|---|---|
| Title | **Names the presentation.** (Avoid using during your presentation.) | The default first slide for most slide applications is typically a Title Slide. While it seems to make sense to put a cover on your presentation, if you really think about it, your slides are not a "book" of your presentation, rather they are specific visuals designed to support your presentation. Automatically using a Title Slide can actually harm your presentation. Remember that you need to begin your presentation with a "Wow" factor, a hook or an attention grabber. Can a Title Slide ever really be dynamic and create that great first impression? No, it provides a Title of your presentation and your name. No "WOW" at all. I advise people to follow the Speech Formula and take control of every aspect of how you begin your speech. To do that well, at no point is there any room for a slide that states your name and the name of the speech. There can be situations, where event coordinators may use a Title Slide as a space holder between presenters. In these situations resist the urge to begin your presentation with an underwhelming opener referring to your name and topic. *(Referred to as Title Slide)* |
| Content | **Presents key information with a descriptive title.** | Content slides are crucial for your presentation. They help you stay on point and they help your audience comprehend vital information. Create Content Slides with care. Break down data using key words. Remember the rule of 4 words/4 lines per slide unless a list of information is being presented. Content slides can have one or two areas of content. The two areas allows you to compare and contrast ideas. To make the slide visually appealing remember you can insert images but do so sparingly and always explain what the image is and why it is there. Don't assume your audience has made the same connection that you did. *(Referred to as Title and Content Slide or Comparison Slide or Two Content Slide)* |

| | | |
|---|---|---|
| Transitional | **Transitional slide to indicate a change from one idea to another.** | Section Header slides are wonderful to use to transition between Main Points. Displaying the Main Points on one slide and showing that same slide to indicate progression from one point to another helps the audience follow the ideas in your speech. Use the Section Header slide every time you change a point and your audience will know the points of your speech by the end. After all, isn't that the point of the presentation? |
| Graphic | **Blank slide used to insert an image, graph or media.** | Sometimes a picture really can be worth a thousand words. If you find that image, use it! Anytime you have an image explain what it is and why you used it. Don't assume the audience will process it in the same way you have. Graphs displaying data can also be extremely helpful in relaying content. Finally, a short video can be a great way to grasp the audience's attention and help them make sense of information. Warning...I recommend having any videos in a separate browser and just display an image of the video on the slide as a place holder. In my experience about 50% of the time videos embedded in presentations fail to play—even when they have been tested on the equipment. I recommend bypassing the potential problem all together, unless you have experience well beyond mine. *(Referred to as Blank Slide)* |

**Table 4.3: Slide Presentation Guidelines**

| Do | Don't |
|---|---|
| Engage the audience—individually and as a group for at least $1/3$ of every slide. | Write full sentences and just read off slides. |
| Cite any ideas that are not your own — both visually and orally. | Turn your back to the audience. |
| Create powerful audience connection using at least one of the 4Ps for each content slide. | Make a sloppy presentation with unexplained images, overly dark colors, and unclear labels. |
| Select a light background with dark letters for readability with the lights on. | Turn the lights down for PowerPoint and this lowers the room's energy level. |
| Include images that match and support theme. | Just flip through the slides and forget about the audience. |
| Interact with content on the slides. Touch the points or key words for emphasis. | Ignore the visual. |

| Do | Don't |
|---|---|
| Before you show each slide, grab attention by thoughtful introduction. | Have misspelled words, lack of titles or content on wrong level. |
| Keep your body facing the audience at *all* times. | Read off the slide word for word. |
| Explain any images. | Make the same mistakes you have seen other people make with visuals. |

The C$^2$ARES Concept for making your visuals work for you and the audience engagement strategies we recommend integrate effective approaches for accommodating multiple learning styles.

## Part 4: The C$^2$ARES Concept

**Criteria for Showing You C$^2$ARES**

Table 4.4: C$^2$ARES

| Check | For each slide | 🅰 Definition |
|---|---|---|
| | **C**ITE | What is your citation? Be sure to include the source site and explain why it's credible. |
| | **C**ALL | When will you call on the audience? Who will you call upon? Keep your audience involved in the transmission of content during each slide. Remember WPPR: Word, Probe, Phrase, Review. |
| | **A**TTENTION GRABBER | How will you intrigue the audience by your transition to this slide content? |
| | **R**EWARD | How do you intend to reward your audience for their participation? (Besides physical objects, rewards can be verbal acknowledgment or gratitude, but sometime during the presentation, sweeten it to include a physical reward.) |
| | **E**NGAGE | What will you do to physically involve the audience in your presentation? You can use a prop that reveals content and requires interaction. You can include an activity that requires at least two audience members to move from their seats. |
| | **S**LIDE | Break down content so it makes sense. Follow the 4 lines/4 words per line rule, and use light background with dark text. |

> ❝ Humans are completely incapable of reading and comprehending text on a screen and listening to a speaker at the same time. ❞
>
> *– Garr Reynolds*

Garr Reynolds said, "Humans are completely incapable of reading and comprehending text on a screen and listening to a speaker at the same time. Therefore, lots of text (almost any text!), and long, complete sentences are bad, bad, **bad**."

This is so true. There is an art to integrating visuals and slides. Remember you must introduce each visual and control the dissemination of the content. This means you must instruct the audience on how to digest the information whether it consists of objects, images, cartoons, key words, clips, lists of information, sounds, or even food.

Remember, the most recent movement captures attention. If someone enters the room, they get the attention and you have to earn it back. If a slide changes, the audience will stop listening to you and read the slide. How and when you present the visuals to the audience matters. The C²ARES Method will help you make your visuals work for you rather than against you.

*Note: C²ARES was developed to help presenters overcome glaring mistakes with slides. Most of these mistakes can also be made with other types of visuals. Sometimes all instances of the C²ARES concept may not apply. For instance, if I hold up an iPhone as a visual, I might say, "This product was made by Apple", however, no citation is needed because it is an object. Apply to the best of your ability.*

## CITE

**Step 1: Distinguish your thoughts from someone else's ideas.**

> For example: "According to Cosby (2017), . . ."

**Step 2: Credit the source in 3 ways.**

1.  Write the citation on the visuals. The correct form is to display the author's name and year in parentheses (Sahagian, 2017) next to the bullet or slide title. Always follow the required formatting rules (APA, MLA, Chicago) for an in-text citation. If you struggle with the formatting rules, this citation style guide provided by the Owl at Purdue is a fantastic simple resource that outlines the different formatting requirments.

2.  Mention the citation to the audience. As you go through the presentation distinguish your thoughts from the research when you discuss someone else's work.

    > For example: "The cover for the June issue of Scientific America proclaimed..."

3.  Create an oral context (the written speech should include this context as well).

    *   Stating a name is not enough. Audience members need to hear qualifications to accept the information as credible. Who is the author? Where was it published? Why do you trust that it's true?

For example: "In his bestselling book, Outliers: The Story of Success (2008), Malcolm Gladwell points out..." Integrate your remarks on his content to show the book's credibility.

"Considered the father of birth order, Australian psychiatrist Alfred Adler (1964) suggests that birth order influences personality."

Here, Adler clearly is a worthwhile source because he is the "father of birth order theory", but throwing names out without explaining why their ideas are reliable can cause audience members to question the legitimacy of your speech. Smith tells us XYZ will not satisfy savvy audience members practicing basic methods of critique.

Share your "research journey" with the audience. We all benefit from other people's experience. As a speaker, you probably will have more experience than the audience members will about your topic. Share that insight. Audiences appreciate it, and it adds to your credibility.

"In my research, one article entitled, XYZ, resonated with me more than the others."

- Expose the bias. Notice how the bias for the publication is used as further support of the point's merit. Be aware if information you include is considered biased by audience members. Certain publications contain an innate bias. For instance, Fox News promotes a conservative agenda; CNN promotes a liberal agenda. Educated people are aware of these biases. Avoid them, unless they serve a purpose in your presentation. If you do use a biased source, you must highlight the bias right away to avoid seeming naïve and/or manipulative.

In the article published XYZ by ABC, even the Huffington Post supported the conservative Senator's proposition.

- Share the titles of any books you refer to, so readers can find them later. Bring the book to use as a prop if you have a copy available.

4. Insert a reference slide. Include a slide displaying all your references near the end of your presentation. Notice I did not say this is the end of your presentation, before you enter your conclusion, reveal your sources to your audience and perhaps comment on one or two of your favorites. Include the list of sources on your slide handout so audience members can investigate further if their curiosity was sparked.

5. Create a slide handout for your audience. Each audience member can easily access your sources and won't need to take detailed notes, so they can focus on your presentation. If you don't distribute handouts ahead of time, let them know at some appropriate point that they will be provided. Think carefully about whether to hand these out prior to the presentation or after. People often get distracted reading presentations during a speech, but they may be helpful for taking notes. Handing things out during a presentation is disruptive and eats precious time.

## CALL

Have you ever had someone just read the slides or a flipchart? How boring! Visuals are a way to involve the audience.

Involve them in the dissemination of the content. This does not mean you ask someone to read all the content. It does mean that you highlight key words or concepts from the slides and involve the audience. Engaging audience members by calling on them to participate sharing the slide content works really well for one-third of the content of each slide.

Call on audience members using the WPPR (Word, Probe, Point, Review) system for each visual that displays words (slides, handouts, poster boards, or props). This technique is guaranteed to keep your audience on their toes, riveted to your points. How does the WPPR system work?

**Table 4.5: Call WPPR (Word, Probe, Point, Review)**

| | |
|---|---|
| **Word** | Choose a key word that you want to highlight. Point to the word, and ask everyone together, "What is that word ___?" If their reply is not loud enough, ask them again. Involve a specific audience member to read a point on each slide. (Alternatively, on an important point you can ask the entire audience to state the word(s) aloud—for emphasis repeat . . . What? (Encourage them to be louder). |
| **Probe** | Ask, "Which of these points do you think is most important?" This works really well with a list. The audience can always read faster than you speak. Let them. This also requires them to engage and think about the content. |
| **Point** | After you share a point, say (or gesture to indicate), "Moving on to the next point . . . Ashton, can you please read." Then explain or provide an example. |
| **Review** (if necessary): | "Skye, what are the 4 techniques to keep your audience awake for your slides?" |

## ATTENTION GRABBER

**3 Disastrous Ways to Start a Speech**

| 1 | Never begin with the words. "Hi, my name is. . ." |
|---|---|

| 2 | Never begin with the words, "Today I'm going to talk to you about. . ." |
|---|---|
| 3 | Never begin your speech with your visual displayed behind you with the topic and your name. |

These introductions all create a boring, predictable presentation. When someone begins their speech like this, a cacophony of "I don't cares," screams in my head.

"I don't care enough to be creative!"

"I don't care enough about myself to properly represent myself in front of a group of people."

"I don't care that my audience is bored to tears."

"I don't care if they think I'm mediocre."

The first words that come out of your mouth are the most important words you'll say. They create the first impression. Grab the audience's attention. You should have a fantastic, spell binding way to gain their attention and their respect. Explore the Types of Visuals chart to stimulate your creativity to identify the best way to do so. The Attention Grabber can vary depending upon the length of the presentation.

*Note: Another term often used for Attention Grabber is "Hook." In this book, we will stick with Attention Grabber.*

### Use Different Types of Attention Grabbers for Different Purposes

1. **Ideas for Short Speeches about Someone Else (Award, Introduction):** If I am introducing someone, a great probing question might work wonders. Here are a few examples:

   "When you were a child, what did you want to become? A superhero? An athlete? An actress? The person I will introduce you to today never imagined he would become the volunteer of the year.

   "Imagine being born with three strikes against you: 1) addicted parents, 2) extreme poverty, and 3) disability . Our speaker today refused to allow these three strikes knock her out, rather she used these traumatic experiences to be stronger, to be kinder and to inspire others."

   "Have you ever had butterflies in your stomach, knowing that something great was about to happen? That's how I feel tonight in anticipation of these great leaders coming together for this event."

2. **Ideas for Longer Speeches You Write:** (For these examples, I will use "public speaking" as the topic.
   - Pass out a sheet of paper and ask everyone to write down what comes to mind when they hear the phrase, "dynamic speaker"? Get the audience to share their responses. (This would be for an audience under 20.)
   - Another time, for a women's group, I delivered a speech dealing with fear entitled, "I'd rather pull my fingernails out than deliver a speech." I began by setting the stage, calmly taking a pair of pliers, placing the pliers on my nail and pulling (making faces) until the audience verbally recoiled. I then asked, "How many of you have that exact reaction when you are asked to deliver a speech?" At the end of the speech, I gave them all nail

files with my company name as a reminder that with help, they can confidently shape their words if asked to deliver a speech, rather than recoil with terror.

- For many years, as an introduction to my class, with his permission, I stole an idea from a friend. I dressed down, sat in the classroom as a student, and waited until ten minutes after the start time as students began to get restless. I then walked to the front and asked everyone to, "Stand up." They did. "Sit down." They did. Again, I said, "Stand up." I turned and wrote, "Supercalifragilisticexpialidocious" on the board. I said, "Repeat after me." I repeated that instruction and word three times. Then I told them to sit down. "Some of you are wondering why you have to take public speaking," I said. Then I asked, "Why did you just move around and say weird words?" A student would answer, "Because you told us to, you are the teacher." "Ah," I reply, "but a moment ago, I was a student just like you. What changed? I stood up and I spoke to an audience. I got you guys to do things you didn't want to do. The way I used words asserted authority, I was able to lead you. James Humes says, 'Public speaking is the language of leadership'. As a result of what we will learn in this class, you can lead people to action. You can change your world. And, if you really focus, you could even change the world."

A marinade is a sauce for soaking a food item before cooking to flavor or soften it. In a speech, an Attention Grabber acts like a marinade. Expose your audience to the Attention Grabber as a way to establish rapport and open their minds so that the ideas are well received. Don't confine Attention Grabbers to the beginning. Use them to gain attention whenever you introduce a new idea. Marinate the group for what's coming next, and it will be well received.

### Tiny Attention Grabbers Introducing Each New Visual

Each visual you introduce to the audience needs an introduction. This technique is an advanced technique. It requires you to be comfortable engaging the audience and dancing with the audience to really incorporate correctly. Presenters need to be aware of their next movement in the speech and prepare the audience.

**Slides:** Do not just click through the slides. Discuss each one and be familiar with their order. I've seen presenters act surprised when they click to the next slide. It should never be a surprise. The speaker should know what's next and get the audience anticipating the content before they see it.

**Prop:** Don't just hold a prop up or simply pass it around. Use more finesse. Let nonverbal cues provide context before you ask a probing question like, "What's your favorite book?" Then, hold up the book or prop and discuss it. Consider this: in general, when you tell someone a story, before you say the first words, does the recipient know whether it is sad or exciting? They should. Why? Your body language precipitates the change in tone. Your words and body language should intentionally do the same for your visuals.

I recommend that Tiny Attention Grabbers forecast the content of each slide and each section of the speech. While transitions are generally used to let the audience process information, Tiny Attention Grabbers create a sense of anticipation for the next thing. Notice the paragraph above this section that begins with, "A marinade . . ." That sentence is an example of a Tiny Attention Grabber.

### Individual Slides (Sub Point like First Slide)

Furthermore, when you use visuals do not just click through the slides. As you transition from one point to another, grab their attention—creatively introduce that slide. The next slide should not be a surprise to you! You should anticipate it and guide your audience to the next idea. I recommend that your Attention Grabber precipitate the content of each slide and each section of the speech.

## REWARD

Think about ways you can reward audience members for their involvement at selected spots in the presentation. You may use something as simple as a smile or recognition—mentioning someone by name generates affinity. But don't limit yourself to these simple things. Go the extra mile by offering tangible rewards now and then. Rewards motivate most people to be more involved and enhance their experience.

Audiences in general appreciate being acknowledged and rewarded, and this tendency seems to increase with age. I've found that the older the average age of an audience, the more they like to be acknowledged and rewarded.

**Rewards can include:**
- a tasty morsel like candy or a cookie
- gift certificate
- money
- certificate to leave early a day?
- company or branded product (e.g., t-shirt, coffee mug or bag)
- whatever your creative mind dreams up

Use rewards to drive attention and retention.

## ENGAGE

Seek creative ways to **physically** involve the audience with either a prop or activity. Engage your audience or at least a few audience members at some point during each section.

Examples:

| | |
|---|---|
| **Prop** | Props can relate to a product or contain key concept or ideas. They can be distributed to various audience members so they appear throughout the presentation at your request. |
| **Role Play** | Asking for a few volunteers to act out a scenario can make content lively and entertaining. |
| **Game** | Key concepts can be incorporated within the context of a simple game. Use this technique to introduce or review content. |
| **Movement** | You can ask volunteers to raise their hand, stand, or move to one side of the room. This stirs energy and involves the audience. |

On their own, slides have minimal content. They only add value when you use them as discussion points. Explain the points on the slide, involving the audience as you go. Randomly ask various audience members to read the next word or point for about a third of the content. Don't have them do all the work—just keep them guessing who you will call on next and when. Before you move to the next slide, create a sense of anticipation by providing a mini attention grabber such as a question. Then reveal the next slide.

If you have a list of information, graph or image remember to give the audience time to read or process the slide. Once they've read and digested the information, they'll take a more active role in the presentation as opposed to passively waiting for your input. When you see they've finished reading, put on your facilitator hat and ask questions to guide them to key points you wish to emphasize. Then begin your discussion.

**Examples:**
1. Which option will be more alluring to the customer?
2. After reviewing this graph, can someone give me three reasons why XYZ is a better option?
3. What do you think _____ means?
4. Which of these is most significant to you?

**Table 4.6: Tips to always follow when creating your slides/visuals.**

| DESIGN | 1 | Choose a background consistent with your message. |
|--------|---|---------------------------------------------------|
| | 2 | Avoid funky colors and fonts. |
| | 3 | Make text large enough for easy reading anywhere in the room. |
| | 4 | Use a light background and dark letters so slides can be seen with lights up. |
| CONTENT | 5 | State your source content in key word format, not full sentences. |
| | 6 | Cite sources within the content of your slides for visibility and a reminder to cite orally. |
| | 7 | Bulleted lists always have at least two items, preferably three or more. |
| | 8 | Keep slide content to four lines or fewer per slide with four words or fewer per line. |
| DELIVERY | 9 | Keep the lights up while you present. |
| | 10 | Use images consistent with content and explain them. |
| | 11 | Use a buddy with whom you have practiced so you can focus on your audience rather then the electronics. |

| PREPARATION | 12 | Prepare for Murphy's Law: What can go wrong, will go wrong. Always have a backup plan—test in room if possible. Have slides on USB stick/ jump drive, and print presentation in case electronics fail. |
|---|---|---|
| | 13 | Distribute a copy (can be as little as one page) of slides but wait at the end to avoid distracting from your message. |

## Part 5: Mistakes People Make

To illustrate this point, I'm going to use a client's slides. I saw the presentation. The individual had great information and delivered a decent speech. But...oh my. The slides had so much room for improvement! Let's analyze one slide to explore how to make it more compelling.

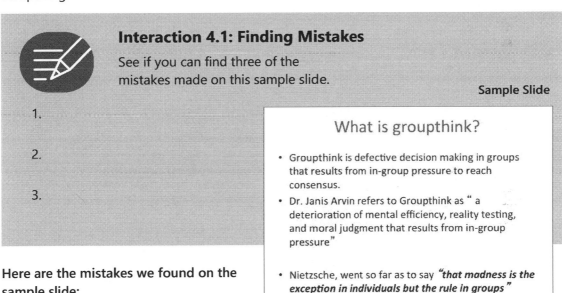

**Interaction 4.1: Finding Mistakes**

See if you can find three of the mistakes made on this sample slide.

Sample Slide

1.

2.

3.

### What is groupthink?

- Groupthink is defective decision making in groups that results from in-group pressure to reach consensus.
- Dr. Janis Arvin refers to Groupthink as " a deterioration of mental efficiency, reality testing, and moral judgment that results from in-group pressure"
- Nietzsche, went so far as to say *"that madness is the exception in individuals but the rule in groups"*

**Here are the mistakes we found on the sample slide:**

1. Titles are not capitalized. Title should read, "What is Groupthink?"
2. Titles don't represent the content accurately. This question listed as the title, "What is groupthink?" is the first main point; whereas the content on the slide relates to the subpoint which is Definintion. Thus the slide title should be "Definition" not "What is groupthink?" Titles should always describe the slide content. If you implement the Speech Formula, your subpoints will consistently be the Titles for your content slides. For instance, in this case the speech shows this skeleton outline:

   I.  What is Groupthink?
      A. Definition
      B. Individual vs. Group Decisions
   II. How can we make better decisions as a group?

Notice how on the corrected version of the slide located in the next section, *How to Improve the Slide*, the sub point is featured to correctly label the slide content, "Definition." The title should consistently feature the sub point as that accurately names the content of the slide.

3. Chunks of information will distract audience and tempt speaker to read slide rather than explaining. Instead, break the information down by creating bullets for key ideas.
4. Citations are inconsistent and wordy. Limit citations on slide to author's last name and the publication date.
5. Lacks images. Visuals such as a cartoon or image of a group listening to a leader would add value to this message .

**How to Improve the Slide**

If this presenter had taken more time to analyze the definition of groupthink, and identify what circumstances provoke it, she would better grasp the concept and be able to speak about it extemporaneously without reading the definition. For instance, in this situation Paulus (1994) defines groupthink as "defective decision making in groups that results from in-group pressure

**Figure 4.2: Break Down Slide Content into Keywords**

Subpoint

Keywords

Main point

to reach consensus." Key words that pop at me in that definition are defective, pressure, and consensus. Having read, analyzed, and written the words I want to use in the speech, when I see this slide featuring these three key words, I can flesh out the thought.

Here's the script I would write:

*Note: In place of a title slide, I'd use an engaging introduction to this speech featuring an Attention Grabber, thesis with questions, quotes and qualifying statements and finally, a review slide featuring the main points of the presentation.*

Begin discussion. *"In order to understand "What is groupthink?" we should begin by exploring what it means."*

Change to the Cartoon slide. Pause.

Ask the audience: *"Can everyone read this cartoon? I found this cartoon on LeadersLab, a company in the UK's website. As you can see, there is a leader. What are the group members saying?"*

Solicit audience participation. *"Yes!"* Response.

*"And, what are they thinking?"* Read various captions or wait for audience response.

Mini Attention Grabber to the next slide: *"This cartoon pretty accurately relays the phenomenon that occurs when groups work together. Let's take a peek at the official definition."* Notice how these words anticipated the coming slide, rather than changing and being surprised which slide appeared!

Change slide to Definition slide: *"Paulus, in his definition of groupthink in the Encyclopedia of Human Behavior (1994), explains that it is characterized by three components: 1. it represents defective decision making in groups."*

Repeat: *"What type of decision making?"* (Wait for audience to say word.) *"Defective!"* Physically point to the word, "Defective" to add emphasis—don't be afraid to interact with the visual.

*"2. The group seeks consensus."* Flip back to Cartoon slide.

Ask, *"In this image, who do you see seeking consensus?"* Some may say group members—by act of complying. Others may say the leader is applying pressure.

Flip slide back to Definition slide and transition to third component. *"3. In order to achieve the consensus, the in-group applies pressure to ideas that don't support the dominant opinion and/or the leader."*

Review the three keywords for groupthink with audience speaking each: *1) defective decision making, 2) consensus is sought, and 3) pressure is applied.*

*Note: To help audience members remember these key words, you could write "DCP" on board or emphasize the key words using this acronym.*

I would supplement the slide with this information. These words are written in my speech. *Back in 1984, Dr. Irving Janis pioneered the initial research on groupthink. He explains that this pressure results in a "deterioration of mental efficiency, reality testing, and moral judgment." Nietzsche went so far as to say, "Madness is the exception in individuals but the rule in groups."*

My cards would provide prompts to make this point (notice they include just key words, not full sentences. An exception to this is writing entire quotes to get the words right but do not do lengthy quotes that you just didn't decipher. Use quotes from your research sparingly):

Sample cue card (4" x 6" or 3" x 5")

> I. **What is Groupthink?**
>
> A. Definition
>
> 1. Research: See PP
> Janis...pioneer...pressure="deterioration of mental efficiency, reality testing, and moral judgment".
>
> Nietzsche="that madness is the exception in individuals but the rule in groups"
>
> 2. Connection: Personal Story Group internship

Your slides and cards provide the perfect combination of direction and key points to deliver the presentation with ease. Trust the process—you have all the information you need.

*Note: 4" x 6" cards give room for more or larger content.*

## Interaction 4.3: Fix This Slide

What is wrong with this slide?

### STEPS TO FORGIVENESS

1) State who and/or what you need to forgive aloud.

   a) This helps in the process of understanding and coming to grips with what the objective is.

2) Acknowledge how you currently feel about the situation. It is best if these are your honest feelings, not the nice, polite things you think you should feel. You need to work from how you really feel. Then you express your willingness to at least be open to the possibility of letting go of those feelings.

3) State the benefits you will get from forgiving. This will mainly be the opposite of what you are currently feeling. Sadness will become happiness, anger will become peace, heaviness becomes a feeling of lightness and so on. If you are not sure about the benefits just choose a few general good feelings which you would like to have for now (happier, more at ease, more confident etc). It helps if you can imagine how much better you will feel when you have forgiven.

4) Commit yourself to forgiving. This is simply stating who you intend to forgive and then acknowledging the benefits which come from forgiving. (martin, william (n.d.). Four Steps to Forgiveness)

Answer:
1. Way too much information
2. Not chunked, no key words
3. Steps not numbered
4. Credibility issues with citation
- The only citation listed for a large amount of content has no year, first name is not capitalized, and citation only requires first initial.
- The citation is assigned only to point #4. Where are citations for the other points?
- Content appears to be copied and pasted on the slide rather than broken down into key words. You cannot copy a paragraph of content from a source and paste it into a slide without referencing it as a long quotation and citing the source.
5. Low contrast between background (lighter) and letters (darker)

Create a new slide that follows the rules.

I hate the way people use slide presentations instead of thinking. People would confront a problem by creating a presentation. I wanted them to engage, to hash things out at the table, rather than show a bunch of slides.

– *Steve Jobs*

## Chapter 4 Review Questions

1. List three reasons why visuals are valuable for both speakers and audience members.

2. List the top mistakes people make creating their slides.

3. List five Do's and Don'ts for making visuals work for you.

4. What is your preferred learning style and how does that reveal itself in your presentations?

5. How can you accommodate multiple learning styles in your speech?

6. Apply the C$^2$ARES Concept using a content slide.

7. Call on audience members using WPPR.

8. List three disastrous ways to start a speech.

9. Identify five tips you will incorporate when you create your slides.

10. Which quote from this chapter resonates with you the most?

## Practice Speech: Interacting with Visuals

**Time Limit:** Two minutes

**Target Audience**

Option one:  You are asked to present a new procedure to your peers in your office. Legislative compliance requires that the protocol is followed. Be sure your peers can correctly follow the procedure after hearing your presentation. Use a procedure that fulfills a legislative requirement so you can practice citing.

Option two: You are asked to present a research article about public speaking to a group you joined to improve your ability to speak in public.  Identify an article and present an overview to the group. Be sure that in your citation you qualify why it is credible information that we should follow.

**Instructions:**

1.  Create a content slide that follows the rules for making your visuals work. You may have a question slide following the content slide.
2.  Explain how you intend to implement the C$^2$ARES Concept using the rubric and reference slide. No more than three total slides:  1. Content Slide, 2. Question Slide, 3. Reference Slide.

| Slide # | For each slide | How would do it? |
|---------|----------------|------------------|
| | **CITE:** | |
| | **CALL:** | |
| | **ATTENTION GRABBER:** | |
| | **REWARD:** | |
| | **ENGAGE:** | |
| | **SLIDE:** | |

3.  Practice deliberately making your stretch goal to implement each of the six C$^2$ARES Concepts
4.  Dynamically present the slide, interacting with your audience as expected.
5.  Record your presentation and evaluate how well you implemented C$^2$ARES.

**Purpose:** To ease into the delivery process by providing a non-threatening venue. Focus on the variety of vocal inflections you use. Project your voice as much as you can. Create excitement by the energy you put into your voice.

**Skills to Practice:** Employ each part of the $C^2ARES$ concept effectively.

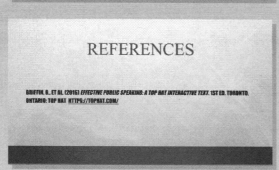

## Sample Story: Making Visuals Work for You

### Script

This is a sample presentation by Makeda Serju and Fabienne Desir with the help of a buddy in the audience. See how well they incorporated the $C^2ARES$ concept.

As Makeda and Fabienne stand before the audience ready to begin, suddenly an audio clip randomly plays from the back of the audience.

### Begin with little skit:

Buddy: Start audio clip from the back of the audience.
Both Makeda and Fabienne look at each other confused. Mouthing the words, "What?" Both shrug their shoulders.

**Begin Presentation:**

Makeda: *Are you really listening to what you are hearing? How good of a listener are you?*

Fabienne: *May I have five volunteers from the audience come to the stage?* Calls on specific individuals.

Instructs volunteers that she will whisper a phrase and each must whisper it into the next person's ear. Fabienne whispered the phrase "blue jeans" in the first volunteer's ear and Makeda announced the message from the last volunteer that travelled down the chain—which was "blue cheese."

Makeda: *See how bad we can be at listening? The first person heard "blue jeans" somehow the message was misheard and the message got messed up.*

Fabienne: Share content for slide #3 being sure to employ C2ARES. See Sample Criteria Listening Skills below.

Makeda: Share content for slide #4 being sure to employ C2ARES. See Sample Criteria Listening Skills below.

**Sample Rubric: Listening Skills by Makeda Serju and Fabienne Desir**

| Slide # | For each slide |
|---------|----------------|
| 1, 2, 3 | **CITE:** According to Edward Griffin in the book *Effective Public Speaking*. |
| 2, 3 | **CALL:** Slide 3: Call Lily...to read, "Social Oriented Listening."<br>Slide 4: Hand out three posters with the definitions.<br>Poster 1: Someone has so much information that they are unable to deal with it.<br>Poster 2: We come into a conversation with ideas about what the other person is going to say and why, we can easily become blinded to their original message.<br>Poster 3: Absence or deficiency in desire, interest and driving force to hear or follow words. |
| 1 | **ATTENTION GRABBER:** Start with the game "Chinese Whispers." |
| N/A | **REWARD:** Reward the individuals who participated in the game and read the points off the slide with a chocolate turtle. Give everyone a little quote on listening.<br><br>"When people talk, listen completely. Most people never listen." –Ernest Hemingway<br><br>"Most people do not listen with the intent to understand; they listen with the intent to reply." –Stephen R. Covey<br><br>"One of the most sincere forms of respect is actually listening to what another has to say." –Bryant H. McGill<br><br>"If you make listening and observation your occupation, you will gain much more than you can by talk."–Robert Baden-Powell<br><br>"Most of the successful people I've known are the ones who do more listening than talking. –Bernard Baruch<br><br>"The art of conversation lies in listening."–Malcom Forbes<br><br>"We have two ears and one tongue so that we would listen twice as much as we talk." –Diogenes<br><br>"You cannot truly listen to anyone and do anything else at the same time." –M. Scott Peck |

| Slide # | For each slide |
|---------|----------------|
| 1 | **ENGAGE:** Ask five members of the audience to come to the front. We whispered into the ear of the first one. during the "Chinese Whispers" game.<br>Definition, Poster Slide 4 |
| all | **SLIDE:** Followed the rules, only key words. |

References

Carnegie, D., & Carnegie, D. (1962). The quick and easy way to effective speaking. New York, NY: Pocket Books.

Cuban, L. (2001). Computers in the classroom, Cambridge, M.A. Harvard University Press. Retrieved from http://www.webpages. uidaho.edu/mbolin/akerele-afolable.htm

Felder, R. & Soloman, B. (2017) Index of learning styles questionnaire. Retrieved from https://www.webtools.ncsu.edu/learningstyles/

Hall, E.T. (1976). Beyond culture, New York: Doubleday.

Hall, E. T. (1984). The dance of life : the other dimension of time. Garden City, N.Y., Anchor Press/ Doubleday.

Hampden-Turner, C., & Trompenaars, A. (1993). The seven cultures of capitalism (Currency Doubleday, New York).

Humes, J. C. (1993). The Sir Winston method: the five secrets of speaking the language of leadership. New York: Quill/William Morrow.

Jacka, J. (2011). The Human Energy Field. ACNEM Journal,30(3), 12th ser. Retrieved July 21, 2017, from https://explore.scimednet.org/index.php/2016/04/02/the-human-energy-field/.

Lickerman, A. (2009) Eight ways to remember anything; Research based strategies to boost your memory and keep it strong. Psychology Today, November 16, 2009. https://www.psychologytoday.com/blog/happiness-in-world/200911/eight-ways-remember-anything

Mandhyan, R. (2016). The heart of public speaking, 2nd ed. CreateSpace Independent Publishing Platform.

O'Hara, C. (2015, August 12). How to Tell a Great Story. Retrieved March 19, 2017, from https://hbr.org/2014/07/how-to-tell-a-great-story

Ralph Richardson (n.d). Azqutoes.com. Retrieved March 14, 2017 from http://www.azquotes.com/quote/602438

Safire, W. (1991, June 16). On Language; Impregnating the Pause. http://www.nytimes.com/1991/06/16/magazine/on-language-impregnating-the-pause.html. Retrieved March 19, 2017.

Shabiralyani, G., Hassan, K. S, Hamad & Iqbal, H.H. (2015). Impact of visual aids in enhancing the learning process case research: District Dera Ghazi Khan. Journal of Education and Practice. Vol6, No 19.

Twain, M., & Twain, M. (1903). The writings of Mark Twain. How to tell a story and other essays. Hartford, CT: American Publ. Co.

Trompenaars, F. and C. Hampden-Turner (1997). Riding the waves of culture : understanding cultural diversity in business. London, Nicholas Brearley.

Winston Churchill. (n.d.). BrainyQuotes.com. Retrieved March 16, 2017, from BrainyQuote.com Web site: https://www.brainyquote.com/quotes/quotes/w/winstonchu111314.html

Vark, A. (2006). Guide to Learning Styles. http://www.vark-le Springfield, MO

Xunzi. Origin of "I hear and I forget. I see and I remember. I do and I understand."? English language & usage. Web site: http://english.stackexchange.com/questions/226886/origin-of-i-hear-and-i-forget-i-see-and-i-remember-i-do-and-i-understand

Zak, P. (2014). Why your brain loves good storytelling. Harvard Business Review. https://hbr. org/2014/10/why-your-brain-loves-good-storytelling

# Chapter 5:
# You Are Your Audience

## Objectives

**By the end of this chapter you should be able to:**

1. Describe why it is important as a speaker to connect with yourself.

2. Explain why taking a personal inventory is vital to your personal awareness.

3. Describe the components of a good personal support system.

4. Identify your most extreme characteristic for each personality test.

5. Share your stories dynamically.

**Part 1: Connect with Yourself**

**Part 2: Social Support System**

**Part 3: Personality Tests**

     Big Five

     Myers Briggs

     Johari Window

**Part 4: Our Stories Matter**

**Practice Speech:** My Favorite Story

**Practice Speech:** Who Am I?

**Practice Speech:** Pitch/Elevator

> " Only when you are aware of the uniqueness of everyone's individual body will you begin to have a sense of your own self-worth. "
>
> – *Ma Jian*

SELF AWARENESS

## *Chapter 5:*
# You Are Your Audience

Years ago at the end of a course, I asked my students what they had learned about communication. One woman, Sharon, raised her hand and said, "I learned to be an audience-centered speaker." With eyebrows raised, I said, "Please explain." She continued.

"I never realized that I was a selfish communicator. As I progressed through the assignments and speeches, I really started to mold my messages increasingly with my audience in mind. Then, one day while speaking to my ex-husband, my world changed. I got it! You see, over fifteen years ago, I went through a divorce. It was painful and tore me apart. He cheated on me. I felt betrayed and hurt. There were constant frustrations with the custody of our son. Now my son is a grown man, and he is getting married in a few months. For the first time in years, I am going to have to face my ex-husband. I was dreading the thought. There are also financial issues that we have to discuss in relationship to the ceremony, and in our experience, this was going to involve arguing and resentments. Knowing these things needed to be addressed, I carefully thought about how to do so. My thoughts suddenly caused me to think of my ex as my audience. Putting my own emotional scarred experience with him aside, I thought of him as a person. A man excited for his only son to get married. I thought about how he must feel about dealing with his ex (myself). I thought about the stresses he must face as the director of a company, I thought about his perspective."

"When I was ready to pick up the phone, the resentment and anger I felt slipped to the background. I dialed the number. He answered, I said "Hi. How are you?" (And meant it.) He responded in kind. I asked how he felt about the wedding and our soon-to-be daughter-in-law. Before I knew it, we had spoken for fifteen minutes without the hostilities that had obscured our dialogue for more than a decade. We moved on to the business we had to discuss and spoke openly and honestly about the commitments we could and could not make in regards to wedding—no accusations or anger. We ended the call as two parents proud of their son."

She hung up the phone and sobbed, realizing it was she who had entered every conversation with this man with such an attitude from her pain there was nothing he could have said that would have appeased her. She had caused this agony for years. Her son told her that his Dad had shared the miraculous conversation they had had. Her son hugged her and cried. He said, "Thank you, Mom. Now I can enjoy my wedding without being stressed about you two." Sharon's eyes welled up again as she vulnerably shared with the class how she had always communicated selfishly, only thinking about her perspective. Her son never was able to enjoy his milestones, like prom or graduation. Even holidays were saturated with resentments. She said she felt years younger. As a nurse, her bedside manner improved; her patients couldn't say enough about her empathy and compassion.

This amazing transformation came about because she learned to consider how her audience would respond, rather than just what she wanted from the interaction.

> 66 Communication is at the core of every dream we have. 99
>
> — J.R. Steele

Consider the times you have arguments and disagreements with others. How often are you speaking with the audience's needs in mind? Imagine how it might affect your life if you could design messages so people would be open to them rather than rejecting them?

In this chapter, we will take a personal journey to explore how to understand our audience. This journey begins by developing a profound sense of self-awareness—better understanding of whom you are. Self-awareness is one of the keys to being a great speaker. The combination of the self inventory, personality tests, and examining your social support system will provide a foundation of better understanding of both yourself and others. We all differ for good reason. How we see the world is powerfully influenced by our environment, but we each have unique strengths and weaknesses that shape our lives on a daily basis.

From this humble perspective, we can begin to include these considerations when we construct messages for influencing others. The more the message matters to us, the more care we should take to consider how it will be received by others. When we do, we come audience-centered communicators. This shift in perspective can make all the difference, in speeches and life. It can be the difference between being hired or fired, between a makeup or a breakup, or being included rather than excluded. This can be a challenge when dealing with one person; considering an entire audience takes even more skill. Each audience is different, and to be effective, you must remain receptive to their needs.

Communication is at the core of every dream we have. Becoming a conscious communicator can empower you to reach your dreams.

# Part 1: Connect with Yourself

Self-awareness is defined by Merriam-Webster dictionary (2017) as the "conscious knowledge of one's own character, feelings, motives, and desires." The self-awareness tools in this section will help you answer questions like these. **How well do you know yourself? What do you think of yourself? What drives you? What is your underlying motivation? How do others experience you?**

Angela Duckworth shared a story at the end of her presentation on Grit at the Broward Speaker's Series (2017). A reporter, in a candid moment asked her for her gut "feeling"—after all the research she has conducted about success, what is the one underlying contributing factor? Duckworth instinctively responded: self-awareness. Growth is everything! The more aware you are, the more you can reach your full potential.

How do you become conscious of your core being? Northwestern University psychology professor Dan McAdams suggests you need to know your own story. He explains, "The stories we tell ourselves about our lives don't just shape our personalities—they are our personalities."

How do you plug into your story? You must be willing to take an honest look at every aspect of your life and how you have come to see things the way that you do, then take ownership of your actions and inactions.

### Interaction 5.1: Awareness Traits

Examine the list of traits below. Which of the characteristics below are traits of an aware person and which are traits of a person who is not aware?

| | Aware | Unaware |
|---|---|---|
| 1. Takes Ownership | | |
| 2. Open | | |
| 3. Trusts Others | | |
| 4. Action Meets Word | | |
| 5. Makes Excuses | | |
| 6. Defensive | | |
| 7. Micromanages Situations | | |
| 8. Talks More than Others Do | | |

*Answer: 1-4 are traits of individuals who are aware; 5-8 are traits of people who are unaware.*

Would you rather have a person who exhibits the traits of an aware or unaware person as your boss? Partner? Friend? It stands to reason that healthier relationships would come from having a greater awareness. Self aware people are open to constructive feedback rather than defensive. In his article, Self-Awareness is the Key to Becoming a Successful Leader, Dan Goleman shares a story of a female engineer whose boss reports that when he would suggest

> ❝ The key to growth is the introduction of higher dimensions of consciousness into our awareness. ❞
>
> — *Lao Tzu*

a way she might improve her work, she'd respond with a "yes, but" and some defensive excuse. The young engineer's skills were acceptable but "unlikely to improve without the ability to hear and respond to constructive feedback (2016)." This ability is a skill that develops when we tune in to ourselves and take an honest inventory. About 95% of the general public think they have good self awareness but in reality only about 10-15 percent do reports organizational psychologist Dr. Tasha Eurich in her book *Insight: Why Were Not As Self-Aware As We Think, and How Seeing Ourselves Clearly Helps Us Succeed at Work and in Life.*

The Harvard Business Review reports (Tjan, 2015) that increasingly business leadership courses realize the significance of tuning into self. When you can resolve issues from the past and take ownership in the present, chances are you can better lead others (Goleman, 2016). This may seem like a crazy question, but when was the last time you took an inventory to learn more about yourself?

## Take an Inventory of Yourself

Typically, inventory refers to "a list of goods and materials held by an organization" but it is also used to define the process of an individual taking stock of themselves. Merriam-Webster (2017) further defines inventory as "a list of traits, preferences, attitudes, interests, or abilities used to evaluate personal characteristics or skills."

Periodically, companies review their inventory to correctly account for their holdings or "assets." Periodic reviews may deliver surprises when forgotten items show up, or others disappear. That's why a system of accounting for tangible goods is considered good business practice. On the home front, insurance agents and financial advisors often encourage their customers to take an inventory of their home. Your personality trait assets are even more valuable than your physical ones. Use the questions below to take an inventory of yourself.

Answer the following questions. Write down your answers or discuss them with a friend—or both. You'll benefit from making this an annual event.

1. What are your five greatest strengths? What are your five biggest weaknesses?
2. When people first meet you, what words would they use to describe you?
3. What words would you use to describe yourself?
4. What three things are most important to you?
5. What are your top three pet peeves?
6. What is your proudest moment? What is your most embarrassing moment?
7. What are your goals for this day, week, month, and year?
8. How organized are you, and how does your organization affect your life?
9. In a typical room filled with people, to what extent are you an extrovert? What does that mean about how you communicate?
10. How open are you to change compared to other people?
11. What is your learning style preference and to what extent? Think of someone close to you. What is their learning style preference?
12. Do you think more globally (big picture) or sequentially (specifics)?

13. What part of your brain dominates your interactions? How does this compare to other people around you?
14. When is the last time you *really* looked into your own eyes in the mirror? If you haven't, do so. Look closely. Did you like what you saw? What made you uncomfortable or comfortable?
15. What is your personal mission statement? Write one if you don't have one.
16. What is funny to you? What do you **not** find funny?
17. What is the nicest thing you have ever done for someone? What is the **nicest** thing someone has ever done for you?
18. What is the **worst** thing someone has ever done to you? And the **worst** thing you did to somebody else?
19. Who is the happiest person you know? Who is the most miserable? What makes them the way they are?
20. Who is the best communicator you know? What makes them great? Who is the worst communicator? What makes them bad?
21. What are your three best moments in your job?
22. What are five things you do to raise your self-esteem and five things you do to harm your self-esteem?
23. What is your biggest fear?
24. What is your personal favorite quality you possess?
25. What is your favorite picture of yourself?
26. What is the funniest thing you have ever witnessed? When have you laughed the hardest?
27. How often do you laugh? How could you laugh more?
28. Whom in your life do you most admire and why?
29. Who in your life admires you? Why?
30. Describe a time in your life when "you being who you are" opened doors for you. When have "you being who you are" closed doors for you?

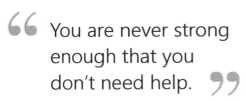

> " You are never strong enough that you don't need help. "
> — *Cesar Chavez*

Were some of these questions difficult to answer? Take the time to get to know yourself better. Have you ever heard the quote by George Bernard Shaw, "Life isn't about finding yourself, it is about creating yourself?" If you haven't already, begin the creation process today. Ask the hard questions. Examine who you are, inside and out. You will have the intel to create the life of your dreams.

## Part 2: Social Support System

What is social support? The Journal of Health Social Behavior defines it as a "support accessible to an individual through social ties to other individuals, groups, and the larger community." As human beings, we depend upon each other. The people we have or allow in our lives influence us greatly. According to researchers social support is one of the most important factors in predicting our success, happiness, physical health and well-being from

> Help others achieve their dreams and you will achieve yours.
>
> — *Les Brown*

young to old, rich to poor, conservative to liberal, (Gallo, et. al., 2005; Clark, 2005; Hale, Hannum & Espelage, 2005; Stice, Ragan & Randal, 2004). Even the National Cancer Institute's Dictionary of Cancer Terms offers a definition (2017): "A network of family, friends, neighbors, and community members that is available in times of need to give psychological, physical, and financial help." They have found that individuals who have a strong social support system have a much better chance of successfully winning the fight against cancer (www.cancer.gov).

It is vital to create a positive social support system. Ryan Cuff poses the question, "Which Came First, the Depression or the Social Isolation?" The absence of social support, Clark (2007) states, can predict the deterioration of physical and mental health among the victims. While not everyone was born into a supportive environment, we can and should consciously work to create a positive network. It is worth your time and energy to explore how to develop and nurture relationships in your life. As I explore this question with clients, often they say they don't have many people in their lives. I always wonder if the lack is based solely on a limited perspective that perpetuates their circumstances. It boils down to being open and willing to allow people in your life as opposed to being closed and unwilling to risk involvement. For instance, one person sees co-workers, whether they like them or not, as participants that actually make up their lives; another refuses to acknowledge that co-workers have any bearing in their life. If an individual who sits next to you for eight hours a day, forty hours a week, has no place in your life, they never will. Neither will the others in the department, or the building or the business, or the block. Those who see co-workers as people with whom they interact, and that like them or not, they matter, have the potential for a support structure to emerge.

The article Social Support and Resilience to Stress (Ozby et al, 2007) reveals that a positive social support provides psychological resilience to adapt well in the face of adversity. In other words, when life offers lemons, our social support system helps us make lemonade! Both quality and quantity of relationships matter. 2400 years ago, Greek historian Herodotus found that "Of all possessions a friend is the most precious." Consider this list of criteria from Table 5.1 to assess your overall level of support.

---

**Table 5.1: Six Criteria to Determine the Overall Level of Social Support (Clark, 2005):**

1. Support from a lover/spouse
2. Support from a group of people/friends
3. Assurance of worth from others
4. Reliable support
5. Guidance and support from a higher figure
6. Opportunity of nurturance

---

The people in our lives influence our lives. Sometimes this influence is positive, sometimes it is negative, but either way, the people around us affect us greatly. Who are the people who influence your life? Let's take a journey to examine this network of people that exist as your support structure.

## Interaction 5.2: Social Support

**Who are the people who make up the characters in your life?**

Please note that you don't have to like or even trust the individuals you list. These are people who "get" your time, for whatever reason. They account for the moments that make up your life. Imagine the tick-tock of the clock...seconds, minutes and hours—to whom do you give those moments? Anyone who captures a portion of your time per week should be listed. Next list the degree of positive influence they have on your life on a scale of 1-10.

Would they agree? Why would your opinions differ?

### PEOPLE IN MY LIFE

(Use a separte sheet of paper, maybe even create a comprehensive list on the computer that you can modify and reflect upon in the future.)

| Name | Rank | Name | Rank |
|------|------|------|------|
|      |      |      |      |

### MY SUPPORT NETWORK

Now refer to the list of people on that list. Visually show your relationship with these individuals by placing their name in the following table. Illustrate how close each relationship is to you by the associated sphere with the inner circle characterizing your closest relationships. Distinguish the following: Friends, Family, Other (work, church, neighbors, organizations, online relationships, or community groups.)

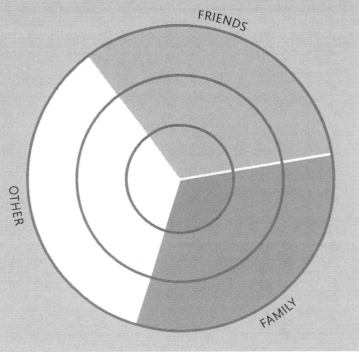

Of all possessions a friend is the most precious. 🙶

— *Herodotus*

**Table 5.2: Personal Support System Chart**

| Type | Definition | Example | Who's in my corner? |
|------|-----------|---------|---------------------|
| Emotional | Expressions of comfort and caring | Someone who makes you feel better because they listen to your problems | |
| Informational | Provision of advice and guidance | A person who can give trusted advice and guidance on an issue | |
| Tangible | Provision of material aid | A person who could give you a personal financial loan - SOS | |
| Belonging | Shared social activities, sense of social belonging | A friend whom you enjoy just "hanging out" | |

Did the same people appear on each list? Did some new names show up on this final list? What type of support do you provide to the people in your life? Live consciously! Sometimes we need help; sometimes we help others—for both large and small crises. What type of help are you requesting? What type of help are you providing? When you take someone's time, is it time well spent? Are your relationships balanced or one-sided? Are you a giver or a taker?

Assess what these exercises say about the people in your life. Strive to obtain the most positive social support system you can attain for yourself. These people's influence will either help or hinder your success. Choose wisely!

In my lifetime, I have delivered hundreds if not thousands of speeches and I also love to run creative ideas by virtually anyone who will listen just to observe the response. Never have I given a speech that has not required access to my social support system. My support system means the world to me. They provide a perspective I cannot attain alone. When you pour over information for hours upon hours during the speech writing process, your perspective is vastly different from members of your audience. They will hear the ideas for the first time during the speech. For me, reviewing my presentation with a member of my support team is a vital resource that helps me gain insight to my audience. I also love to run creative ideas by my support team. They often contribute and it gets even better! I can't count the times friends have provided props or information. Often a simple pep talk makes all the difference. Great public speakers aren't afraid to ask for help and input, because they know it adds insight and perspective they can't obtain alone.

## Part 3: Personality Tests

Do you know how you rate on different personality tests like the Big Five or Myers Briggs? For instance, are you an introvert or an extrovert? To what extent? Introverts and extroverts experience the world quite differently. Here's a question that can help you comprehend the fundamental difference: do people take your energy or do people give you energy? Introverts expend energy while interacting with others while extroverts enhance their own energy by absorbing it from others. This fundamental personality difference comes into play everyday, in almost every interaction we have. Personally, I can attest to how much my extroverted personality impacts my actions. My sister Laura and I score on extreme ends of the scale; she is an introvert, I am an extrovert. She once wisely observed, "If something happens to you and you share it with someone else, it's as if it never happened." I listened and shook my head as I replied, "Yes. That is it exactly!" We live in a world that celebrates extroverts, argues Susan Cain (2013), who wrote *Quiet: The Power of the Introverts in a World that Can't Stop Talking*. She believes we dramatically undervalue introverts and shows how much we lose in doing so. She charts the rise of the Extrovert Ideal throughout the twentieth century and explores how deeply it has come to permeate our culture. Artist Roman Jones comically depicts the predicament introverts face in his cartoon Dr. Carmella's Guide to Understanding the Introverted.

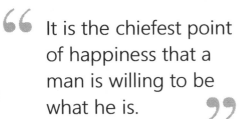

> It is the chiefest point of happiness that a man is willing to be what he is.

— *Erasmus*

*Note: Extroversion and Introversion are by far the most popular preference people and businesses use to assess personality differences in each other. However, when people discuss these differences they often think of it incorrectly. To really understand the core difference between introverts and extroverts consider where do you derive your energy? Researchers like Marti Olsen (2002) have actually shown that the difference comes from how introverts and extroverts process stimuli.*

*A good rule of thumb to determine if you are more of an introvert or extrovert is to consider if people take your energy or give you energy. If being with people energizes you, you are an extrovert; if they drain you and suck your energy, you are an introvert. Now, take the test to determine to determine to what extend you fall in either category.*

*Beyond the primary dimension of introversion and extraversion are many other characteristics that can help us understand others and ourselves. Let's explore three different personality tests to help you grasp the intricacies that make you tick.*

Do you know your how you rate on personality tests? For instance, are you an introvert or an extrovert? To what extent? Do you think more sequentially or globally? Are you calm or high strung?

If you have taken personality tests before, are they current? We change with time. I recommend taking a few tests designed to heighten your self-awareness. . . today. To reap the best results from taking these tests, keep these ideas in mind.

# Dr. Carmella's GUIDE TO UNDERSTANDING THE INTROVERTED!

By Roman Jones ©2012

## 1. WHAT IS INTROVERSION?

INTROVERTED PEOPLE LIVE IN A HUMAN-SIZED HAMSTER BALL.
(NOT REALLY, BUT YOU KNOW WHAT I MEAN)
THE MAJOR TRAIT OF A TRUE INTROVERT, AS OPPOSED TO SOMEONE WHO IS WITHDRAWN, IS HOW THEY GAIN THEIR ENERGY.

EXTROVERTED PEOPLE GATHER THEIR ENERGY FROM THEIR SURROUNDINGS.

THEY ABSORB THE "GOOD VIBES" OF THE PEOPLE AROUND THEM AND THUS NEED A LOT OF SOCIAL INTERACTION.

INTROVERTED PEOPLE MAKE THEIR OWN ENERGY AND, RATHER THAN TAKING IT FROM OTHERS, GIVE IT ON SOCIAL CONTACT.

THIS MEANS THAT THEY NATURALLY FIND MOST INTERACTION EXHAUSTING AND NEED TIME TO RECHARGE.

BECAUSE THIS ENERGY IS A LIMITED RESOURCE, THEY TEND TO SEE EXTROVERTS AS OBNOXIOUS PREDATORS OUT TO STEAL THEIR SWEET, SWEET ENERGY JUICES.

THAT'S WHY THEY HAVE THE HAMSTER BALL OF PERSONAL SPACE.

## 2. HOW TO INTERACT WITH THE INTROVERTED

JUST BECAUSE SOMEONE IS INTROVERTED DOESN'T MEAN THEY DON'T LIKE COMPANY.
INTERACTION IS JUST EXPENSIVE AND THEY DON'T WANT TO SPEND IT ON SOMETHING ANNOYING (READ: WASTEFUL)
HERE'S WHAT YOU DO:

SAY HELLO, BE POLITE AND RELAXED, SHOW THAT YOU RECOGNIZE AND APPROVE OF THEIR PRESENCE.
IT IS IMPORTANT FOR INTROVERTS TO FEEL WELCOME - THEY WON'T SPEND THEIR PRECIOUS ENERGY ON SOMEONE WHO DOESN'T WANT THEM AROUND.
IF YOU HAVE INTERESTING/IMPORTANT NEWS TO MENTION, MENTION IT. JUST DON'T PRESS FOR GOSSIP.

THEN GO BACK TO WHATEVER YOU WERE DOING.
NOW THE INTROVERTS KNOW THAT YOU ARE FRIENDLY AND OPEN TO INTERACTION BUT WILL NOT PUSH THEM INTO SPENDING ENERGY IF THEY HAVE NO NEED TO.

TAH-DAH! THAT'S ALL THERE IS TO IT!

## REMEMBER:

- RESPECT PERSONAL SPACE (HAMSTER BALL)
- ENERGY IS LIMITED
- DON'T DEMAND TO HAVE ENERGY SPENT ON YOU WHEN IT'S NOT PARTICULARLY NEEDED
- DON'T TAKE SILENCE AS AN INSULT - IT ISN'T!
- INTROVERTS GET LONELY, TOO

THAT'S IT, FOLKS!
BE SURE TO HUG YOUR INTROVERTS TODAY!
(WITH PERMISSION, OF COURSE.)

## Personality Test Instructions

1. Focus on what the test is measuring. Explore what each text actually measures. Clarify the meaning of specific words.

2. Focus on your specific results. Where exactly did you fall on the scale, not just what classification you are, but to what extent? If you are extreme (rank in the top 25% or bottom 25% of any dimension), **beware!** This offers you a great strength but also poses a huge weakness. Learn how to use these so they become your strengths, **not** your weakness.

3. Focus on how you differ from others. Think about how you think. Consider how innately different your process and response is compared to other people.

4. Focus on what you don't know or what you can learn. So many people take the test, stating, "I already knew I'm an extrovert." Great! Hopefully you do, but that is not the point for taking these tests. The purpose is to learn the degree to which you are an extrovert in comparison to others operating around you. Consider how this affects your life for better or worse. Identify specific instances where these attributes revealed themselves.

*Note: This is a great opportunity to practice telling a story which is an important quality to have as a speaker and as a communicator – see Part 4: Our Stories Matter.*

## The Big Five Personality Test

### Take the Test Now
Below are a few different free tests you can take.
- Big Five Project: http://www.outofservice.com/bigfive/
- Truity: https://www.truity.com/test/big-five-personality-test
- Psychology Today: https://www.psychologytoday.com/tests/personality/big-five-personality-test

### Background
In 1936, two psychologists, Gordon Allport and H. S. Odbert, put the Lexical Hypothesis into practice, a hypothesis searching to articulate the differences among human personalities (Digman, 1990). With decades of help from various scientists and psychologists, what began as a list of 17,000 adjectives describing personalities eventually boiled down to the five broad traits that we have today. Studies have even shown that the five dimensions available can uniquely profile the 10 personality disorders listed in the

**Figure 5.1: Big 5 Personality Traits**

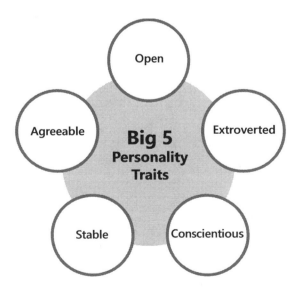

> 66 I think self-awareness is probably the most important thing towards being a champion. 99
>
> — *Billie Jean King*

Diagnostic and Statistical Manual of Mental Disorders, 5th. Edition DSM-5. This manual is published by the American Psychiatric Association and is the standard classification of mental disorders used by mental health professionals in the United States.

Caveat: Often people who score low in openness to new experience tend to get upset. Saying things like, "What do you mean, I'm not open to new experiences? Just today I tried XYZ." This always makes me laugh as someone who is truly open to new experience would ask, "I'm closed minded how?" In today's world, which is far different from 1936 when these traits where named, to be "closed minded" has a negative connotation. The intent of Allport and Odbert was to ask, "Do you seek the same or variety? Do you prefer vanilla ice cream each time or try a different flavor?" Refrain from putting a value judgment on any of these traits. Ask instead, "how does this show up in my life?"

### Purpose

The purpose of this test is to describe human personalities with five broad dimensions of personality.

### Measures

The five personality traits measured by the test are:

1. Openness to Experience - appreciation for art, emotion, adventure, unusual ideas, imagination, and curiosity.
2. Conscientiousness - a tendency to show self-discipline, act dutifully, and aim for achievement; planned rather than spontaneous behavior.
3. Extraversion - energy, positive emotions, assurgency, and the tendency to seek stimulation and the company of others.
4. Agreeableness - a tendency to be compassionate and cooperative rather than suspicious and antagonistic towards others.
5. Neuroticism - a tendency to experience unpleasant emotions easily, such as anger, anxiety, depression, or vulnerability; sometimes called emotional instability.

### Myers Briggs Personality Test

**Take the test now:**
- Truity: https://www.truity.com/test/type-finder-research-edition
- 16 Personalities: https://www.16personalities.com/free-personality-test

### Background

Today, the MBTI tool is the world's most widely

**Figure 5.2: Meyers Briggs**

## 4 MBTI
### Dichotomies

**Where do we get our energy?**

Extroversion ⟺ Introversion

**How do we take in information?**

Sensing ⟺ Intuition

**How do we make decisions?**

Thinking ⟺ Feeling

**How do we organize our world?**

Judging ⟺ Perceiving

used and recognized personality tool. Katharine Cook Briggs and her daughter, Isabel Briggs Myers shared a lifetime passion of studying personality. Influenced by various observations, particularly how Carl Jung's ideas aligned with their own ideas about personality, the women developed the test with a shared vision. World War II was going on at the time, to support the war efforts, thousands of men and, especially women, joined the workforce and found themselves in jobs that did not suit them. Briggs and Myers believed knowing the personality preferences would help identify which war-time jobs they would feel most at ease in thus helping these individuals acclimate into the industrial workforce

> 66 There are three people in yourself— who people think you are, who you think you are, and who you really are. 99
> — *William Shakespeare*

and ultimately helping the war effort (Myers, 1995 & 2017). With the war won, their mission broadened. They wanted to promote world peace by enabling individuals to grow through an understanding and appreciation of individual differences in healthy personalities and to enhance harmony and productivity in diverse groups (Marselle, 2012 & Myers, 1995).

### Purpose

The purpose of this test is to measure psychological preferences found in the perception of the world and in decision-making by means of questionnaire.

### Measures

At the heart of Myers Briggs theory are four pairs of preferences. Do you prefer to deal with:

People and things (Extraversion or "E"), or ideas and information (Introversion or "I").
Facts and reality (Sensing or "S"), or possibilities and potential (Intuition or "N").
Logic and truth (Thinking or "T"), or values and relationship (Feeling or "F").
A lifestyle that is well-structured (Judgment or "J"), or one that goes with the flow (Perception or "P").

Remember these preferences are on a scale, you can score much more sensing than intuitive but almost equal on the judgment and perception continuum. To quote Carl Jung, "There is no such thing as a pure introvert or extrovert. Such a person would be in the lunatic asylum."

### Johari Window

**Take the test now:**
Below are two different free tests you can take:
- http://kevan.org/johari
- http://kevan.org/nohari

### Background

Back in 1955, Joseph Luft and Harry Ingham created a model to demonstrate awareness of your communication with interpersonal relations (Luft, 1969 & 1970; Luft & Ingham 1955). "It is a behavioral model which aims to boost group relations through individual self awareness and mutual (group) understanding" (Trainer, 2014). For decades, individuals, management, and researchers have used it to better understand our perceptions interacting with others. The

Johari Window is a conceptual tool for illustrating the interaction between what is known/unknown to oneself and to others.

The associated online interaction provided above, asks you to solicit feedback from others, it can be quite interesting and a good way to demonstrate how to request feedback from those with whom we interact. The first test asks others to select five words from a list of positive words that they would associate with you. You can solicit feedback from multiple people and enter your own opinions and your window will expand incorporating the observations using the Johari Window model. The other test is a Nohari Window, this has negative words, if you are courageous enough to open yourself to the negative associations people assign to you see how this can help you gain personal awareness.

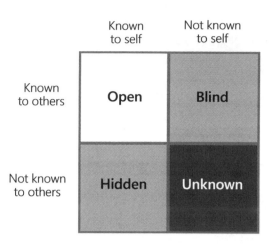

Figure 5.3: The Johari Window

Be advised that this activity does not fully represent the intent of Luft & Ingham's model. To fully grasp the model, explore some of these resources.

### Resources

Changing Minds: http://changingminds.org/disciplines/communication/models/johari_window.htm

Silicon Beach Training: https://www.siliconbeachtraining.co.uk/blog/the-johari-window

Allan Chapman, Businessballs: http://www.businessballs.com/johariwindowmodel.htm

Armstrong, (2006) considers this model to be one of the most useful ways to improve communications through disclosure and feedback. Other researchers have expanded upon the Johari Window to create other tools that help users improve their self-concept (Esposito, Mcadoo, & Sher, 1978).

### Purpose

The purpose of the test is to help people better understand their interpersonal communication and relationships. Individuals can solicit feedback from others, thus improving the accuracy of their perceptions.

### Measures

Charles Handly calls this concept the Johari "House" containing four rooms.

We take our personalities with us everyday, every place we go, every interaction we have. The results of these tests should help you fine tune your level of self-awareness. No dimension should come as a shock. Pay particularly close attention to the degree you scored in each dimension. In my college classroom, by the time we reach the third week and the students explore who they are by taking these tests, I can pretty well predict the results. For instance,

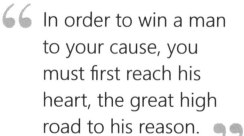

66 In order to win a man to your cause, you must first reach his heart, the great high road to his reason. 99

– *Abraham Lincoln*

| **Room One** is the part of ourselves that we see and others see. | **Room Two** is the aspect that others see but we are not aware of. |
|---|---|
| **Room Three** is the most mysterious room in that the unconscious or subconscious part of us is seen by neither ourselves nor others. | **Room Four** is our private space, which we know but keep from others. |

the student who raises their hand to answer every question is not an introvert, whereas the one that I have to draw out a response from each day is most likely not the extrovert. The student who has missed two classes and been late three times will not score high on conscientiousness. Explore how these characteristics find their way into your life. Often times, our greatest strength can be our greatest weakness. For instance, I score in the ninetieth percentile as an extrovert on the Big Five. This trait lends itself to my chosen career as a speaker, passionate public speaking coach, and instructor. In meetings, as I have matured and gained insight into my personality, my behavior has completely changed. Before, my extraversion would cause me to easily jump in and contribute to discussions. Sometimes I wondered why others didn't speak up. I just rolled right over them. Now... I shut up and listen carefully to the great minds in the room. Just because it might be easier for me jump in doesn't mean I always should—once, maybe twice per meeting is plenty. Sometimes, I even use my extraversion to help others find their voice. For instance, "Lloyd, I'm curious to hear your take on this issue." Our personalities are a part of who we are; we can do with them as we best deem fit. Navigate yours to take the course you want.

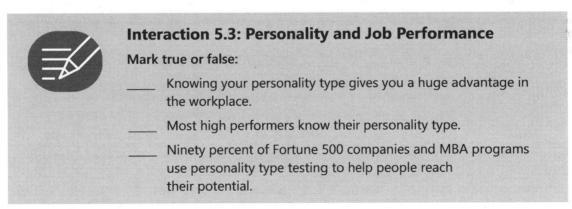

### Interaction 5.3: Personality and Job Performance

**Mark true or false:**

_____ Knowing your personality type gives you a huge advantage in the workplace.

_____ Most high performers know their personality type.

_____ Ninety percent of Fortune 500 companies and MBA programs use personality type testing to help people reach their potential.

*Answer: All three are facts!*

## Part 4: Our Stories Matter

"It's like everyone tells a story about themselves inside their own head. Always. All the time. That story makes you who you are. We build ourselves out of that story." This quote penned by Patrick Rothfuss from The Name of the Wind, highlights why our stories matter to ourselves as well as others.

**Words are how we think; stories are how we link.**

*– Christina Baldwin*

What is your story? Are you telling the right one? And are you telling it to the right people? We become attached to our stories. If you listen carefully, our stories reveal the heart of who we are and what we care about most. Jeremy Hsu, in his Scientific American article (2008) entitled "The Secrets of Storytelling: Why We Love a Good Yarn", writes, "Our love for telling tales reveals the workings of the mind."

Throughout history, stories have served a crucial societal function (Mott, 2016). Jean Clottes, "a respected authority on cave art" believes that "Wherever you find modern humans you'll find art (Mott, 2016)." The United States National Gallery of Art in its educational programs highlights that "Every Picture Tells a Story." Telling stories is a fundamental way people communicate. But why? What's in a story?

Storytelling is what connects us to our humanity. Author, Sharon Lippincott who is the founder of The Heart and Craft of Lifestory Writing explains, "Story is the operating system of the human brain. We think in story." Stories can elicit powerful emotional responses; they are powerful tools. They can help us find faith and purpose. In Saving Mr. Banks, Walt Disney exclaims, "That's what storytellers do. We restore order with imagination. We instill hope again and again." Stories can also be used to create unity and solidify groups of people. Writing for Psychology Today, Pam Allyn (2010) notes,

> "Story connects us all. Children, adults, all of us everywhere can use the magic of story to find aspects of ourselves in others, and of others in ourselves. Story reminds us that connectedness to the world does not always mean some have more and some have less, but that we all have stories and that is what brings us together."

The ancient art of storytelling has made its way to the boardroom. We tell stories all the time, to our boss, our employees, and our customers. Our stories serve to motivate, justify, and convey personal information about ourselves. Nonprofit organizations specifically require leaders who are excellent storytellers. How else can one be persuaded to give their time, energy and heart? The story makes it a cause. Abraham Lincoln said, "In order to win a man to your cause, you must first reach his heart, the great high road to his reason."

Stories are a fantastic device in a speech because they provide a universal language. They can help us bridge natural divides that often separate us, like culture, age, and even religion. Nick Morgan says, "stories create 'sticky' memories by attaching emotions to things that happen." Stories connect us to each other. Christina Baldwin says, "Words are how we think; stories are how we link." Leo Widrich, author of The Science of Storytelling: Why Telling a Story is the Most Powerful Way to Activate our Brains explains that a good story can make or break a presentation, article, or conv ersation. But why is that? It seems our brains are wired that way. Jeremy Hsu's (2008) research found that "most scientists are starting to agree: stories have such a powerful and universal appeal that the neurological roots of both telling tales and enjoying them are probably tied to crucial parts of our social cognition." Unlike facts and figures, stories trigger activity in our brains. An unknown author said it much more succinctly, "There are two ways to share knowledge. You can push information out. You can pull them in with a story." Researchers at Princeton found "a story is the only way to activate parts in the brain so that a listener turns the story into their own idea and experience" (Stephens, Silbert & Hasson, 2010). No wonder stories are so powerful. In her chapter advising readers to master the art of storytelling, motivational speaker and author Carmine Gallo (2016), author of Talk Like TED, explains that, "a well told story gives leaders a strong advantage in today's increasingly competitive marketplace."

Events happen. It is up to us to use our profound powers of observation to see our experiences as a story and share them with others. Look for the stories in your life. To do so, you must see yourself as interesting and valuable enough to have worthwhile stories to share. We all do!

> " Tell me the facts and I'll learn. Tell me the truth and I'll believe. But tell me a story and it will live in my heart forever. "
>
> *—Native American Proverb*

Brené Brown is a research professor at the University of Houston. She has spent a decade studying vulnerability, courage, authenticity, and shame. In her TED talk "The Power of Vulnerability" (2010) seen by nearly 30 million people world wide, she challenges people "to embrace our vulnerabilities and imperfections so that we can engage in our lives from a place of authenticity and worthiness." Nowhere is this more necessary than when we tell our stories. But how can we develop this skill?

Businessman and author, Michael Hyatt (2017) in his article "What Story Are You Telling Yourself?" encourages readers to create more empowering inner narratives by following five steps:

1. **Become aware of the Narrator.** Half the battle is simply waking up and becoming conscious of the commentary running through our minds. Most people are oblivious to it. It is especially important to be alert to it whenever we experience adversity or trauma. Ask: Am I telling myself a story right now?

2. **Write down what the Narrator says.** When the story starts playing, take a minute and jot it down. Try to get it word-for-word. It could be, "I'm not a gifted public speaker." Or, "I'll never reach my goals." Or, "He'll never go out with a person like me." Whatever the story is, get it down. Ask: What is the story am I telling myself right now?

3. **Evaluate the story the Narrator is telling.** It's easy to confuse the Narrator's voice with the Truth. But the Narrator is only offering one perspective, based on previous experiences and—too often—fear. We don't have to accept the version of reality the Narrator is telling, especially if it's disempowering and prevents us from reaching our goals. Ask: Is this storyline just a limiting belief?

4. **Affirm what you know is true.** You can either live life based on past experiences, current feelings, or the Truth. As one of my mentors often says, "Most people doubt their beliefs and believe their doubts. Do just the opposite." Ask: What do I know to be true?

5. **Write a new script.** We don't have to be passive spectators in our stories; we certainly don't have to be victims. Our choices matter—more than we think! They can affect the outcome. Ask: How can I make the choices that create the best possible story?

Once you notice your stories, seek to include relevant ones in every speech you give. The fascinating field of narrative psychology examines how our stories influence our personality (McAdams, 1993; Sarbin,1986; Vassilieva, 2016). In his book, *The Stories We Live By* (1993), Dan

McAdams, one of the pioneers in this field, persuasively argues that we are the stories we tell. In other words, stories are far more than just words; change your stories, change your world. Why not try it? Imagine that McAdams is correct, that understanding and revising our personal stories can open us to new possibilities in our lives. Dan McAdams (1993) makes a rather profound statement (pg.11 in his book),,

> If you want to know me, then you must know my story, for my story defines who I am. And if I want to know myself, to gain insight into the meaning of my own life, then I, too, must come to know my own story. I must come to see in all its particulars the narrative of the self—the personal myth—that I have tacitly, even unconsciously, composed over the course of my years. It is a story I continue to revise, and tell to myself (and sometimes to others) as I go on living.

Our stories are a significant part of delivering a speech. Our story literally affects our ability to stand in front of an audience. Before any of the speakers who once shook with terror at the thought of speaking in a group, mastered the art, their story first changed from "I can't to I can." Or, as Henry Ford puts it, "Whether you think you can or think you can't, you're right." Our performance directly relates to our story about ourselves as speakers, and the stories we share can either make our point or detract from it. Our story can create a connection with the audience, or it can reveal an ugly underbelly they aren't interested in hearing. Choose your stories wisely.

 Speakers who talk about what life has taught them never fail to keep the attention of their listeners.

— *Dale Carnegie*

# Chapter 5 Review Questions

1. Why it is important as a speaker to connect with yourself?

2. What question in your inventory was the most interesting for you to answer? Which question was the most difficult to answer?

3. What can you do to enhance your social support system?

4. Which of the personality tests is the most known?

5. What is the difference between an introvert and an extrovert?

6. Which is more important: Identifying which trait you are or identifying where you fall on the scale?

7. Identify your most extreme characteristic for each personality test.

8. Which test held the most significance for you? Why?

9. Identify at least two ways that stories can serve as powerful tools.

10. Identify a story in your life that could use a facelift. Follow Hyatt's five steps to create a more empowering narrative. (The practice speeches will provide specific guidelines to do so.)

11. Which quote from this chapter resonates with you the most?

## Practice Speech: My Favorite Story

**Time Limit:** 90 seconds

**Audience:** You are at dinner with a group of friends and/or family. Someone references an event and you have the perfect story to augment the conversation.

**Instructions:**

1. Choose a story you love! What's your favorite story? Why do you like it?

2. Consider your audience.

3. Identify the reason for sharing. What is the moral of the story?

4. Write the story. Include vivid details: who, what, where, when, how and why. Find the right amount, not too much, not too little. Be sure you include a hook, emphasize the conflict, and conclude with impact. Be vulnerable open up about your experience.

5. Practice speaking the story. Tell it often.

**Purpose:** Examine your stories; rewrite the script if necessary. Practice your ability to speak about yourself personally. Practice the art of telling a story.
Skills to practice: DP2: Project, DP5: Pause, DP6: Engage, DP9: Dance.

**Resources:**

- How to Tell a Great Story: https://theartofcharm.com/self-mastery/how-to-tell-a-great-story/?hvid=3q1eB7
- WikiHow: Tell a Story: http://www.wikihow.com/Tell-a-Story
- Harvard Business Review: How to Tell a Great Story https://hbr.org/2014/07/how-to-tell-a-great-story

**Example:** Sorry, this is your story! It just doesn't work if you tell somebody else's.

## Practice Speech: Who Am I?

**Time Limit:** Three minutes

**Audience:** You have decided to take the trip of a lifetime, sailing as a passenger through the Greek Islands for a month without anyone you know. Nine other people that have chosen the same vacation. You come together for a meet-and-greet. Directly afterward, you attend an orientation where each passenger must deliver a short speech by briefly explaining who they are and sharing a significant story that was instrumental in molding their character.

**Instructions:**

1. Think of your life on a timeline.

2. Consider your audience.

3. Identify the key moments you will highlight.

4. Create some tension by revealing a struggle you had and how you resolved it.

5. Construct the story being sure to share vivid details: who, what, where, how and why. Be vulnerable open up about your experience. Include a hook, emphasize the conflict, and conclude with impact. Consider if it is the right length.

6. Practice telling the story as often as possible.

**Purpose:** Examine your stories; rewrite the script if necessary. Practice your ability to speak about yourself personally. Practice the art of telling a story.

**Skills to Practice:** DP2: Project, DP5: Pause, DP6: Engage, DP9: Dance.

**Example:** Sorry, this is your story! It just doesn't work if you tell somebody else's.

### Practice Speech: Pitch/Elevator

**Time Limit: 60 seconds**

**Audience:** You are walking down the hallway at work and see the elevator doors begin to close. You hurry and just manage to stop the doors from closing. As they reopen, you're stunned to see the owner of the company you have been dreaming of working for standing on the elevator. Thank goodness, you are on the 36th floor. You have sixty seconds to inspire the owner to read your resume and request an interview.

**Instructions:**

1. Determine your purpose. What do you want to have happen by the end of the pitch? An interview? Submitting a business card? A sale?

2. Write the elevator speech.

   a. Set the Stage. Smile – Attention Grabber. Killer first line.

   b. Who are you? What do you do? Be enthusiastic!

   c. What makes you unique? What's next? Share contributions you have made or problems you've solved. Provide an example. Consider audience. What makes you the best?

   d. Engage with a question. Call for action!

3. Establish a deliberate practice to nail this pitch!

4. Tailor your pitch to different audiences.

**Purpose:** To fine tune your personal branding pitch.

**Skills to Practice:** DP1: Set the Stage. DP2: Project DP3: Assess and Cope DP6: Engage, Engage, Engage

**Resources:**

- How to Write a Killer Elevator Pitch - https://theinterviewguys.com/write-elevator-pitch/

- Your Elevator Pitch Needs an Elevator Pitch - https://hbr.org/2014/12/your-elevator-pitch-needs-an-elevator-pitch

# References

Allyn, P. (2010, March 02). Storytelling Connects us All. Retrieved April 20, 2017, from https://www.psychologytoday.com/blog/litlife/201003/storytelling-connects-us-all

Armstrong, T. (2006). Revisiting the Johari window: Improving communications through self-disclosure and feedback. Human Development;Summer2006, Vol. 27 Issue 2, p10

Attitudes and Cancer. (n.d.). Retrieved April 04, 2017, from https://www.cancer.org/cancer/cancer-basics/attitudes-and-cancer.html

Brown, B. (2010). The power of vulnerability. Retrieved April 20, 2017, from https://www.ted.com/talks/brene_brown_on_vulnerability

Cain, S. (2013). Quiet: the power of introverts in a world that can't stop talking. London: Penguin Books.

Chapman, A. (2011). Johari window. Retrieved April 01, 2017, from http://www.businessballs.com/johariwindowmodel.htm

Cooper, B. B. (2017, May 29). Are you an introvert or an extrovert? What it means for your career. Retrieved July 23, 2017, from https://www.fastcompany.com/3016031/are-you-an-introvert-or-an-extrovert-and-what-it-means-for-your-career

Digman, J.M.(1990) Personality structure: Emergence of the five factor model. Annual Reviews of Psychology. 41, 417-40

DSM-5. (n.d.). Retrieved July 23, 2017, from https://www.psychiatry.org/psychiatrists/practice/dsm

Esposito, R. P., Mcadoo, H.& Scher. L. (1978) The Johari Window test: A research note. Journal of Humanistic Psychology, Vol. -18, No. 1, Winter, 1978, pp. 79-81.

Eurich, T. (2017). Insight: Why Were Not As Self-Aware As We Think, and How Seeing Ourselves Clearly Helps Us Succeed at Work and in Life. Random House Inc.

Gallo, C. (2016). Talk Like TED. Pan Books Ltd.

Gallo, L. C., Bogart, L. M., Vranceanu, A., & Matthews, K. A. (2005). Socioeconomic status, resources, psychological experiences, and emotional responses: A test of the reserve capacity model. Journ200al of Personality and Social Psychology, 88, 386-399.

Goldberg, L. R. "The development of markers for the Big-Five factor structure." Psychological assessment 4.1 (1992): 26. <http://dx.doi.org/10.1037/1040-3590.4.1.26>

Herodotus (n.d.) BrainyQuotes.com. Retrieved March 18, 2017, from BrainyQuote.com Web site: https://www.brainyquote.com/quotes/quotes/h/herodotus379319.html

Hsu, J. (2008, July 23). The secrets of storytelling: Why we love a good yarn. Retrieved April 20, 2017, from https://www.scientificamerican.com/article/the-secrets-of-storytelling/

Hyatt, M. (2017). What story are you telling yourself? Retrieved April 20, 2017, from https://michaelhyatt.com/what-story-are-you-telling-yourself.html

Inventory. (n.d.). Retrieved July 23, 2017, from https://www.merriam-webster.com/dictionary/inventory

Jones, R. (2015). Dr. Carmella's Guide to Understanding the Introverted[Cartoon]. Retrieved from http://romanjones.deviantart.com/art/How-to-Live-with-Introverts-Guide-Printable-320818879

Lin N, Simeone RS, Ensel WM, Kuo W. Social support, stressful life events, and illness: A model and an empirical test. J Health Soc Behav. 1979;20:108–19.

Luft, J. (1969) Of Human Interaction. Palo Alto, CA. National Press

Luft, J. Group processes: An introduction to group dynamics. Palo Alto, Calif.: National Press Books, 1970.

Luft, J., & Ingham, H. (1955) The Johari Window as a graphic model of interpersonal awareness University of California, Los Angeles, Extension Office Proceedings of the Western Training Laboratory in Group Development, 1955.

Marselle, T. (2012) MBTI® history and tributes to Isabel Briggs Myers and Mary McCaulley. Retrieved July 23, 2017, from http://www.becomewhoyouare.net/MBTI-history-and-tributes-newest-ver.html

McAdams, D. P. (1993). The Stories We Live by: Personal Myths and the Making of the Self. Guilford Press.

Morgan, N. (2015). How to think about storytelling. (2015, May 14). Retrieved April 20, 2017, from http://www.publicwords.com/2015/05/14/how-to-think-about-storytelling/

Mott, J. M. (2016, January 01). A Journey to the Oldest Cave Paintings in the World. Retrieved April 20, 2017, from http://www.smithsonianmag.com/history/journey-oldest-cave-paintings-world-180957685/

Myers, I. B. (2017) The Myers & Briggs Foundation - MBTI® Basics. Retrieved April 01, 2017, from http://www.myersbriggs.org/my-mbti-personality-type/mbti-basics/

Myers, I.B., Meyers, P.B. (1995) Mountain View, CA. Gifts differing: Understanding personality type. Mountain View, CA. Davies-Black Publishing.

National Gallery of Art. (n.d.). Retrieved April 20, 2017, from http://www.nga.gov/content/ngaweb/education/teachers/school-tours/every-picture-tells-a-story.html

Olsen-Laney, M. (2002). The introvert advantage: How to thrive in an extrovert world. Workman Publishing.

Shostrom, E.L. The Personal Orientation Inventory. San Diego, Calif .: Educational and Industrial Testing Service, 1966

The Johari Window. (2002). Retrieved April 01, 2017, from http://changingminds.org/disciplines/communication/models/johari_window.htm

Trainer, A. 2014. The Johari window model and relationship management. https://www.siliconbeachtraining.co.uk/blog/the-johari-window

Powell, A. (2016, September 20). Children need touching and attention, Harvard researchers Say. Retrieved April 04, 2017, from http://news.harvard.edu/gazette/story/1998/04/children-need-touching-and-attention-harvard-researchers-say/

Sarbin, T. R. (1986). Narrative Psychology: The storied nature of human conduct. Praeger.

Stephens, G. J., Silbert, L. J., & Hasson, U. (2010, August 10). Speaker–listener neural coupling underlies successful communication. Retrieved April 20, 2017, from https://www.ncbi.nlm.nih.gov/pmc/articles/PMC2922522/ Wilson, C., & Moulton, B. (2010). Loneliness among Older Adults: A National Survey of Adults 45+. Prepared by Knowledge Networks and Insight Policy Research. Washington, DC: AARP.

Tjan, A. K. (2015, February 11). 5 ways to become more self-aware. Retrieved July 22, 2017, from https://hbr.org/2015/02/5-ways-to-become-more-self-aware

Vassilieva, J. (2016). Narrative Psychology: Identity, Transformation and Ethics. Springer.

Widrich, L. (2012, December 05). The Science of Storytelling: Why Telling a Story is the Most Powerful Way to Activate Our Brains. Retrieved April 20, 2017, from http://lifehacker.com/5965703/the-science-of-storytelling-why-telling-a-story-is-the-most-powerful-way-to-activate-our-brains

# Chapter 6:
# Your Audience Writes the Speech

## Objectives

**By the end of this chapter you should be able to:**

1. Draw Maslow's hierarchy of needs.

2. Distinguish between the primary audience analysis,the secondary audience analysis and formal audience analysis.

3. Consider how you can respectfully communicate with people who have differing values, beliefs and attitudes.

4. Descibe the components of a good personal support system.

5. Explain what it means to be an audience centered communicator.

6. Describe the significance of establishing a meaningful connection (lock) between the audience, yourself and the content.

**Part 1:** What Drives Us? Maslow's Hierarchy of Needs

**Part 2:** Tracking Values, Beliefs, Attitudes and Actions

**Part 3:** Be Aware and Beware: Analyze Your Audience

**Part 4:** The Holy Trinity: You, Your Audience, Your Message

> "Words have incredible power. They can make people's hearts soar, or they can make people's hearts sore.
> – Dr. Mardy Grothe"

*Chapter 6:*
# Your Audience Writes the Speech

## Part 1: What Drives Us? Maslow's Hierarchy of Needs

Have you ever watched someone do something and questioned their motives? There are reasons we as people are motivated to action. Literally, nearly everything we do from "Saying Hi!" to our decision to further our education or drop out, take the job or hand in our notice, fall in love, marry, have children, lie, cheat, even speak in front of an audience. Let's explore some of the best ideas about why we as people do what we do.

Abraham Maslow (1943, 1954) spent an enormous amount of time thinking about what drives us as human beings. After much thought, Maslow determined that we are all driven by needs. He tried to categorize these needs and he found that the best way to represent them was in a hierarchical pyramid. Maslow found that people are motivated to achieve certain needs and that some needs take precedence over others. The base of the pyramid represents the deficiency needs and the top levels are known as growth or being needs.

### Physiological needs

The base of the pyramid represents the most important needs; the things that we could not live without for long. The term he gave these was physiological needs—primal needs such as air, water, sleep, food, and even sex.

**Figure 6.1: Maslow's Hierarchy of Needs (1943)**

BEING NEEDS

Self-actualization

Esteem Needs

Belonging needs

Safety needs

Physiological needs

DEFICIT NEEDS

Imagine your air supply is cut off right now. What will you do to survive? Imagine a child or someone you love, a child, parent or grandparent is starving, unable to find food to survive. The longer someone goes without, the stronger the need will become. For instance, if you skipped one meal, by the fourth skipped meal you will become almost desperate for food. What do you do? How do you react? Human survival instinct will most likely kick in, and we'll do anything we can to survive. Once the physical needs are met, Maslow explains (1943) that we must address our safety needs.

### Safety needs

The World Bank (2016) reports that 10.7% of the population of the world lives in "extreme poverty"—meaning food and clean water are a daily challenge to secure, not to mention health care. In real numbers, this translates into 767 million people who live on less than $1.90 a day. Half of those living in "extreme poverty" are under 18 years old. Poverty is even more prevalent, according to a new Pew Research Center (Kochbar, 2015) report found that 71% of the world's population lives on less than $10 a day. How much do you live on a day? Those of us fortunate enough to seldom stress about meeting our basic physiological and safety needs should be extremely grateful. Maslow (1954) explains that once the deficiency needs are met one can focus on the growth needs.

### Belonging needs

Next, Maslow discusses belonging needs (1943). As human beings, we need each other (Mineo, 1998). Did you know that if a baby is left untouched, it could die?

Debrah Bruce (2003) in her book *Miracle Touch* explains:

> "A "touch-less" society can lead to failure to thrive and death with newborn babies. The perils of a touch-less society became apparent in the early 1900s, when Dr. Luther

Emmett Holt (1910), known as one of America's first and finest pediatricians, decided that parents were spoiling their children by cuddling and holding them too much. Good parents took notice and immediately followed his order, beginning a trend of "hands-off" parenting. Within just a few years, doctors across the nation started to notice a dramatic increase in infant deaths—particularly in seemingly healthy babies. It soon became apparent that these infants experienced "failure to thrive," simply because they were not getting enough human contact through touch. There are hosts of studies of babies in orphanages concluding that those infants who suffered from touch deprivation achieved only half of the height normal for their age."

Many other studies support this research from the famous Harlow (1959) experiment that used monkeys to see how "touch" affected their psyche. They found (Harlow 1959) that early maternal deprivation could be reversed in monkeys only if it had lasted less than 90 days, and estimated that the equivalent for humans was six months. After these critical periods, no amount of exposure to mothers or peers could alter the monkeys' abnormal behaviors and make up for the emotional damage that had already occurred. When emotional bonds were first established was the key to whether they could be established at all.

*Note: Harlow's studies have received great criticism for cruelty to the monkeys. This began the movement for protection of animals in research.*

More recently, studies have examined the quality of touch given by caregivers in orphanages and by mothers correlates to child development (Finio, et. al., 1985 & Poland & Ward, 1994).

Most everyone has had an experience where their belonging needs have suffered, perhaps through a divorce, a move, or the end of a friendship. As an adult, take the time to ensure these needs are met.

### Esteem needs

Maslow states that the next level is self-esteem needs (1943). Over the past few decades, the topic of raising ones self-esteem has been widely discussed—just look at the self-help section of a bookstore. People seek to grow as human beings, they often look for books on self-esteem improvement. Seeking to raise their self-esteem can't necessarily hurt, but according to Maslow, it just might be futile if ones belonging needs are not met. Notice that our need to belong, to have a place that we fit in, must be met before our sense of self can flourish. As an adult, it is up to you to fulfill your need to belong. Perhaps developing a great social support system can help you thrive as an individual. This might mean you have to push yourself to get involved with a group, an activity, a church, or a philanthropic cause. Some good advice is to smile...be approachable and you might open the door to a new friendship.

Self-esteem is the way you think about yourself. There are things that you can do to raise your self-esteem as well as things you can do to lower your self-esteem. Remember discussing the things you do to raise or lower your self-esteem during the Self Inventory?

In discussions with people and in my own life, negative self-talk is at the top of the list of ways to raise or lower self-esteem.

For example, setting manageable goals or having a general direction on something can be a way to raise your self-esteem. Exercise goals can be a win-win situation: exercise reduces stress, improves your appearance, and keeps your body healthy. You look better and you feel

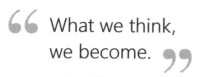

> ## What we think, we become.
> — *Buddha*

better. Reaching an exercise goal is a major accomplishment that enhances your sense of self-worth. People often report that feelings of self-worth are raised by furthering their education or simply trying new things to broaden their world of experience. Over the years, I have learned the tremendous power of words. I repeatedly return to these words, almost as a mantra, to remind myself of the need to manage my thoughts.

"Watch your thoughts, they become words;
watch your words, they become actions;
watch your actions, they become habits;
watch your habits, they become character;
watch your character, for it becomes your destiny."
— *Author*

*Note: While widely attributed to an array of people from Ralph Waldo Emerson, Lao Tzu, Frank Outlaw, Gautama Buddha, Bishop Beckwaith, Father of Margaret Thatcher, Quote Investigator found that it was first published in a Texas newspaper feature called "What They're Saying" in May 1977. The saying was ascribed to the creator of a successful U.S. supermarket chain called Bi-Lo, Frank Outlaw.*

Profoundly believing in the power of words, several years ago, a friend of mine and I began to have a retreat in early January where we explored our New Year's Resolutions. What began as a list, developed into a report. The goals turned from a simple list to categories and subcategories with completion ratios. Last year's New Year's Resolutions was 12 pages long, and I was proud to reach 78% of the goals on my list. This year, I'm aiming to reach 85%. Our lives are radically different, and I believe a large portion of the change results from the accountability this activity promotes. This year I even published an article, *Goal Plan: Five Days to an Actualized Year* and created an online Facebook Group named Goal Plan: Actualize Your Year—feel free to join—enjoying a group of like-minded individuals who seek to plan and reach their goals.

**Self-actualization Needs**

At the top of the pyramid, the final need that Maslow (1962) explains is self-actualization Maslow (1970) loosely defined self-actualization as "the full use and exploitation of talents, capacities, potentialities, etc." These can include: morality, creativity, spontaneity, problem solving, lack of prejudice, acceptance of facts. Others see self-actualization as a feeling of being/having enough.

To me, self-actualization is the desire to reach your full potential; to be all that you can be. Isn't it a philosophical notion? I can't determine whether another person is self-actualized, because I don't know what he or she is capable of. I do know that we as human beings barely scrape the surface of what we are capable of. According to Maslow, when our other needs are met, we strive or perhaps we are free, to reach this final point of self-actualization. Do you think most people reach self-actualization? Or do they mostly spend their lives attempting to meet the more basic needs? Maslow stated: 'I think of the self-actualizing man not as an ordinary man with something added, but rather as the ordinary man with nothing taken away.'

Who is someone that you would think would be self-actualized? Many people suggest

Gandhi, Mother Theresa, Oprah, Madonna, Donald Trump, Adolph Hitler, or Margaret Thatcher. It is impossible from the outside to judge the degree of self-actualization a person attains. We are all driven by needs. Maybe the need to belong drives you to be a household name, but getting there does not mean you're at the top of the pyramid. A legendary case of this is Marilyn Monroe. Although she was one of the most photographed persons of all time, her unfilled need to be accepted and loved drove her to suicide.

### Characteristics of Self-Actualization

In his book *Motivation and Personality* (1970), Maslow studied 18 people he considered to be self-actualized. These individuals included some great minds like Abraham Lincoln, Thomas Jefferson, Albert Einstein, Mother Teresa, and even Margaret Thatcher. He was able to identify common characteristics of the self-actualized individual. These characteristics are:

1. They perceive reality efficiently and can tolerate uncertainty;
2. Accept themselves and others for what they are;
3. Spontaneous in thought and action;
4. Problem-centered (not self-centered);
5. Unusual sense of humor;
6. Able to look at life objectively;
7. Highly creative;
8. Resistant to enculturation, but not purposely unconventional;
9. Concerned for the welfare of humanity;
10. Capable of deep appreciation of basic life-experience;
11. Establish deep satisfying interpersonal relationships with a few people;
12. Peak experiences;
13. Need for privacy;
14. Democratic attitudes;
15. Strong moral/ethical standards.

Sometimes I wonder if self-actualization can be obtained in one area of your life, but not in another. For instance, you could be a great parent, but a poor businessperson. Consider the athlete Michael Phelps. There's no doubt that he is an outstanding athlete, but as a role model and businessman, he has failed miserably. He agreed to endorse products and received great sums of money capitalizing on his "gold medal" athleticism. He enjoyed the prestige that came with being an athletic role model, but the photograph of him smoking a bong at a party destroyed the image he was paid to convey. Yes, he apologized, but those in the swimming world know that this incident was far from the first time he was caught making bad choices. He lost millions of dollars in sponsorship money, and his credibility was shot for many as a role model. Self-actualized? As a swimmer and athlete, absolutely; as a businessman and role model, he missed some huge opportunities that he could have capitalized on at the time; perhaps he will create new business opportunities in the future.

**Evaluating Maslow's Hierarchy of Needs**

Now I have a few questions for you regarding Maslow:

**1. Where do you fall? What needs do you find yourself striving to attain daily?**

Which level of the pyramid are you currently concerned about? For me, I am so fortunate to not have to be routinely worried about physiological and safety needs. I'd like to believe that my belonging needs, which were left quite unfulfilled as a child and which I sought, often unsuccessfully to fulfill in my early adult life are finally at a healthy place. For many years, I worked on self-esteem, but because my belonging needs were unfulfilled, my work efforts seemed to fall on barren ground. Once I was able to surround myself with a fantastic social support system and open myself to experience the love and support offered, my esteem blossomed and actually bloomed. I'm still experiencing smelling the flowers and continue to prune the plants and am moving into the area of self-actualization. I am finding that reaching this level has a significant amount of believing in yourself to the core. Self actualization is truly a leap of faith, and when all the other needs are truly met, one is able to catapult to that final stage. I'm currently playing with the catapult!

**2. What the heck does Maslow have to do with public speaking?**

Answer: Hopefully you answered that it is important to know not only where you fall, but also where your audience falls on the scale. Some of the biggest faux pas in history occurred because a speaker spoke above the audiences' needs. For example, consider Marie Antoinette's famous "Let them eat cake" statement. While not factually correct, the common myth supports this point. France experienced a tremendous financial crisis leaving many desolate. Marie Antoinette was given the name "Madame Déficit" due to her lavish spending and her opposition to the social and financial reforms. Had she been able to communicate compassion to her people struggling to survive at the base of the pyramid, rather than flaunting excess, she might not have lost her head.

A similar faux pas came from the whole "Just Say No!" program (Dukoupli, 2016). While First Lady Nancy Reagan was speaking in an impoverished neighborhood, a frustrated mother posed a question to her. The mother was concerned for the well-being of her children, and wanted to know what she should tell her children to say when they get approached by drug dealers on their way home from school. Mrs. Reagan unceremoniously responded, "Just say no." The news media responded depicting her as "disconnected" with the inner battle this mother faced. In a defensive move, Mrs. Reagan's team responded by launching the "Just Say No" program in an effort to save face, but Mrs. Reagan opened her eyes to the problems that existed in our inner cities.

Other examples that infuriated the general public include: in the wake of the Katrina disaster, Condolesa Rice's excursion to buy shoes on Fifth Avenue (Rice expresses regret in her memoirs, *No Higher Honor, 2011*), and Michael Browning asking the camera crew as the New Orleans catastrophe escalated, "How do I look?" His concern should have been for the unmet needs of the thousands of people suffering in the city, not his appearance. *Undercover Boss* is an American reality television series, based on the British series of the same name. Each episode depicts a person who has an upper-management position at a major business, deciding to go undercover as an entry-level employee to discover the faults in the company. The manager/owner always seems to be profoundly impacted by interaction with the line personnel. They return to headquarters and make significant changes. Why? Because they opened themselves to experience the needs of those with a very different experience.

When it comes to a speech, you will not have time to play Undercover Speaker; you have one time to get it right. This is why it is important to take the time to understand where your audience is coming from and what needs are driving their thoughts and actions.

### 3. How good do you think Maslow's theory is?

Does it help you better understand your life and how to interact with the world around you? That is the role that theory plays in the social sciences.

In the previous chapter, we explored a few theories, and we will be looking at more. Hopefully you will be researching and using quality theoretical work as the basis of your research in speeches. To me, a theory is like trying on a pair of sunglasses. There are many different types of sunglasses. By filtering out specific light frequencies, tinted lenses highlight certain colors you might not have noticed before. Some sunglasses draw out specific colors that might have been missed entirely. Looking at a theory is like looking through a filtered lens; it causes us to see some things more clearly or notice things that might have been passed over without wearing the glasses.

What personal strengths, weaknesses or limitations can you can find through the lens of Maslow's hierarchy? Maslow can help explain your needs and where you are in life and can help you better understand other people. As for weaknesses, some claim that the way that Maslow looks at it is a hierarchy, meaning that you can't move on to a higher need until another is met; but some think that we address many needs simultaneously, in a more holistic way. Enjoy theories for how they can expand your insights, but always take the time to evaluate them, considering their innate limitations.

*Note: If you would like to further explore Maslow's Hierarchy of Needs, Saul McLeod does a phenomenal job of breaking down Maslow's ideas and his life's work on SimplePsychology.org.*

*In a survey conducted from 2005 to 2010, Tay & Diener (2011) tested Maslow's theory by analyzing the data of 60,865 participants from 123 countries, representing every major region of the world. Turns out, Maslow was right, the results found while the order varied by culture, these universal human needs exist regardless of cultural differences.*

## Part 2: Tracking Values, Beliefs, Attitudes and Actions

Define the following words:

*Values*

*Beliefs*

*Attitudes*

*Actions*

> **Draw a tree.**
>
> Label: roots, trunk, branches and fruit.
>
> Match: values, beliefs, attitudes and actions.

We often hear about attitudes, beliefs, and values but what do these terms actually mean? Values, beliefs, and attitudes comprise a system of thinking, whether conscious or unconscious, that drives our behavior. The clearer we are, the greater we understand our structure, and hence our lives can be more productive.

The Merriam-Webster dictionary (2017) defines these terms as:

**Value:** relative worth, merit, or importance or a thing or idea

**Belief:** an opinion or conviction, confidence in the truth or existence of something

**Attitude:** feelings about things, values and beliefs, proclivities, or tendencies

**Actions:** things people do to support or achieve their values, beliefs, and attitudes

**Roots** are the equivalent of the values. They are those ideas or concepts we perceive to have the greatest merit or worth. We each place specific values on different ideas. Our values are deep within us and not always apparent to outsiders.

**Trunk** represents the belief structure. When we meet new people, often we can sense their belief system based on things they say. Take for example the statement: "I believe that smoking cigarettes is irresponsible." Or, "Smoking should be allowed in public places, what's the big deal?" We often share our beliefs with those we encounter.

**Branches** represent the attitudes, growing up and down, left and right. I like/don't like smokers, I want to help/punish them.

**Fruit** represents what people do; the actions, the taste of the tree, what it produces. These are our attitudes. Perhaps because of former smokers' disdain for smoking, they may avoid making friends or dating a smoker because they don't want to breath in the toxic smoke. On the other hand, a person who is nonchalant about it might enjoy the company of smokers and might grab a cigarette with them outside an establishment.

So what does your fruit taste like? Does it taste sour? Does it taste sweet? The taste of the fruit is a direct result of the roots and beliefs.

Depending on the topic, the same values may lead to different beliefs, attitudes, and actions. People are human and humans vary. As the Red Queen says in Alice in Wonderland "Why, sometimes I've believed six impossible things before breakfast" (Dodson, 1865).

### Where Do Values, Beliefs, and Attitudes Come From?

Using Maslow, where do your values, beliefs, attitudes, and actions originate? Some point out that if one's physical and safety needs were threatened, deprived, or exploited, most certainly one's values would be impacted (take for example those who lived through the Depression tend to save money—their value for doing without stuck with them throughout their life). Outside of primary needs being threatened, our values, beliefs, and attitudes are predominantly influenced by our belonging needs. Remember your sphere of influence, the place you called home? How much choice did you have into which family you were born? Now consider some of the people in your life. Who would you be today, how would your life be different, if as a baby you had been brought up exposed to another sphere of influence?

### Thanksgiving Dinner

Have you ever experienced a Thanksgiving Day dinner? If you haven't experienced a Thanksgiving meal, is there a traditional dinner you partake in that is a shared experience within your culture? Think of that meal as we continue this discussion. What is your favorite food item on the table? Was it the juicy turkey, the sweet potatoes, stuffing, cornbread, macaroni and cheese, mashed potatoes or pecan pie? It makes you hungry just thinking about it, doesn't it? Can you smell it?

Have you ever experienced Thanksgiving or a traditional holiday meal at somebody else's house? What was that experience like? When I ask this question in a workshop, I always chuckle at the physical response of my participants. Their faces scrunch up; they look mortified and respond, "It was messed up." When asked why it was "messed up," the general response is that it wasn't like what they were used to. The potatoes had a spice in them, they served pasta, or the stuffing was from a box! "They didn't even sit down at a table together." Then I ask these wrinkly-nosed individuals if the people who hosted the meal thought it was messed up. They shake their heads and say, "No, they thought it was right on."

So why is this common experience of a traditional holiday meal so vastly different from table to table? It's all a matter of what we're exposed to. If you grew up eating creamy smooth mashed potatoes with nutmeg in them, when you sit down expecting Thanksgiving dinner and receive lumpy mashed potatoes, you freak out! This is not what you're used to. We see images portraying the traditional Thanksgiving dinner and think we are all experiencing the same thing until we realize that other people just don't know how to do it right!

Then I ask, "At this celebration, was there an item at that table you actually liked? Maybe it was different or even ("Shhh!") better than your mom's?" Suddenly heads begin to nod. They respond, "Yes they had sweet potato pie or a casserole that was stupendous!"

Can you see how the Thanksgiving table represents a metaphor for life? Whether you realize it or not, whether your eyes are "wide shut" or "wide open" with every choice you make, you are essentially creating the dishes you will serve on your "table of life." What are you

A mind that is stretched
by a new experience
can never go back to
its old dimensions.

*– Oliver Wendell Holmes*

serving? Are you going to recreate the dishes exactly as they were prepared by your "sphere of influence" (your family of origin), or are you going to consciously select which ones you will take and perhaps add a little "something" to make it your own? Or are you going to throw out everything and come up with your own meal and make seafood gumbo instead of turkey? Ultimately, you are the chef in your own kitchen. Choose your menu wisely for each and every day you serve these dishes to everyone you encounter.

Can you imagine a parent who would not wish more for their child, than what they were given? That if they could afford more opportunity for their child, they would not offer it to them? Have your parents in their own way tried to do so for you? Maybe they were successful or perhaps they failed. Parenting is not easy, and no one does it perfectly. Realize the impact their influences have had upon you to date and consciously choose your course. Keep in mind that every person's perspective is limited. To make the best decisions, exploring other points of views and ways of doing things can be invaluable. So, what choices will you make in creating your life?

What does this Thanksgiving Table metaphor have to do with communicating? When you envision your audience and consider the words you will use to connect with them, know that they face the same limitations you do and have their own experience and preferences. Do your best to leave space for them to be who they are. That will enhance your chances for communicating.

How do you make this happen? It's not that difficult. Do you remember when I asked the question "Have you ever experienced a traditional Thanksgiving dinner?" And then followed it up by allowing those who hadn't to substitute a meal they could relate to? It is that simple. Thanksgiving is actually a holiday that is celebrated in many different cultures from Korea, Ghana, Germany, India, China, Canada, and even Barbados. If this book was being published first in a country that did not celebrate Thanksgiving like Hungary, I would first ask who had celebrated a New Year's Celebration. Be aware of the fact that even if most people in a given group share and experience, not everyone necessarily has. Leave room for people who have not experienced your dominant experience to continue with the conversation rather than being excluded. Imagine you have **never** experienced a Thanksgiving Day dinner and a speaker makes one of the following questions/statements. To which do you best respond?

1.  You've all had Thanksgiving Day dinner.
2.  What's your favorite Thanksgiving dinner item?
3.  How many of you have experienced a Thanksgiving Day dinner?

Which question would leave the audience member feeling included rather than excluded? Hopefully you answered the last option! Assumptions were not based upon the majority of the group. The audience member(s) "assumed" to share the exact same experience as the group majority. Let's take a closer look at "assumption," defined as "a thing that is accepted as true or as certain to happen, without proof." How do you feel when someone makes an assumption about you? During speeches, people frequently make glaring assumptions and do not even notice. Here are a few examples:

**Religion:** Not everyone shares the same belief structure. Unless you are at a religious institution chartered to create shared meaning and understanding of a belief structure, don't assume others share your belief or lack of belief in a higher power. According to the Hartford Institute of Religion Research and a demographic report by Pew Research *(Wormald, 2015)*, more than 40 percent of Americans "say" they go to church weekly. As it turns out, however, less than 20 percent are actually in church. In other words, more than 80 percent of Americans are finding more fulfilling things to do on weekends *(Ridgaway, 2013)*. Furthermore, in a public audience, ideas about religion held by of people from other cultures are sure to vary drastically.

*Note: When I originally wrote the first sentence in the paragraph above, I initially used the word "church" instead of "religious institution." Immediately I realized that word was not audience-centered and changed it. Why? I grew up going to "church"—this was my experience of a religious institution. The vocabulary erupts from within me based on my experience. Others may refer to a temple, mosque, cathedral, synagogue, chapel, etc.*

Simple statements like: "When you pray" or "Jesus answers prayers" or "What did you do for Christmas?" make an inherent assumption. Conversely, people who do not practice religion should be careful to consider those who do. "Don't you enjoy those lazy Sundays sleeping in until ten?" To an avid churchgoer, which in the United States is reportedly 37% of the population, this would be an assumption, causing them to disagree and perhaps question your credibility.

*Note: Sharing your personal experience as your own is fine, just don't portray your belief as true for all and allow others space to have their own beliefs. For example: "I can remember the first time I went to the church of which I am now a member." Or, "I recently visited my fiancé's family. As an atheist I never even think about going to church, but for her, family was the Sunday event." Now there is no need to reveal either of those tidbits of information unless it is in context with a personal story you are sharing. Can you see how statements like these don't make an assumption that everyone prays or is an atheist?*

**Politics:** Unless you are on the campaign trail, be very careful about imposing your political beliefs about policy, pundits and candidates. Such statements can distract from your message. Audience members are likely to discredit your opinions if yours don't jive with theirs. Unless the purpose of the speech is to examine such issues, stay neutral. There is no need to reveal any irrelevant viewpoint.

**Behaviors:** Mostly likely, your habits differ from those of audience members. Beware of making silly assumptions about your routine that distract from your message. Maybe it is about texting or Facebook—chances are, depending upon the audience, some use it and some oppose the use of social media. If you want to bring up a potentially controversial issue, why not ask the audience a question about their behaviors? That gets them involved and participating in the speech, which increases audience engagement. This is an effective alternative to referring to their use of social media with a blanket statement like, "I'm sure you all love smart phones, how can we live without them today?" Rather, ask, "Who in here has a smart phone?" Look around to seek confirmation. If someone fails to engage, engage that person directly. Once you have obtained consensus, make your point.

Assumptions can stem from nearly any topic: drinking, hygiene, travel, experiences like going to the beach, or working countless hours. The truth is, experiences differ greatly, each and every day. You can refer to your experience, but be sure not to assume shared understanding of that experience with your audience. Leave room for their experiences. This marks the difference between an audience-centered approach and a speaker-centered one. In this way, the audience writes the speech.

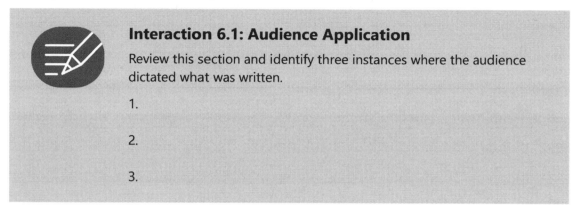

**Interaction 6.1: Audience Application**

Review this section and identify three instances where the audience dictated what was written.

1.

2.

3.

**Figure 6.2: Model of Communication**

speaker (sender)          message          audience (recipient)

**The Lock**

Remember the communication model that we used? You have the speaker, the message and the recipient (audience). Now that you know your limitations, strengths, and weaknesses as the speaker, your understanding of audience members can improve. That knowledge helps you realize that each audience member confronts limitations too. Understanding this better equips you to design a message that will take the best that you have and connect it with the audience.

To help us take the crucial step of learning more about our audience, we conduct an audience analysis. Most books on public speaking discuss what I'm going to refer to as your Primary Audience Analysis. To truly connect, I believe there is a Secondary Audience Analysis, which will create a "lock" or connection between you and your message to the audience. Finally, if you have the opportunity create a Formal Questionnaire do so, the results can be a fantastic edition to your speech. Let's explore these three types of audience analysis.

## Part 3: Be Aware and Beware

### Audience Analysis

One of my favorite sayings is the quote just shared above, "The audience writes the speech." What do you think this statement means?

One way to let the audience write the speech is to allow their anticipated reactions to influence every word you write. I like to think of the audience as a little bird on my shoulder. I mentally confer with them as I write. I ask myself questions like "How will my audience respond to this point? Can this statement offend anyone? How can someone interpret this message another way? Is this example relevant to this particular audience, or is there a better, more relevant example available? How can I check with the audience to ensure my point resonates?"

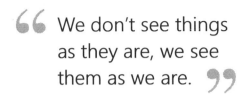

> We don't see things as they are, we see them as we are.
>
> – Anaïs Nin

**Primary Audience Analysis**

In order to answer these types of questions, you must know who your audience is. The answer to these questions will vary, depending upon many factors about your audience.

Before you even begin to select a topic, conduct a cursory audience analysis. This preliminary audience analysis asks the basic question, "Who is my audience?" Think like a marketer—know who they are! Before a product goes to market, an intense marketing analysis is conducted. Speakers' market research methods may include inspecting a given audience using specific criteria designed to provide market segmentation (the identification of portions of the market that are different from one another.) By undergoing this analysis, the needs of potential customers can be better satisfied. Companies take marketing very seriously as they must understand and satisfy their customers' needs better than the competition, so should speakers.

As a speaker, you must also satisfy the needs of the customers, in this case your audience. How? Throughout your speech, you will have to earn the ear of your audience members. Be careful, we as individuals tend to prefer our own internal dialogue. How often have you daydreamed during a presentation or conversation? During a speech, there are many reasons audience members may find to resist or focus on other things. Why does this natural tug-of-war exist?

1. **Incongruent Opinions:** Audience members each have their own values, beliefs, and attitudes based upon individual experiences. Remember how you learned more about what makes you "you" in the last chapter? Each audience member has a specific personality, complete with idiosyncrasies, just like you! As a speaker, it is up to you to understand that and take it into account in the process.

2. **Noise:** Remember how in Chapter 3 we discussed internal and external noise that you always compete with? Let's revisit these for a moment. There is external noise like a lawn mower outside or the clinking of dishes as servers remove them from the table. We also have internal noise and/or psychological noise. We can come into the speech with life stresses filling our thoughts or we can have preconceived ideas about what the other person is going to say and why. We can easily become blinded to their original message.

Think about the last time you heard a speech. Did those inner voices distract you? As a speaker, you must be more interesting and more compelling than all your audience's "stuff!" That is not easy to do. Everyone's stuff is important to them, as it should be. So how do we compete? Think like a marketer! Ask five to seven questions designed to learn who they are. These questions will help you get outside yourself and get into your audience's heads. Like a marketer, these questions should be based upon:

- Demographics - Determine who you audience is by examining how old they are, their race, religion, gender, family size, ethnicity, income, and education.

- Geographic's - Consider where your audience originates from and how those factors can impact how they respond to your message. A hot climate versus a cold climate. Growing up in a third world country versus a first world country.

- Psychographics - People spend their money and time very differently. Consider how they think and what they value and how this can impact their understanding of your message.

- Behavioral - Often times people are required to attend a presentation by their boss or for certification. Their motivation to listen is something that you should be aware of as you prepare. Sometimes you have the ability to glean some of the answers to these questions from the organizer of the event, however always develop your own set of questions and spend some time thinking about perspective audience members and just trying to get into their minds and make room for their perspectives. The act of doing so will greatly mold your approach to your message so that it has a better chance of being well received.

Often times, the reasons the audience has come together will help you determine the approach. For instance, a group of business people holding a networking meeting focuses on growing their businesses, primarily to make more money. A group of recovering addicts meets to focus on healing themselves and overcoming addiction.

**Primary Audience Analysis**

Write at least five questions about your audience. For example:

1. Who is the oldest member of my audience, and who is the youngest?

2. What do their hands say about them (calloused, work hard physically or softer, manicured, more protected)?

3. Whose view of religion will most align with mine vs. whose religious view will differ most from mine?

4. Are there more males or females?

5. How many different languages are represented in the audience?

6. How is a typical Saturday night spent?

7. How much do they want to be listening to this speech?

The act of asking these questions heightens your awareness of your audience. Remember, these questions are not based upon your topic but rather have to do with the demographics, geographics, psychographics and behaviors of anticipated audience. Will you literally obtain the answers? No! The act of asking the question is the most important factor into his activity. Considering the audience at such a specific level will influence your approach in the design of your message.

**Why Your Audience Analysis Matters: A Story of Two Audiences**

Once I was delivering speeches to various organizations regarding the fear of public speaking. After a speech to a group of executive women, a woman approached me asking if I would speak to a group of girls at the center where she worked. They were high school girls who had been arrested. The center was trying to intervene and teach life lessons to help them change course. The girls I was asked to speak to were the group "leaders."

Consider how the answers to my Primary Audience Analysis questions differed for these two audiences. The same questions were asked the answers differed, which dramatically altered my approach to my delivery.

**Table 6.1: Audience Analysis**

| Executive Women | Juvenile Girls |
|---|---|
| **What is the age range of the audience, median age?** 30-65; 50 | **What is the age range of the audience, median age?** 14-18; 16 |
| **What cultures are represented? Which are under represented?** Predominantly Anglo and Jewish, some Hispanics, a few Blacks. Fort Lauderdale, Florida is a very diverse population. | **What cultures are represented? Which are under represented?** Going into this speech I truly did not know. Turns out, it was Anglo and Hispanics. Fort Lauderdale, Florida is a very diverse population. |
| **What are they seeking to "get" from this group?** Business/money/relationships **From this speech?** Ability to generate more money/business/confidence | **What kinds of problems fill their mind?** I can only imagine...WOW! BOYS, FB, family, school, friends...media. |
| **What religions? Any non-Christians?** Christianity, Islam, Judaism, Buddhism, Hinduism, New Age, Agnostic | **What religions? Any non-Christians?** Christianity, Islam, Judaism, Buddhism, Hinduism, New Age, Agnostic |
| **What would make them feel good?** Success? **What would make them smile?** Kindness, consideration? | **What would make them feel good?** Security? success? **What would make them smile?** Kindness, consideration? |
| **What is their personality?** They joined this group so they have to have some sense of personal development—go getters! | **What is their personality?** They have landed themselves in hot water, so they have to have major problems, issues I can't even imagine. But they are in the leadership group so they are trying to change, seek a new way! |

| Executive Women | Juvenile Girls |
| --- | --- |
| **What is the income level?** Probably middle to upper middle, some wealthy, a few struggling. | **What is their home life like? Is it safe?** I can only imagine. Probably safe for some and not for others. |
| **What would make them feel good?** Add a joke and acknowledgment to both. | **What would make them feel good?** Add a joke and acknowledgment to both. |

The message was the same for both audiences, but how I constructed the message was completely different because of my primary audience analysis. For the Executive Women, I dressed in a business suit. I made sure I had a manicure and a pedicure. I believe I even borrowed a Coach bag from a friend. This group was extremely well-groomed and they noticed these details. I didn't want this "stuff" to influence their perception of me or more importantly, my message. "I'd rather pull my nails out then deliver a speech" was the advertised topic. I began the speech by taking out a pink pair of pliers and feigning that I was pulling out my longest nail. When the audience recoiled, I laughed and asked, "So which would you prefer. . . deliver a speech or pull out a nail? At the end of the speech I gave each a nail file that had my company's name as now they could shape their message rather than pull out their nails.

When it came time to speak to the juvenile girls, I was so nervous. Having done my audience analysis, I couldn't imagine why these girls would care about delivering a speech—if they didn't care, why would they want to listen? I knew my message well. When I arrived, my dress was much different than the Women's Executive group—I wore slacks and a shirt. I didn't run out to get my nails polished and certainly didn't borrow a Coach bag. In fact, I didn't even begin by standing in front of them—to this day, this is the only speech I have ever delivered sitting. I didn't even sit at the head of the table. We just began talking, I asked lots of questions trying not to sound like an interrogator. I listened with both ears! I asked about their program, their day, their future plans. Eventually one young lady shared that she was going to the community college in the fall. Guess what? I taught at that college, maybe she could take my class! Soon she revealed that indeed she had received a scholarship and was speaking at an event to thank the committee who awarded it to her. BAM! I had a way to connect. Without my attention to my audience analysis, I very well may have just stood in front of that audience and done my speech, same as the Executive Women's group, after all, that's all that was asked of me. The coordinator approached me after the presentation and thanked me so much. She expressed that while she believes having speakers come in to inspire these young impressionable women was valuable, almost all just got up and spoke and failed to connect with them at all. As a result the girls didn't get much from the presentation. Be sure this doesn't happen to you. Conduct an audience analysis and mold your message to the needs of that particular group. The juvenile girls probably couldn't care less about overcoming their fear of public speaking! As a result, I began the speech by just getting to know them, because if they didn't feel that my topic was important or relevant, why would they ever listen? My Secondary Audience Analysis helped me be able to tune in to their needs.

I once met a great salesman. When I asked him why he was successful, he explained that it was simple; he had to identify his customer's "hurt." If he could identify where the business was hurting, he could determine if his equipment could resolve the hurt. His job, as he saw it, was like a doctor's: to help the company feel better. If the company was not hurting, they didn't need his equipment, so he was friendly and moved on. But if they were hurting, he offered a remedy...thus making a sale and a satisfied customer. Likewise, when an audience gives you their time, focus and attention, isn't it best if they can be better as a result? So find the audience's hurt! What can you offer to help them feel better?

The audience should be better off for having heard your words. Strive to leave the audience with some useful information. Make it worth their time. Author Nick Morgan has a quote I take to heart, "The only reason to give a speech is to change the world." Your words should have the capacity to change the audience member's life. Your job is to find the key information and convince them that it will indeed change their life. Finding the benefit is different from understanding why it is important. Do your research on your topic. Find the exciting, valuable information, then develop a strategy to tell why it is worth the audience's time.

When you deliver a speech, your audience members give you the gift of their time. Appreciate the gift; thank them by offering content that can benefit their lives. Treat these moments as something special and worthwhile. Be sure your audience will be better for having heard your words. When you answer the question, "How can the audience benefit from my words," build from the previous question that discusses the importance. By finding the benefit, you resolve the "hurt." Does it matter to you if the audience connects to your words? It should. When it matters to the speaker, an audience always knows. Heart and soul is difficult to hide from an audience. If you care about the needs of the audience more than your own, you will construct a message that is audience-centered, one that connects with each individual member. Let's put this in perspective.

Answer this question: How many audience members are you prepared to **not** care about... to lose?

Is 50% too much or too little? How about 25%? Suppose you had an audience of 25 people—are you okay with not reaching five? How about two? One?

Over the years, when I ask these questions I always hear different responses. Few accept less than 50% but quite a few are satisfied with 50%. From my perspective, I find this intriguing, because the attitude permeates into the speech. The same people who shrugged their shoulders unconcerned about how many they would lose, accepting the fact that they would lose a percentage of the audience, are the same ones who lost audience members in their speeches! Their body language and intent was perceived by the audience, which responded accordingly. Audiences instinctively read the intent of the speaker. Once you are willing to do your best to consider each audience member, you have taken the first step in connecting your message to the audience. How do we construct such a message?

Be committed to make it worth their time!

 Find out what's keeping them up nights and offer hope. Your theme must be an answer to their fears. 

– *Gerald C. Myers*

Care enough about each audience member to select a message that can reach each one. Incorporate all that you have learned about your audience from your audience analysis. We do this by carefully answering three questions.

**Find Good Answers to These Questions**

Clarify why your words are worth their time. These questions are instrumental in connecting you to the message while ensuring your audience too can connect to the message. While these questions are closely aligned, they each serve a specific purpose.

*Note: In order to answer these questions correctly, you must have completed your research and identified the sources you plan to use.*

1. **Why is this topic important to my audience?**
   When you go to answer this question, think about what you have gained from your research. What "hurt" can this information cure? Was this new information significant to you? How? Why? Asking these questions helps the most pertinent information to surface so you can then target those key ideas.

2. **How can the audience benefit?**
   If you speech is 10 minutes and you deliver it to twenty people, that is 3.3 hours of time given to you as a gift. Use the every second your audience afforded you with care, treat it as a special commodity. Explore your research to determine what value the information can have for audience members. Remember how we discussed WIIFM? The What's In It For Me Concept? Use your own interaction with the content, what did you find most valuable? Now consider your audience, will they too identify with the parts that you did? Are there other parts that will resonate with them?

   When I think about my words benefiting my audience, I always think about the gift of time audience members bestow upon me by being in my audience. I want to make the message worth their time. Consider this:

3. **What new information will they learn?**
   From the incredible amount of material available, be sure to select information your audience does not already know. Imagine someone chose to deliver a speech on the ABC's to a literate audience. How would you respond? No matter how clever or dynamic, it would be a waste of everyone's time, right? Offer your audience substance, something they don't already know.

**Play Devil's Advocate!**

Once you have good answers to these three questions, ask a buddy to play devil's advocate, challenging and probing you, asking questions that try to shoot your material down. As you defend your position, consider the logic that surfaced. If it was insightful, factor the insight into further responses to these questions. Perhaps you were unable to respond, and you had no defense. Reconsider your topic, or at least your connection to it. Think—have you done enough research? Do you believe this information has value? Is it worthwhile to your audience and you? If you do, you should be able to justify your position with logical arguments. If you don't believe the information is worthwhile and valuable, do you honestly believe your audience will?

*Note: The Audience Analysis section is fundamental to designing a good speech. The whole purpose is for the audience to get the message. In the next chapter, The Speech Formula, the audience analysis will be presented with a bit less detail.*

**Formal Audience Analysis**

If you have the opportunity to create a survey and literally ask your potential audience members questions before the speech, do so. What a fantastic opportunity to really include your audiences ideas and thoughts about your topic in your presentation. These questions should be related to your topic. Don't go overboard and ask too many questions. If you have this opportunity, it is vital that you include the results in your presentation. Audience members are quite keen on having the presentation specifically tailored to them.

## Part 4: The Holy Trinity: You, Your Audience, Your Message

You are now prepared to begin constructing your message. If you are connected to yourself and your audience, you are essentially connected to your message. Construct the message, keeping all that you have learned in mind. Use this information to select the words you use and shape your message. Construct your messages from an audience-centered perspective. This way, your audience writes the speech by way of the Holy Trinity: you, your audience and your message.

 The only reason to give a speech is to change the world.
– *Nick Morgan*

## Chapter 6 Review Questions

1. How much control do we have over our sphere of influence? Explain.

2. Why are belonging needs listed before self-esteem needs?

3. How can Maslow's Hierarchy of Needs be used as a vital part of the speech process?

4. What was the purpose of the Thanksgiving dinner table scenario?

5. What assessments are used to create your Primary Audience Analysis?

6. Write five questions that could be used for a Primary Audience Analysis.

7. What are three questions answered in your Secondary Audience Analysis.

8. What is the significance of the difference between the two?

9. When should you conduct a formal audience analysis?

10. Which quote from this chapter resonates with you the most?

## Practice Speech: Same Speech, Two Audiences

**Time Limit:** 3-5 minutes

**Topic:** Choose a topic, issue, or experience in which you have some expertise. If you have none, choose the drinking age.

**Audience #1:** The Kiwanis club closest to your house needs a speaker for their weekly meeting. They are trying to gain insight into people in their community.

**Audience #2:** The local YMCA has a community fair that young adults will attend to gather tips about life. You have been invited to present a session.

**Instructions:** Conduct a Primary Audience Analysis and Secondary Audience Analysis for both of these audiences.

**Purpose:** Examine how your Primary Audience Analysis questions illuminate why audiences need to be approached differently even with the same topic.

**Example:** Provided in the chapter between the Executive Group of Women and Juvenile Girls.

Topic _____

| Primary: Kiwanis | Primary: YMCA |
|---|---|
| 1. | 1. |
| 2. | 2. |
| 3. | 3. |
| 4. | 4. |
| **Secondary: Kiwanis** | **Secondary: YMCA** |
| 1. Why is the topic important? | 1. Why is the topic important? |
| 2. How will they benefit? | 2. How will they benefit? |
| 3. What will they learn? | 3. What will they learn? |

# References

Bruce, D. F., & Krieger, D. (2003). Miracle touch: a complete guide to hands-on therapies that have the amazing ability to heal. New York, NY: Three Rivers Press.

Bruce, D.F. (2013 How can lack of touch lead to babies' failure to thrive? - Children's Health. Retrieved May 08, 2017, from https://www.sharecare.com/health/kids-teens-health/lack-of-touch-failure-thrive

Dokoupil, T. (2016, March 07). Nancy Reagan's war on drugs. Retrieved May 08, 2017, from http://www.msnbc.com/msnbc/nancy-reagans-biggest-failure-the-war-drugs

Finlon, M. A., Drotar, D., Satola, J., Pallotta, J., Wyatt, B., & El-Amin, D. (1985). Home Observation of Parent-Child Transaction in Failure to Thrive: A Method and Preliminary Findings. New Directions in Failure to Thrive, 177-190. doi:10.1007/978-1-4684-5095-8_12

Goleman, D. (2016, July 22). Self-Awareness is the Key to Becoming a Successful Leader. Retrieved July 22, 2017, from https://www.inc.com/linkedin/daniel-goleman/want-succeed-first-become-self-aware-daniel-goleman.html

Harlow,H.F. (1959) "Love in Infant Monkeys," Scientific American 200 (June 1959):68, 70, 72-73, 74.

Holt, E. (1910). The Care And Feeding Of Children. AJN, American Journal of Nursing, 10(6), 444. doi:10.1097/00000446-191003000-00025

Kochhar, R..(2015), "A global middle class is more promise than reality: From 2001 to 2011, Nearly 700 million step out of poverty, but most only barely." Washington, D.C.: Pew Research Center, July.

Littlejohn, S. W., Foss, K. A., & Oetzel, J. G. (2017). Theories of Human Communication. Long Grove, IL: Waveland Press, Inc.

Maslow, A. H. (1943). A Theory of Human Motivation. Psychological Review, 50(4), 370-96.

Maslow, A. H. (1954). Motivation and personality. New York: Harper and Row.

Maslow, A. H. (1970a). Motivation and personality. New York: Harper & Row.

McLeod, S. A. (2016). Maslow's Hierarchy of Needs. Retrieved from www.simplypsychology.org/maslow.html

O'Toole, G. (n.d.). Watch Your Thoughts, They Become Words; Watch Your Words, They Become Actions. Retrieved May 08, 2017, from http://quoteinvestigator.com/2013/01/10/watch-your-thoughts/

Polan, H. J., & Ward, M. J. (1994). Role of the Mother's Touch in Failure to Thrive: A Preliminary Investigation. Journal of the American Academy of Child & Adolescent Psychiatry, 33(8), 1098-1105. doi:10.1097/00004583-199410000-00005

Powell, A. (1998), Children need touching and attention, Harvard researchers say. Retrieved May 10, 2017, from http://news.harvard.edu/gazette/1998/04.09/ChildrenNeedTou.html

Rice, C. (2011). No higher honor: a memoir of my years in Washington. New York: Crown.

Ridgaway, T. (2013, November 30). Statistics don't tell the whole story when it comes to church attendance Retrieved May 10, 2017, from http://churchleaders.com/pastors/pastor-articles/170739-statistics-don-t-tell-the-whole-story-when-it-comes-to-church-attendance.html

Tay, L., & Diener, E. (2011). Needs and subjective well-being around the world.Journal of Personality and Social Psychology, 101(2), 354.

World Bank. 2016. Poverty and Shared Prosperity 2016: Taking on inequality. Washington, DC: World Bank. doi:10.1596/978-1-4648-0958-3. License: Creative Commons Attribution CC BY 3.0 IGO

Wormald, B. (2015, May 11). America's changing religious landscape. Retrieved May 10, 2017, from http://www.pewforum.org/2015/05/12/americas-changing-religious-landscape/

Writer, L. G. (2016, October 26). Description of how marketers can use Maslow's Hierarchy of Needs. Retrieved May 10, 2017, from http://smallbusiness.chron.com/description-marketers-can-use-maslows-hierarchy-needs-39333.html

1977 May 18, San Antonio Light, What They're Saying, Quote Page 7-B (NArch Page 28), Column 4, San Antonio, Texas. (NewspaperArchive)

# Chapter 7:
# Speech Formula

## Objectives

**By the end of this chapter you should be able to:**

1. Identify the five parts to a dynamic speech.

2. Explain how the primary audience analysis can be so beneficial even if you literally don't ask audience members the questions.

3. Describe how the primary audience analysis differs from the secondary.

4. Identify when a formal audience analysis would be most beneficial. How?

5. List the five rules for creating a statement that has a clear purpose.

6. Identify when a formal audience analysis would be most beneficial. How?

> " It takes one hour of preparation for each minute of presentation time. "
>
> *– Wayne Burgraff*

## *Chapter 7:*
# Speech Formula is the Secret to the Perfect Speech

Let's begin this chapter by activating your prior knowledge. Think about speeches you have heard or delivered, suppose someone asked you to create a list of ingredients for a speech. What would your list be?

**Interaction 7.1: Speech Ingredients**

What are the ingredients for a good speech? Examine speeches you have heard and speeches you have presented, construct a list of ingredients you think belong in a speech.

## Part 1: How it Works

**Introduction**

The Speech Formula contains five key ingredients: Audience Analysis, Purpose Statement, Introduction, Body, and Conclusion. This chapter describes the ingredients in detail. Please note, this list of ingredients supplements the speech writing process, but is not the process itself. For example, a recipe has both a list of ingredients and instructions for combining them. The same is true for a speech. This chapter focuses on ingredients. The next chapter, Putting It

All Together, will cover the process of assembling the speech. Some readers learning style may be global and others sequential. For the global learners, you may prefer taking a look at the "big picture" or the process presented in Chapter 8 first. For sequential learners, learning about the necessary ingredients first should work best for you. Here's an example: We use Sources from our research in the Body of the Speech Formula. Research is conducted in the Planning Stage of the Process. Thoroughly understanding what goes into a speech and the process of creating a speech is complex. It involves an itinerant (back and forth motion) process. Therefore, elements must be addressed more than once.

### Tell, Show, Do, Apply

To get the most out of this chapter, we will incorporate the Tell, Show, Do, Apply strategy to help you master the Speech Formula.

1. **Tell:** Each Ingredient of the Speech Formula is explained in detail in a separate section.

2. **Show:** At the end of each section, a sample speech entitled, "Listening Can Change Your Life" demonstrates how one speech used the Speech Formula and how the Speech Formula comes alive as it's used.

3. **Do:** Become familiar with the Speech Formula by writing your own informative speech.

4. **Apply:** Practice using the Speech Formula. You may find it helpful to use the speech writing application located at www.speechformula.com. Create an account and plug in the promotional code: MyBestSpeech. You can use the Sample Listening Speech content to create your first speech and familiarize yourself with the application, but I recommend you use your own content. Although the website is a fee-based service, everyone gets to write one free speech to try it!

### Choosing a Topic for Your Practice Speech

### Suggested Topics and Sources Identified for Your Informative Speech

To get the most out of this chapter, identify a topic for a speech you need to prepare or choose a topic that you would like to use. If you need some ideas, here is a list of great topics for an informative speech. These topics are interesting and compelling to a wide variety of audiences as they explore our human condition, for instance, forgiveness, financial freedom, excuses, negotiation and time management all are great topics. Below are topics associated with experts who offer some of worthwhile work in the field.

### Table 7.1: Practice Speech Topics

| Topic | Expert |
| --- | --- |
| **Birth Order Theory** | **Alfred Adler** |
| **Culture** | **Edward T. Hall**, *Context*<br>**Geert Hofstede**, *Cultural Dimensions* |
| **Finding Your Voice** | **Elisabeth Noelle-Neumann**, *Finding Your Voice*<br>**Irving Janis**, *Spiral of Silence & Group Think* |

| Grit | Angela Duckworth, *The Power of Passion and Perseverance* |
|------|------|
| Habits/Grit | Stephen R. Covey, *7 Habits of Highly Successful People* |
| Happiness | Marci Shimoff, *Happy for No Reason* |
| Lying | Pamela Myers, *How to Spot a Liar* |
| Love | John Lee, *Styles of Love*<br>Robert Sternberg, *Triangular Theory*<br>Gary Chapman, *5 Languages of Love* |
| Marriage | John Gottman, *4 Horsemen of the Apocalypse* |

## Research Guidelines for Your Practice Speech

In case you were thinking of just speaking off the top of your head, guess what? Research is always a good idea. Depending upon the topic you selected, here are a few guidelines.

**Suggested topics:** Identify five references you can include as you build your speech. Remember, be credible, do your research, each of these topics has quality research from people who have dedicated their lives to advance the field. Even if you feel as if you know a lot about a topic, save your insights to connect with the audience. Rejoice in their findings, advance your credibility by sharing with your audience and crediting their efforts.

**Scholarly topics:** If you are the expert, invited to discuss your expertise, be sure to share insight as to how you came to your conclusions. Scholarly research is dependent upon developments in the field, scholars are trained to respect and share ideas from their peers.

**Non Scholarly topics:** If you're presenting, for example, reasons why a new park is needed, you'll have different resources than a scholar would use. Perhaps identifying local reports from school or city, even census data for your community would be beneficial. Substantiate your vision with data.

Great! Now that you have a topic that you can use to interact with the Speech Formula, let's get started. Review the Speech Formula in its entirety before we break it down section-by-section, element by element .

SPEECH FORMULA

## Table 7.2: Speech Formula

| Audience Analysis | Purpose Statement | Introduction | Body | Conclusion (Intro backwards) |
|---|---|---|---|---|
| **Primary:** Who is my audience? Not about topic! | **1. Use words,** "By the end of my speech my audience will..." | **Attention Grabber** Special, interesting & provocative have them at "Hello!" | Which organizational strategy works BEST to support my purpose? **Select Organizational Strategy** | **Review Main Points** Last opportunity to ensure audience got your points! |
| Ask questions re: demographics, psychographics or behaviors. | **2. Dream!** GO BIG! What would you like to occur? | **Thesis** | **Create a Skeleton Outline:** I.   II.   A.   A.   B.   B. | **Restate Thesis** |
| **Secondary:** WIFM, connects speaker, message and audience. | **3. KISS:** Keep it simple, 1 idea, no 'and's or conjunctions. | **1. Relate:** Ask probing questions | **Fill out Skeleton Outline** For each sub point break out: 1. Source 2. Connection | **3. Return to Thesis Statement** |
| 1. Why is this topic important to them? | **4. Use active verbs**— something you can physically do! | **2. State:** State your thesis.Modify your purpose statement. | **1. Source:** Write what you will say to your audience about your sub point. Include quality research and be credible, cite. | **2. Return to Thesis Statement** |
| 2. How will my audience benefit from my words? | **5. Do not share in this form with audience.** You will repurpose for your thesis statement | **3. Quote:** Use a quote written by someone famous to support value of speech. | **2. Connection:** For each sub point, make the information come alive by making it fun and interesting using the 4Ps Personal Story, Probe, Physical Activity, Prop 3D) | **1. Relate:** Ask probing questions. |
| 3. Will they learn something new? | | **Preview Main Points** One sentence, literally copy/paste your Main Points! | **Transitions:** Create transitions to guide the audience from one point to another. | **Return to Attention Grabber** It's an art; bring them full circle! |
| **Formal:** Conduct a pre-speech questionnaire. | | | Write out source, connections and transitions for each sub point. | **Call to Action** (Persuasive speech only) |

# Part 2: Audience Analysis

<table>
<tr><td colspan="1" style="background:#333;color:#fff">Speech Formula</td></tr>
</table>

**AUDIENCE ANALYSIS**

**Primary:** Ask five specific questions regarding the audience demographics, psychographics, or behaviors.

*Note: These questions have nothing to do with the topic only the audience.*

**Secondary:** Connect speaker, message, and audience. Get into the heart and mind of your audience. Speak from an audience-centered perspective.

1. Why is this topic important to them?
2. How will my audience benefit from my words?
3. Will they learn something new?

*Note: These questions examine your research to identify the most significant content that will appeal for your audience based upon your insights.*

**Formal:** Explore what your audience thinks and feels about your topic. Include the data in your presentation as an effective strategy to connect the content to their specific needs.

**Construct 5 – 10 questions you can ask the audience regarding your topic.**

*Note: These questions have everything to do with how your audience perceives your topic. You can easily create a survey on www.surveymonkey.com or a similar website and electronically share with your audience.*

## Audience Analysis

As we emphasized in the previous chapter, if you are serious about reaching your audience, you must consider them with every decision you make and every word you choose while creating your speech. Just like you, each audience member has their own ideas, values and beliefs, and a distinct personality. It is up to you, the speaker, to design a message they will respond positively to. Knowing your audience is a crucial step. The Speech Formula features three different types of Audience Analysis to help you fine-tune your understanding of your audience and select words that will resonate with them.

*Note: You will see the Audience Analysis referenced several different times in this book. For instance in the previous chapter, a case was made for the significant role it plays in helping speakers build an awareness of how their audience is actually instrumental in formulating every word of your speech. Here we will describe the process in more detail. If you are reading this book sequentially, feel free to jump to the last part of this section, Formal Audience Analysis.*

## Primary Audience Analysis

A Primary Audience Analysis asks you to identify 6-8 questions to familiarize yourself with your audience. These questions focus on your audience, not your topic. Like a marketer, we use demographics, psychographics, behaviors, and geography to identify pertinent questions to help us get into the mind of audience members.

*NOTE: These questions are asked, not necessarily answered. If anything, ask the person who invited you to speak for audience details, and surmise the answers yourself as you prepare.*

### Primary – Demographic

Demographics refer to selected population characteristics. An audience comprised of all women is much different from an audience with only men. Think. Consider how a speech would differ for these two audiences. Suppose you were writing a speech about health insurance benefits. Would the main points be the same for these two audiences? What questions would a man have? Would a woman's questions be the same? Perhaps the message would be the same, but would you package it differently? If so, how? How would your message vary if your audience were a group of individuals with advanced degrees? Suppose they were primarily comprised of high school graduates? What if the group came from Haiti? Does your message change? It should. It is up to you to do your homework in order to relate to your audience and consider their perspective—after all, the speech is for them, **not** you!

### Primary – Geographic

Location. Location. Location. Different parts of the world, country, region, and even town represent specific characteristics. Where are you giving your speech? And where are attendees coming from? Even rock stars like Madonna, Elton John, or Usher will consider geography while performing. They will adjust their performance based upon information they receive. They may tell a story about visiting a local venue or driving down a specific highway or road or yell to the crowd to conjure up residents from Palm Beach, Miami, Coral Springs. They interact with their audience, making each member feel special, as if they are considered! Now consider these major productions which have a product that is explicitly choreographed. If they alter their message to include the audience, so should you. Even if you are a salesperson going around the block to visit another company, make an effort to alter your message to accommodate your location.

### Primary – Psychographic

To reach psychographic segments, consider differences in patterns in the way people spend their money and time. The primary focus concerns the consumer's attitudes, interests, and opinions and the way in which these affect their buying activities (for your purposes buying into your message). Is this a sports-oriented group? Are they fashion conscious? Perhaps they are churchgoers, or wine drinkers, or listen to blues or heavy metal music. Each variable represents a value one has in their life. Someone who rides a motorcycle on the weekends shares a certain lingo and lifestyle with other riders. Perhaps politically the group leans to the left or right. How would a conservative audience respond to your message as opposed to a liberal one?

### Primary – Behavioral

Here one should consider the buyers' knowledge of and attitude toward a product. What are the benefits a given audience seeks, and how willing are they to buy into the concept? Do they want to be in the audience or are they required to sit there for hours?

This is only a brief overview of some basic principles marketers use to design messages that resonate with consumers. You, too, need to think like a marketer if you want your audience to "buy" into your message. So how can we more easily create this connection?

Think about your message like a marketing executive. What benefits does a given audience seek and how willing are they to buy into the concept? This is only a brief overview of some basic principles marketers use to design messages that resonate with consumers. You, too, need to think like a marketer if you want your audience to buy into your message. These tips will help create connection

Asking intuitive questions heightens your awareness of your audience. Ask at least six to eight good questions about your audience that can attain meaningful insight. Remember, limit the questions to the proposed groups demographics, behaviors, psychographics, or geography—not about your topic. The purpose of these questions is to learn about the audience. The act of asking the question is the most important factor in this activity. You may not obtain a "final answer" but the fact that you considered the audience at such a specific level will influence your approach in the design of your message. Explore the sample list of questions on Table 7.3, you are welcome to create your own or integrate any of these.

**Table 7.3: Sample List of Questions**

| Primary – Demographic | Who is the oldest member of my audience? Who is the youngest? |
|---|---|
| | How many pairs of shoes does the average audience member own? What brands are represented in their wardrobe? |
| | Are there more males or females in the audience? What's the break down? Why? |
| | What birth order are my audience members? |
| | How many are from families that have a co-culture (two different cultural influences)? |
| | Did their parents go to college? Graduate? |
| | How much does religion influence their thoughts? |
| | What religions are represented in the group? |
| Primary – Geographic | How cold or hot does it get? |
| | Are they from this area or visiting/relocating? |
| | How large is the home they grew up in? |
| | What do their hands say about them? |
| | Was it safe to walk around where they grew up? Where they live now? |
| | Do they walk often? Where? |
| | When was the last time they took public transportation? |
| | Do they enjoy where they live or want to move? |
| | How friendly are the people in the area known to be? |

| Primary – Psychographic | How often do they drink alcohol? |
| --- | --- |
| | How often do they go to church? |
| | How would they define their social class? |
| | How they spend a typical weekend? |
| | Do they vote? How important is it to them? |
| | What media do they plug into to? |
| | Are they more likely to text or pick up the phone and call? |
| | Do they log into Facebook daily? Weekly? |
| | When is the last selfie they published on social media? |
| | What is their favorite restaurant? |
| | What's their favorite brand? |
| | Where do they vacation? |
| | Do they have a financial advisor? |
| | What sport do they follow? |
| | What is the last concert or theatrical show? |
| **Primary – Behavioral** | Why was I asked to speak at this event? |
| | How motivated are the participants to listen? |
| | Are they likely to listen voluntarily or by assignment? |
| | Are they likely to respond positively? |
| | Am I asking them to be open to a new idea? |
| | Does this group tend to be loyal ? |

## Secondary Audience Analysis

The Secondary Audience Analysis is all about identifying the most crucial information from your research about your audience. This will create a strong connection between the speaker, the message, and the audience—it gives the speech a heartbeat. To accomplish this, we ask three key questions about your research. Why is the topic important? How will they benefit? What new information will they learn?

1. Why is this topic important to my audience? (Be sure to be include highlights from your research.)
2. How will they benefit from the information?
3. What new information will they learn?

Answer each question carefully and provide a specific in-depth answer. You should be able to clearly identify your topic in each of your answers, as opposed to a generic statement like, "It will help them." These questions bring the most relevant and important content to the surface and help you tailor content to each unique audience. While these questions are closely aligned, they each serve a specific purpose. Your answers should reveal fascinating key ideas from your research.

### Formal Audience Analysis

Perhaps you are asking the question: If we are spending all this time thinking about the audience, why not just speak directly to them and learn? Not a bad idea. If you can gain advance access to the audience, do so with a Formal Audience Analysis. Create specific questions designed to scrutinize the audience's behaviors. The results of the analysis can help you prescribe the best antidote for that particular audience and allow you to tailor your speech to their preferences. If you have the opportunity to solicit audience input prior to an event, seize the moment. Take the opportunity to learn who your audience is and what their needs are so you can create the best What's In It For Me (WIIFM)! A good rule of thumb is to include basic demographic information and questions that explore your audience's ideas, experience or believe about the content. If you are going to do a Formal Audience Analysis, do it early enough to incorporate the results into your message. The audience is typically trilled to see their responses incorporated into the presentation. Every time I conduct a Formal Audience Analysis, I am amazed to find I learn more than I thought I would.

## Sample Speech: Listening Can Change Your Life

### Audience Analysis

#### Primary Audience Analysis
1. What is the youngest member   of my audience vs. the oldest?
2. Are there more males or females?
3. How many is English their second language? How many co-cultures?
4. How many other religions than Christian are represented?
5. What income levels are represented in my audience? Who is the wealthiest, who is the poorest?
6. Who in my audience is most like me? Most unlike me? Why? How?
7. Is anyone in my audience living an alternative lifestyle? How?

#### Secondary Audience Analysis
1. Why is this topic important to them?
   *Listening is the most essential part of communicating.*

2. How will my audience benefit from my words?
   *They can engage in every conversation they have better, making the person they speak with feel **great** and learn to learn more from others. Become better observers of the world. Get over themselves **more**.*

3. What new information will they learn?
   *A tangible skill set to listen **better**.*

#### Formal Audience Analysis
1. How important is listening to the communication process?

### Interaction 7.2: Audience Analysis

Complete your Primary, Secondary and Formal Audience Analysis.*

**Primary:** Write six questions to explore who your audience is, use demographics, psychographics, geography and behaviors, to form questions.

1.

2.

3.

4.

5.

**Secondary:** Answer the following questions:

1. Why is the topic important to my audience?

2. How will they benefit?

3. What new information will they learn?

**Formal:**
Write 3-5 questions about your topic to explore your audience's views and experiences.

# Part 2: Purpose Statement

| Speech Formula | |
|---|---|
| **PURPOSE STATEMENT: Establishes a clear goal!** | |
| Follow these five rules to develop your Purpose Statement: | 1. Begin with the phrase, "By the end of my speech my audience will..." <br> 2. Dream **big!** What result would you like to create? <br> 3. Keep it simple: One idea, no **ands** or conjunctions. <br> 4. Use active verbs—something you can physically do. <br> 5. Do not share this statement in this form with the audience. It's for your use only! <br><br> Your Purpose Statement will be repurposed and modified to become your thesis statement. |

The Purpose Statement is the most important part of the speech for you, the author. It provides a clear, guiding light for what should go into your speech and what should not. Have you ever listened to a speech that never seemed to get to the point? Or perhaps you have worked on a project and regardless of how hard you work, you just go in circles. The problem may be that a clear decision of what should be accomplished and a roadmap of how to get there were non existent. Too often people start writing their speech without a clear idea of what they want to accomplish. As a result, words are formulated, stories are told but in the end, the audience is unable to form a cohesive idea about what the speech was actually about. I've seen clients immediately discuss their Attention Grabber before they even know the points of their speech. So many students motivated by the number of required pages or business executives by the number of length of the speech rather than the purpose. When you construct a purpose driven speech you can expand or contract the speech at any point. Start SMART and the rest of the speech will flow seamlessly. Author Alvin Toffler states, "You've got to think about the 'big things' while doing small things so that all the small things go in the right direction."

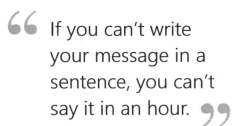

> If you can't write your message in a sentence, you can't say it in an hour.
> – *Dianna Booher*

Don't be alarmed if developing your purpose statement takes considerable time and thought. These statements are typically broad general statements that describes the overall intent. Don't make the mistake of simply combining your main points and call it your purpose statement—those are your points, a purpose statement envelopes all your points in one broad statement. Many experts on goal setting emphasize the need for the goal to be quantifiable and measureable, consider how will you know if the audience actually attained the goal. Be sure it has energy and is something that your audience will embrace. Once you establish your purpose it should be crystal clear to you. If someone were to ask you what is your purpose, it should fall off your tongue—you should be driven to fulfill it. If you have to look at a paper to remember what it is, it either fails to have the significance it should or your motivation for delivering the speech is lacking. Write a purpose statement that inspires you to do your best and one that you are excited to fulfill in the delivery to your audience. There are five rules to write a purpose or objective statement, take the time to be sure you understand and follow each rule.

**Follow these five rules to develop your Purpose Statement:**

1. Begin with the phrase, "By the end of my speech my audience will . . ." This focuses your attention on the outcome. It's crucial to begin by focusing on what's most important.

2. Dream big! Imagine that you could grant a wish to each audience member regarding your topic. What result would you like to create? How would the information you share improve their life? What would you offer each audience member if you could? Convey this in your dream. To hear this message anyone should want to listen to your speech; it should be inspirational.

3. Keep It Simple Stupid (KISS!). Limit this statement to one idea, not multiple points. It should not contain conjunctions (and, but, for, or, yet). Think of it as the title above a list of your main points. This single sentence should describe the outcome rather than specific points you will cover. Eliminate the excess words, "be able to" just go to the dream.

4.  Use an active verb—something you can physically do! You may only select one verb. Avoid these words: know, understand, or learn. For a list of active verbs refer to Table 7.4.

5.  This purpose statement is a tool for you, not intended to be shared with the audience. You will convert this content into for your thesis statement by changing the beginning phrase.

**Table 7.4: List of Active Verbs**
Discover the best word to use for your Purpose Statement.

| | | | |
|---|---|---|---|
| Abandon | Decide | Guide | Prepare |
| Abolish | Deduct | Handle | Present |
| Accelerate | Delegate | Help | Preside |
| Achieve | Delineate | Identify | Process |
| Acquire | Deliver | Illustrate | Produce |
| Act | Describe | Imitate | Program |
| Adapt | Design | Implement | Promote |
| Add | Detect | Improve | Provide |
| Adjust | Determine | Increase | Pursue |
| Administer | Develop | Induce | Question |
| Advance | Devise | Influence | Realize |
| Analyze | Diagnose | Inform | Recommend |
| Answer | Dictate | Inspire | Reconcile |
| Approach | Direct | Instigate | Record |
| Arrange | Discard | Interpret | Redeem |
| Ascertain | Discover | Investigate | Reduce |
| Assemble | Display | Lead | Regain |
| Assess | Dramatize | Maintain | Relate |
| Attain | Edit | Manipulate | Relax |
| Avert | Engage | Measure | Report |
| Budget | Enter | Mediate | Represent |
| Build | Equip | Mentor | Research |
| Calculate | Establish | Mobilize | Respond |
| Catch | Estimate | Monitor | Respond |
| Classify | Evaluate | Motivate | Reveal |
| Coach | Examine | Negotiate | Review |
| Command | Expand | Observe | Schedule |
| Communicate | Expedite | Obtain | Select |
| Compile | Experiment | Offer | Submit |
| Compose | Explain | Operate | Summarize |
| Conduct | Flout | Order | Supervise |
| Conserve | Formulate | Organize | Supply |
| Consolidate | Furnish | Oversee | Support |
| Construct | Gain | Perceive | Synthesize |
| Control | Gather | Perform | Systematize |
| Coordinate | Generate | Persuade | Teach |
| Counsel | Give | Pick | Treat |
| Create | Grasp | Pile | Unite |
| Deal | Grow | Predict | Vanquish |

Here are a few examples of purpose statements first written without applying the rules and then rewritten after the rules are applied.

**Table 7.5: Purpose Statements**

| BEFORE | AFTER |
|---|---|
| By the end of this speech my audience will be able to tell when someone is lying and why they are lying. | By the end of this speech my audience will detect lies. |
| By the end of this speech my audience will understand what anger management is and steps in controlling it and avoid escalating situations that have anger. | By the end of this speech my audience will respond wisely to anger. |
| By the end of this speech my audience will know how to follow up on a sales lead and close a deal and follow a structured sales process. | By the end of this speech my audience will engage prospects to buy. |
| By the end of this speech my audience will find a way to manage stress and know the benefits of laughter | By the end of this speech my audience will enjoy the positive benefits of laughter. |
| By the end of this speech my audience will understand and know how to negotiate everything from going to the movies to a raise for the job. | By the end of this speech my audience will negotiate effectively in their every day lives. |

## Sample Speech: Listening Can Change Your Life

By the end of my speech, the audience will listen more competently.

## Interaction 7.3: Purpose Statement

**Write a purpose statement for your topic.**
By the end of my speech my audience will _____

# Part 3: Body

| Speech Formula |
| --- |
| **BODY: Drives the speech. It is the reason for the speech as it reveals the crucial information about the topic.** |
| Select the organizational strategies that best support your purpose statement to organize your main points and sub points.<br>Main points: _____<br>Sub points: _____ |
| **I./II. Main Point** (must have 2 main points)<br>Breaks down topic. Category title for sub points. Should be easy to remember, organized. |
| **A./B. Sub Point** (must have 2 sub points)<br>Provides name (description) for your research like "Definition" or "Types." Breaks down Main Point. |

**1. Source:**
Drives the speech; reveal "jewels" of information you have discovered. Share/cite source (display on PP cite orally/paper/PP).

**2. Connection:**
4Ps = Super Speech (Personal Story, Probing Questions, Physical Activity, Prop) What type of connection will you select to connect with your audience? The 4 Ps are crucial to help your audience make sense of the information.

**Transitions/Connectors/Sign Posts**
Act as a tour guide, explaining where you are and where you are going. Don't hesitate to **share** your organization.

The success of your speech is determined by the effectiveness of your organizational strategy. Organization requires logic. If you develop the communication tools discussed in this section, the benefits will be far reaching. They can change your life, your relationships, and your direction—ultimately, your success. Consider this: the organization of your thoughts influences the quality of your connections. The extent to which organization occurs in your thought process influences what you say, what you do, and how you do it! Design your messages with care. The Speech Formula will guide you in selecting the best organizational strategy for your speech.

### Select Appeal Types

Merriam Webster dictionary (2017) defines "appeal" as "the power of arousing a sympathetic response." Carefully think about these two questions and select the degree of emotion you want your audience to feel and how strongly you want to inspire them to act.

1. What type of emotional response do you want to evoke with your speech?
2. What actions do you want the audience to take in response to your message?

When it comes to organizing your speech there are an infinite number of opportunities at your disposal. Few speakers study the options and wisely chose the best to meet their purpose. Of the many strategies available, choose the one best suited to achieve your desired response. Examining the emotional and motivational appeal you desire can help you chose a strategy that will strengthen your message so that it has the desired impact upon your audience.

Your answers to the two questions above will guide your choice of organizational strategies. Keep in mind that some strategies are better suited for speeches that are more informative and some work better for persuasive ones. Some strategies allow for greater emotional appeal too. Organizational strategies strengthen your message. Choose wisely based on your desired results.

**Figure 7.1: Appeal Types**

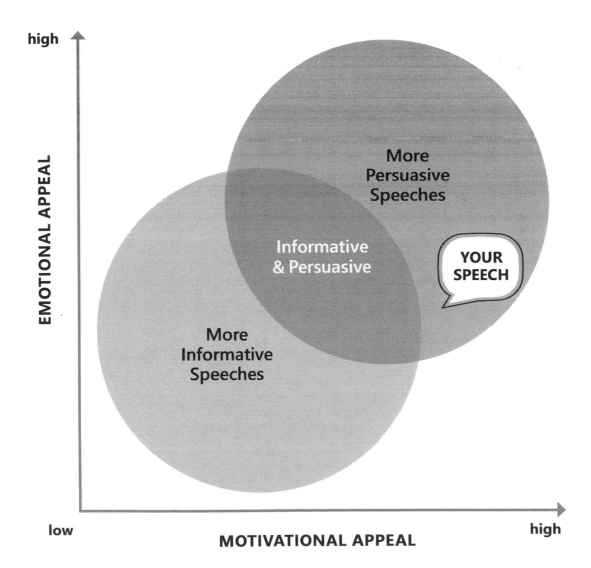

The degree and type of emotional and motivational response you want to evoke in your audience dictates your choice of speech type. Not all speeches require high emotion and/or high motivation. For instance, a speech made to announce something would generally be less emotional and motivational than a sales pitch or sermon. The latter is intended to evoke more emotion and move the audience to action.

**Figure 7.2: Speech Type by Appeal**

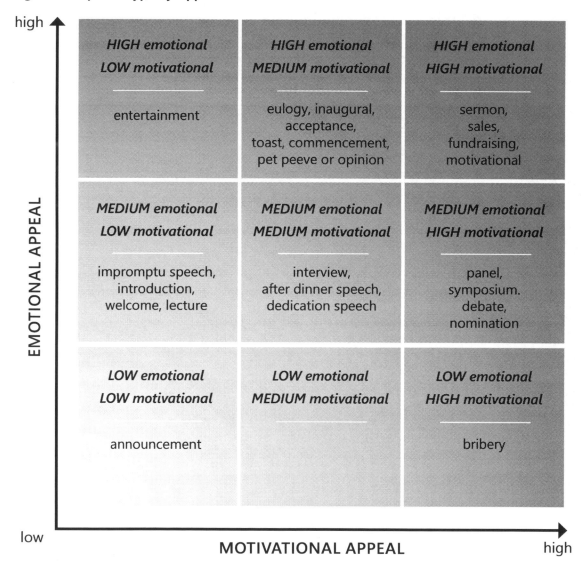

## Organizational Strategies

### Name

Organization is vital to communication. The less organized your ideas the more difficult it is for someone to understand your reason for communicating; the more organized your ideas, the easier it is to make sense of your message. Imagine you are in a room. Everything inside the room is piled into one humongous heap. What would you have? A heap of stuff right?

## Figure 7.3: Organizational Strategies

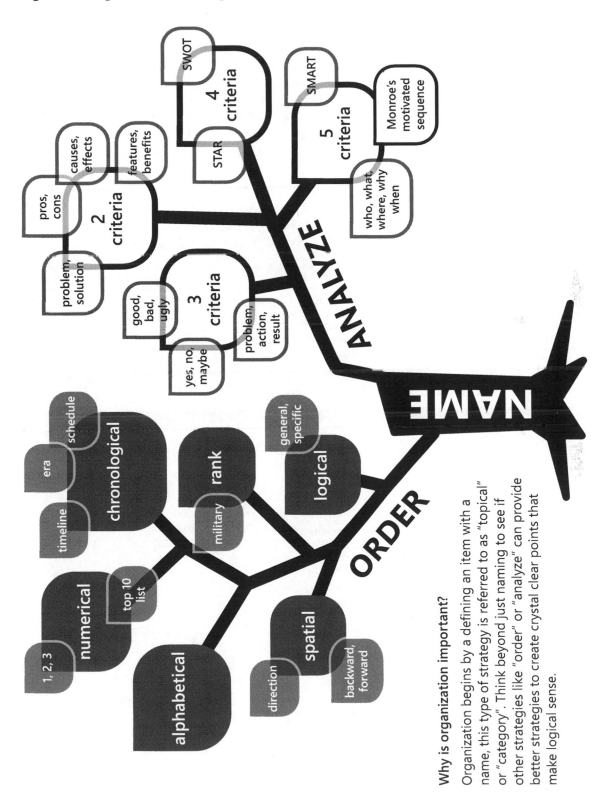

**Why is organization important?**

Organization begins by a defining an item with a name, this type of strategy is referred to as "topical" or "category". Think beyond just naming to see if other strategies like "order" or "analyze" can provide better strategies to create crystal clear points that make logical sense.

It would make no sense. Now suppose you took one item off that pile, you examined it and realized, "Ah this is a chair." So you placed it into a designated area. You grabbed another item off the heap after a look, you realize that it was a desk. You placed the desk next to the chair and labeled the area, "Furniture". Two other item you found were a projector and a computer, these you placed in a new area and labeled it, "Technology". Item by item, piece by piece your naming each item from the heap allows the heap to go disappear and a form to take place. Why? Because you organized each item; organization began by identifying… naming and finding like items to create categories thus creating structure where none existed. Often times when you go to write a speech, you have so many ideas it may seem like an overwhelming heap of "stuff". If you take the time to methodically consider each idea or piece of research, giving each a name and categorizing them, order will triumph. Isn't this what scientists do when they identify a new organism? They systematically place it into the right Kingdom and find the appropriate species. By doing so scientists are able to make sense and give meaning to our world. The same is true for your thoughts, if your thoughts are a mess take the time to quantify them, giving name to each and creating categories that make sense.

**Strategy for Main Points:** When we organize, the process begins by naming—in a speech, often times, these are ideas that stem from your research. For instance you can have a definition, myths, facts, steps, tips, do's, don'ts, types—the list is endless any word that you can find to make sense of a body of research—these are typically your Sub Points. Once named, you can then decide which system of organization will help to create clearer meaning for your audience—these become your Main Points. Objects or ideas can be organized by placing in a particular order or by analyzing features of the object or idea. While we can organize ideas in an infinite number of ways, some work better than others.

Once named, you can then decide which research fits into categories. You can then decide which system of organization will help create clearer meaning for your audience—these become your Main Points. Writing about organization can be confusing, right? Let's help these ideas make sense with this example.

**Topic:** Let's say you have a speech about banning junk food from vending machines on school property.

**Research:** Here's what your research produced (feel free to conduct an Internet search to see what you find):
- disruptive behavior in classroom
- childhood obesity statistics
- Canadian ban worked = after 2 years kids were 2 lbs lighter
- limitations of ban
- case studies
- opposing points of view
- history

Can you find ways to create categories for these individual pieces of research? For instance wouldn't the first two bullets become Reasons? And, couldn't the Canadian ban and case studies go together to create Proof? I bet you could also merge limitations and opposing points of view with Reasons to create Why to Ban and Why Not to Ban.

Notice you have to really think about your research and how to best organize it. The list of strategies organized in the Table 2 and Table 3 below should be a great help.

Your speech is only ten minutes long, while all this information is interesting, you don't have enough time to include all of it. Begin by reviewing the organizational strategies you have at your disposal to use and what your ultimate purpose is.

**Purpose:** By the end of my speech my audience will vote to ban junk food in public schools. (Persuasive speech with a high motivation appeal and medium emotional appeal)

Now let's see which strategies we can use to organize all this information with the categories we have.

| Option 1 | Option 2 |
|---|---|
| I. **Problem** (You could display the problem in two different ways.)<br><br>A. History<br><br>B. Debate (Why to ban/Why not to ban<br><br>A. Problem 1: Harms the learning environment<br><br>B. Problem 2: Promotes bad habits<br><br>C. Problem 3: Sickens our children<br><br>II. **Solution**<br><br>A. Ban Junk Food (Sugary drinks, chips, fried foods and candy bars)<br><br>B. Case Studies | I. **Reason 1: Hurts the learning environment**<br><br>A. Sugar high<br><br>B. Lack of energy<br><br>II. **Reason 2: Promotes bad habits**<br><br>A. Meals<br><br>B. Snacks<br><br>III. **Reason 3: Sickens our children**<br><br>A. Physically (Obesity/Diabetes)<br><br>B. Psychologically (Self image/bullying) |
| **Option 3** | **Option 4** |
| I. **What is the ban?** (Structure – explain what it is)<br><br>A. Cafeteria Nutritional Guidelines<br><br>B. Vending Machines Guidelines<br><br>C. Lunchbox Guidelines<br><br>II. **How will it impact our communities?** (Function – explain how it will work)<br><br>D. Learn more in the classroom<br><br>E. Reinforce better life skills and habits<br><br>F. Reduce childhood obesity and associated diseases | I. **Features**<br><br>A. Cafeteria Nutritional Guidelines<br><br>B. Vending Machines Guidelines<br><br>C. Lunchbox Guidelines<br><br>II. **Benefits**<br><br>A. Learn more in the classroom<br><br>B. Reinforce better life skills and habits<br><br>F. Reduce childhood obesity and associated diseases |

| Option 5 | Option 6 |
|---|---|
| **I. Good** | **I. Causes** |
|   A. Community—Want to chose for themselves |   A. Cafeteria Food Nutritional Guidelines |
|   B. Children—Typically they love sugar and chips and carbs |   B. Vending Machine Options |
| **II. Bad** |   C. Habits at Home |
|   A. Reason 1: Harms the learning environment | **II. Effects** |
|   B. Reason 2: Promotes bad habits |   A. Classroom Behavior |
|   C. Reason 3: Sickens our children |   B. Childhood Obesity Epidemic |
| **III. Ugly** |   C. Avoidable Diseases |
|   A. Before | |
|   a. Canadian Case Before Started | |
|   b. Historical images from local school year book before vending machines and junk food prevalence (30/20/10/5/1) Show | |
|   B. After | |
|   a. Canadian Case After Ban – lost .05 per year of the ban. | |
|   b. Historical images show 10/5/1 and now when junk food was allowed. | |

Now which of these would you propose to actually use? Which strategy will convince your audience the ban should be implemented? Does your audience impact which one you decide? What if you were delivering the speech to the school board versus school kids versus the Parent Teacher Association? Would your choice differ? Realize when it comes to organizing your speech, you have many options and the one you select will impact how well your audience receives your message. Chose your strategy wisely. Explore the organizational strategies available to you.

**Order**

**Strategy for Main Points:** Typically, speeches that strive for a lower persuasive appeal and less emotion lend themselves to using an order strategy to organize the content. Let's explore the list.

*Note: Exceptions exist, for instance an announcement (informative) typically uses Analysis of five criteria, Who, What, Where, When and Why. Both informative and persuasive speeches can use a sequential numerical strategy. Three Basic Principles about Exercise (Informative). Three Reasons Why You Should Begin an Exercise Routine Today (Persuasive).*

## Table 7.6: Order Subcategories

| Subcategory | Definition | Strategy for Main Points |
|---|---|---|
| Numerical | Expressed as a number or numbers. Often ideas are driven by steps or need; therefore, we represent the ideas with a number to assign meaning to the logical placement. Using numbers can help. | Sequential (1,2,3),<br>Motivated Sequence (Step 1, Step 2, Step 3)<br>Order of Importance (Most or Least) (Top 10 List - David Letterman 10, 9, 8 etc.)<br>Dewey Decimal System (100 , 200, 300, etc) |
| Alphabetical | A system where strings of characters are placed in order based on the position of the characters in the conventional ordering of an alphabet | Letter (A, B, C) |
| Chronological | The arrangement of events or dates in the order of their occurrence. | Timeline (1800, 1900, 2000)<br>Era, (Big Band, Rock, Hip Hop)<br>Schedule (Morning, Afternoon, Evening) |
| Rank | Relative position, value, worth, complexity, power, importance, authority or level in the hierarchy of a given system. | Military (General, Captain, Lieutenant)<br>Corporate (President, Vice President, Manager)<br>Government (President, Vice President, Secretary) |
| Spatial | Of or relating to space. | Direction (I. North, II. South, III. East, IV. West)<br>Orientation (I. Top II. Middle III. Bottom) (Head/Shoulders Knees, Toes)<br>I. Internal II. External (Inside/Outside)<br>I. Vertical (Y) II. Horizontal (X)<br>I. Backward II. Forward |
| Logical | A reasonable or sensible way that something happens or would happen. | I. Ingredients, II. Utensils, III. Directions;<br>Color: I. Blue II. Red<br>Size: I. Small II. Medium III.Large<br>I. General II. Specific |

**Analyze**

**Strategy for Main Points:** Analyzing your content is especially important when constructing persuasive speeches intended to evoke a strong emotional response. Look for relationships between your points and make sure each one supports your purpose. These strategies can empower your message. Analyze strategies typically work more effectively for persuasive speeches but some strategies can be effective with informational strategies. Consider how or if you could use each strategy for your given purpose.

## Table 7.7: Analyze Subcategories

| Subcategory | Definition | Strategy for Main Points |
|---|---|---|
| 2 Criteria | Analyzing content by examining two different criteria in order to reveal specific features of the object or idea. | I. Problem II. Solution<br>I. Features II. Benefits<br>I. What it is (Structure)? II. How it is used (Function)?<br>I. Possibilities II. Consequences<br>I. Do's II. Don'ts<br>I. Before II. After<br>I. Pros II. Cons<br>I. Strengths II. Weakness<br>I. Causes II. Effects<br>I. Reasons II. Alternatives, |
| 2 Criteria (cont.) | | I. Compare II. Contrast or I. Similarities II. Differences<br>I. Works II. Doesn't Work<br>I. Good News II. Bad News<br>I. Yes II. No<br>I. Backward II. Forward<br>I. Macro (Big Picture) II. Micro (Small Picture) |
| 3 Criteria | Analyzing content by examining three different criteria in order to reveal specific features of the object or idea. | I. Good II. Bad III. Ugly<br>I. Good II. Better III. Best<br>I. Yes II. No III. Maybe<br>I. Problem II. Action III. Result (PAR) |
| 4 Criteria | Analyzing content by examining four different criteria in order to reveal specific features of the object or idea. | I. Strengths II. Weaknesses III. Opportunities IV. Threats<br>I. Profit II. Sales III. Market Share IV. Growth<br>I. Situation II. Task III. Action IV. Result (STAR)<br>I. Tell II. Show III. Do IV. Apply |
| 5 Criteria | Analyzing content by examining five different criteria in order to reveal specific features of the object or idea. | I. Who II. What III. Where IV. Why IV. When<br>**Monroe's Motivated Sequence**<br>1. Attention<br>2. Need<br>3. Satisfaction<br>4. Visualization<br>5. Action |

Carefully consider the various types of strategies available for organizing your speech. Use your purpose statement and the type of response you hope to evoke from your audience to select the most effective strategy. To identify the most effective strategy, I recommend choosing three strategies you could use for this speech. Then review your purpose statement and determine which is best.

Explore the various strategies available. As you can see, some strategies work better for those speeches designed to have high emotional and motivational appeal and others work better for less. Choose one best suited for what you are trying to accomplish.

## Interaction 7.4: Choose the Best Strategy for This Purpose

Suppose you had a speech whose purpose was: By the end of the speech my audience will donate twenty dollars to help find a cure for cancer. Choose three strategies you could use—which would work best?

Suppose you had a speech whose purpose was: By the end of my speech my audience will appreciate classical music. Choose three strategies you could use—which would work best?

### Main Points

Depending upon the organizational strategy selected you may or may not need to edit the points to reflect the exact words you will say. For instance if you selected these strategies, these words empower your message, they do not need to be edited.

| | |
|---|---|
| I. Features | I. Problem |
| II. Benefits | II. Solution |

Other strategies require you to edit the content. For instance, if you use a Timeline strategy, you have to enter the specific times relevant to your content or if you are using Order of Importance, you will need to list the ideas in the correct order. Unless asking a question, avoid using full sentences. Categorize the idea.

| | | |
|---|---|---|
| I. World War I | I. Most Important | I. What is grit? |
| II. World War II | II. Semi Important | II. How can we be grittier? |
| III. Cold War | III. Least Important | |

I will always remember a seminar I attended at a National Communication Association conference. The seminar featured a panel of three presenters. The first two discussed their interpretation of the theory; the final presenter discussed the Good, the Bad and the Ugly of the theory. The first two presentations were weak, featuring unclear points. In contrast, the final presenter built on a clear, powerful organizational strategy that left a lasting impression. Choose your organizational strategy to simplify your message and clarify your points. Years ago when I was teaching high school, one English teacher employed a spatial organizational strategy to teach students how to write a paragraph.

## Table 7.8: Select Organizational Strategies

### INFORMATIVE

**Order Strategies**

- Letter (A, B, C)
- Timeline (1800, 1900, 2000)
- Era (Big Band, Rock, Hip Hop)
- Schedule (morning, afternoon, evening)
- Military (General, Captain, Lieutenant)
- Corporate (President, Vice President, Manager)
- Government (President, Vice President, Secretary)
- Direction (north, south, east, west)
- Orientation (top, middle, bottom; head, shoulders, knees, toes)
- Internal, External (inside, outside)
- Vertical (Y), Horizontal (X)
- Backward, Forward
- Ingredients, Utensils, Directions
- Color (blue, red)
- Size (small, medium, large) general, specific macro (big picture), micro (small picture)

**Analyze Strategies**

- Causes, Effects
- Works, Doesn't Work
- Who, What, Where, Why, When

### INFORMATIVE AND PERSUASIVE

**Order Strategies**

- Sequential (1, 2, 3)
- Motivated Sequence (step 1, step 2, step 3)
- Order of Importance, Reasons Why
- Most to Least; top 10 list, ie. David Letterman 10, 9, 8, etc.)
- Dewey Decimal System (100, 200, 300, etc.)
- Chronology

**Analyze Strategies**

- What is it? (structure) How is it used? (function)
- Strength, Weakness
- Compare, Contrast, or Similarities, Differences
- Good News, Bad News,
- Yes, No
- Backward, Forward
- Pros, Cons
- Problem, Action, Result (PAR)
- Strengths, Weaknesses, Opportunities, Threats
- Profit, Sales, Market Share, Growth
- Situation, Task, Action, Result (STAR)
- Well, Maybe, But...
- Formal/Informal

### PERSUASIVE

**Order Strategies**

- Order of Importance, Reasons Why
- Most to Least; top 10 list, ie. David Letterman 10, 9, 8, etc.)

**Analyze Strategies**

- Problem, Solution
- Features, Benefits
- Possibilities, Consequences
- Do's, Don'ts
- Before, After
- Pros, Cons
- Causes, Effects
- Reasons, Alternatives
- Works, Doesn't Work
- Good News, Bad News,
- Yes, No
- Good, Bad, Ugly
- Good, Better, Best, Yes, No, Maybe; Problem, Action, Result (PAR)
- Monroe's Motivated Sequence
  - Attention
  - Need
  - Satisfaction
  - Visualization
  - Action
- What it is (structure)?
- Why is it important (functionality)?
- Well, Maybe, But...
- Formal/Informal

Using a sandwich, she began with the top bun representing the introduction sentence, the meat of the paragraph is made up of supporting, evidential or detail statements that answer the main reader's questions about the topic sentence. Additional sentences that support the meat or clarify the main point can be seen as the cheese and condiments. The bottom bun featured a concluding statement wrapping up the paragraphs topic or summarizing the main points. By using this strategy, this high school improved the writing portion of the standardized test results by more than 40%. Students learned how to write a successful essay because of an instructor creatively implementing the use of an effective organizational strategy. Think what the right organizational strategy can do for your speech!

**Figure 7.3: How to Write a Paragraph**

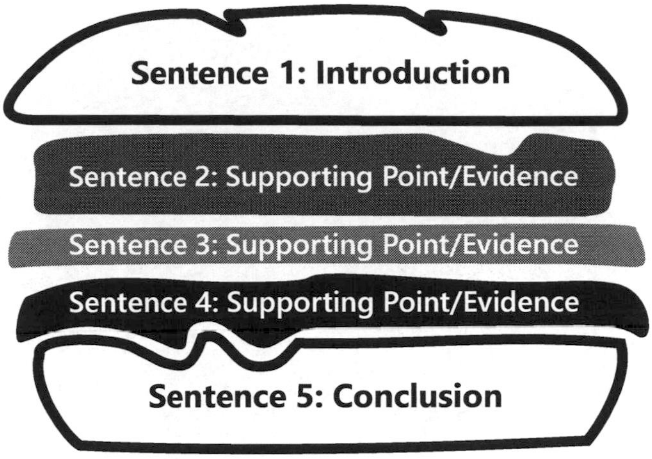

Sentence 1: Introduction
Sentence 2: Supporting Point/Evidence
Sentence 3: Supporting Point/Evidence
Sentence 4: Supporting Point/Evidence
Sentence 5: Conclusion

### Sub Points

No doubt you have lots of information you can include in the speech. Your Sub Point essentially gives a name to the research or event you are explaining. Sometimes a topical strategy, like Definition or Types or Myths, works best for sub points if you just want to name the point you are discussing. Other times, a more defined organizational strategy can provide additional clarity to your message. Take for instance using: Before and After, Timeline or Do's Don'ts. Consider the strategies available, compare to your selected content, and add them. Edit them as necessary. Use strategies like Do's or Don'ts or a numeric system like Top Three Reasons Why—these can really help clarify your message. Always hunt for your best option.

*Note: When outlining, you must have at least two points per level, i.e., a I and II, an A and a B and a 1 and a 2. You can have more points. . .A, B, C, but never just one isolated point.*

---

**Sample Speech: Listening Can Change Your Life**

**Skeleton Outline:**

I.  What is listening?
    a.  Definition
    b.  Myths
    c.  Facts

II. How can we improve our listening skills?
    a.  Awareness
    b.  Tips

### Interaction 7.5: Body Skeleton Outline

**Construct a skeleton outline for a speech for your speech topic.***
Write your Skeleton Outline (Outline your Main Points and Sub Points—use Roman Numerals add any additional points you need as necessary.)

**Recommendation:** To simplify the process of using the Speech Formula to write this first speech, use these main points as your organizational strategy: I. What is ____? and II. How is it used?

I. What is love?

II. How can we find the love we want?

If your selected topic has more than a word, like, "why marriages fail" as opposed to "happiness", modify it. For instance notice how the second option is a much better outline:

I. What is a marriage?

II. How do we stay married?

I. Why do marriages fail?

II. How can we build lasting relationships?

Construct a skeleton outline for a speech for your speech topic.*

I.
    A.
    B.

II.
    A.
    B.

### Source

Your sources or research—jewels of information you plan to share—drive the speech! The object of the speech is to have this content affect the audience. Thus, this key information is the entire reason for the speech. Given the effort a speech requires, the information should be great. Great information is relevant to the audience and credible. Not all information is created equal, particularly with the advent of fake news and viral social media shares that often go unchecked and perpetuate incorrect information. Offer your audience more than a simple internet search. Even if you are an expert in a field, back up your opinions with quality research. How can we determine the degree of credibility? First, you must investigate to see if your source is credible. Have high standards! What criteria do you use to determine whether or not you should believe something and whether or not you should share the information with others? Not every piece of information you find, no matter how much it may work to make a point, gets to go into your speech. Take a close look at the information you wish to use and see if it can pass a credibility test. You have to determine your level of credibility. Exactly how credible does information need to be to make it into your speech? On one end of the spectrum is the most credible, peer reviewed, professional respected industry journal. On the other end of the spectrum is a website that promotes biased information and has no author. It is up to you to determine if it is worth sharing with an audience. This free online tool may help you decide: www.credibilitychecker.com

Credible sources should have an author, be published by a credible publisher, avoid any known biases, be published within the last five years (unless a "seminal work" or foundational theory in a field), and contain references. Use these criteria to evaluate the credibility of each source you plan to use.

When you construct your Source /Research section using a credible source, write out the exact words you will say to your audience. Write them out and then read them aloud to ensure that your intended message hits the target—if you practice this, the words will fall off your tongue. Do not just outline a few key words and think you will say everything brilliantly when you are in front of the audience and nervous. Write the exact words out.

## Interaction 7.6: Body Skeleton Outline

How can you identify if information is credible or not on the internet? Conduct an internet search on this question and see what criteria you can identify. Establish a plan to ensure that you will check your information to determine if it is credible.

**Plan**    Step 1:

Step 2:

Step 3:

Table 7.9: International Public Speaking Institute Credibility Checker

| Who is the **author**? | **When** was it published? | What type of **citations** are featured? |
|---|---|---|
| ☐ Widely-cited Author(s) | ☐ Within 5 years | ☐ Reference page or Footnotes |
| ☐ Credentialed Author(s) | ☐ Over 5 years but seminal work | ☐ Statistics, reference, raw data source |
| ☐ Famous Author(s) | ☐ Over 5 years but historical use | ☐ None |
| ☐ Author(s) not known | ☐ Date unknown | |
| ☐ Does the author have a slant or known bias? | | |

| Who **published** the source? | How **credible** is the information? |
|---|---|

☐ **3rd Party**
   Peer Reviewed
   Academic Books
   Mainstream Media
     • Respected Publisher
     • Major Newspaper
     • Popular Magazine
     • Local Newspaper
   Government Publication
   Professional (Industry) Publication

☐ **Self Published** Book
   Company Publication or Website
   Printed Pamphlet
   Edited Community Website
   Wiki Page
   Individual Blog

☐ Does the publisher have a slant or known bias?

☐ Primary

☐ Secondary
   • Study of studies
   • Paraphrased

*© 2011 J.R. Steele, M.S. All Rights Reserved.*

## Connection

The information and research you share with your audience is the reason for your delivery. Nevertheless, if you do not connect with your audience and make your points come alive, you will lose them. Use these four Ps to keep your audience engaged.

| **Personal Story** | **Probing Questions** | **Prop** | **Physical Activity** |
|---|---|---|---|

Study and master the use of each of these. In a comprehensive speech—more than an announcement or speaker introduction—be sure to effectively incorporate each of the four "Ps." These will most likely be the points of greatest audience connection. Make them great, have fun, and be creative.

Table 7.10: 4 Ps

| CONNECTION | ADVISE |
|---|---|
| **Personal Story** | Personal stories should be specific, relevant to the topic, and strengthen your speech in some way. They should include names, dates, and places. Be sure they do not overpower your speech to become the focus. Remember it is not about you, but about breaking the information down so the research makes sense to the audience and the story creates a personal connection. **Be careful to keep the story brief for a short speech.** |

| CONNECTION | ADVISE |
|---|---|
| Probing Questions | Get the audience to think about your topic in a way that's relevant to them. Consider all topic perspectives. |
| Prop | Make sure the prop is relevant to the topic and will help your speech. Ex: books, videos, pictures, charts. |
| Physical Activity | Get the audience to interact with your speech. Get them moving and active. Ask them to answer questions, write things down, move to a place in the classroom. |

## Sample 4 Ps Applied to Speech Topic: **Love**

| CONNECTION | EXAMPLE |
|---|---|
| Probing Questions | Which couple has the greatest relationship you could ever imagine? Why is it so fantastic? Is it the way they look at each other? The things they do for each other? Or the simple smile of satisfaction that rests upon their face? |
| Prop | Give the audience a heart and ask them to decide what they want to do with it. Either be open to love or close themselves off from love. |
| Physical Activity | Place MYTH on one side of the board and FACTS on other side. Ask three audience members to come forward. Make a statement and ask the participants to move to the side they agree with. |
| Personal Story | Story about my boyfriend Renee, describe how we met and how I feel about him and how my family feels. **Please include using specifics.** |

## Sample 4 Ps Applied to Speech Topic: **Obesity**

| CONNECTION | EXAMPLE |
|---|---|
| Probing Questions | Imagine your child is obese. Would you want them to suffer from serious conditions or try to adopt a healthy lifestyle? |
| Prop | Give the audience a paper child and ask them how they would like to raise their child. Let them eat either whatever they want or help promote a healthy lifestyle. |
| Physical Activity | Give the audience a check and ask them to write down how much more money an obese person has to pay in medical expenses compared to a healthy person. |
| Personal Story | Story about weight gain and how I overcame it by making healthy choices. |

Sample 4 Ps Applied to Speech Topic: **Law to Combat Global Warming**

| CONNECTION | ADVISE |
| --- | --- |
| **Probing Questions** | Ask the audience to think about a world with extreme weather conditions, extinction of animals, and widespread food/water shortages. Be more specific—tornados, droughts, maybe grab a few headlines... |
| **Prop** | Bring in a globe and point to areas that have devastating climate effects due to global warming. |
| **Physical Activity** | Get the audience to circle the number on the scale of 1-10 to what degree they are concerned about global warming. For those that are concerned, ask them to write down at least one way they try to reduce the temperature. If not, why not? Have them line up in order of their level of concern. |
| **Personal Story** | Share a story about how you have witnessed changes to temperatures in your lifetime. OR share a story about a documentary or activity that made you concerned about the issue of global warming, describe how it has made you feel. |

**Personal Story**

Personal stories should be specific, including names, dates, and places. Make sure they are relevant to the topic and strengthen your speech without overpowering it and becoming the focus. Remember, it is not about you, but about presenting information so the research makes sense to the audience. But it also does let the audience connect with you on a personal level.

Research shows another powerful reason to include stories in our presentation. Dale Carnegie makes a valid point, "Speakers who talk about what life has taught them never fail to keep the attention of their listeners." Mark Twain (1895) wrote an essay entitled, "How to Tell a Story." Give it a read. Author James Joyce believes all people are interesting: "The difference between people who seem interesting and people who don't is their ability to turn their experiences into compelling stories." There is an art to telling a story; sometimes called the "art of charm." It might be worth researching and practicing to develop the skill. Good stories include details and emotion to establish rapport. Keep it simple, highlight a struggle, and don't brag (O, Hara, 2014).

Did you know that neurological science has shown that facts and figures activate two brain centers while stories activate seven? Stories trigger emotional responses, and when the brain is more engaged, the stories are more memorable. Stories inspire us to act!

When you tell a story, allow yourself to be vulnerable. Including relevant names, dates, and contextual background, helps you connect emotionally with your audience. Paul Zak (2014), founding director of the Center for Neuroeconomics Studies at Harvard

**PERSONAL STORY**

- Use details: Who, What, Where, Why, When, How

- Be sure they support your purpose—careful they do not distract!

- Consider: What does the story say about you? Do you want to say that to the audience?

University explains this phenomenon in his article, "Why your brain loves good storytelling." "As social creatures, we depend on others for our survival and happiness. A decade ago, my lab discovered that a neurochemical called oxytocin is a key 'it's safe to approach others' signal in the brain. Oxytocin is produced when we are trusted or shown a kindness, and it motivates cooperation with others. It does this by enhancing the sense of empathy, and our ability to experience the emotions of others. Empathy is important for social creatures because it allows us to understand how others are likely to react to a situation." In this sense, it is important to reveal a bit of oneself to your audience. Scientifically, it creates audience connection.

### Probing Questions

People are selfish by nature. Prompting the audience to recall a personal story relating to your topic is even more powerful than telling a personal story of your own. To elicit these stories, we Probe, and ask systematic questions to guide them to a particular memory or conclusion. For example, "Can you remember your favorite childhood toy?" Or, "Who is the happiest person you know?" (Pause) "Who is the most miserable person you know?" (Pause) "How happy are you?" Notice that after each question, you must allow the audience time to connect with their memory. You will see the reaction on their face. If you don't want the audience to respond orally, tell them that ahead of time.

**PROBING QUESTIONS**

- Audience member's story... go for details!

- Ask questions to guide them

- Selfish nature = their story is more powerful

**Example:** *Who is the happiest person you know? Who is the most miserable? How happy are you?*

### Prop

As we discussed earlier, props can add impact to your message—as long as they are relevant to the topic and will help your speech. Go beyond a PowerPoint video or image. For example, use a book, object, model, picture, or chart. Putting forth the extra effort shows you care and adds another dimension to the speech. Over the years, I've seen and used some great speech props that also involve the audience. One versatile one is to hand out a little sheet of paper and asking them to respond to a simple question relevant to your presentation. For a speech on Happiness say, "Write three things that make you happy." For a presentation on Sales Goals say, "Write the number of widgets you plan to sell this year!" Or hand out an inspiration quote that supports your speech. You could hand out a few paper keys to people who respond during your speech. The keys open up tips or key review information at the end of the presentation. For a speech protecting sharks against slaughter for shark fin soup, a fantastic prop was incorporated. Each audience member was given two cards: Scared and Not Afraid. She explained to the audience that she was going to reveal various images. For each image they were to hold up their card indicating how they felt about each image: Mosquito, Human, Pills, Spider, Party, Snake, Dog, Sports Car, Crocodile, Palm Tree and a Shark. She then showed a

**PROP**

- Supports the purpose

- 3D

**Example:** *book, object, model, picture, chart, costume, person.*

*Note: Go beyond PowerPoint which should contain an image or video—this is 3D.*

report that of all the items shown, sharks were the least dangerous with fewer people dying. What an awesome way to involve the audience, getting them to consider the topic and for many, alter their perceptions about how dangerous sharks are.

<table>
<tr><td>

**PHYSICAL ACTIVITY**

- **Call on specific volunteers or entire audience**

- **Provide clear instructions (test)**

- **Supports the purpose, makes the content come alive!**

**Example:** *May I please have 3 volunteers? (Ask them to do something with content, select a correct answer, role play.)*

*Note: Someone in the audience, other than yourself **must move**.*

</td></tr>
</table>

**Physical Activity**

Use your space wisely. Get the audience to interact with your speech. Set a personal goal to have at least two audience members move from their seat during the presentation. Ask a few questions. Have True or False posters on opposite sides of the room and have people answer by moving to the True or False poster. If you have a white board, use it! Maybe play a game on the board. Can you get them to stand at their seats and do something to support your content? I once saw a speech on laughter and the presenter asked everyone to stand and put their hands over their head, breathe and expel their breath and lower their arms by saying "Ha, ha, ha, ha." Everyone was laughing and relaxed. It was a great use of thirty seconds and thoroughly engaging. A goal speech had the presenter asking everyone to stand and do a squat. Everyone did. She then asked to do a squat with one leg. No one did well but she assured them that if they practiced daily they could, and then she demonstrated. That interactive exercise made a great point. A speaker discussing Time Management brilliantly asked all participants to stand. She took out a stop watch and asked them without looking at any devices, to gauge how long a minute was.

*Note: Sometimes you can combine a prop and physical activity. Also, often a probing question often works wonderfully with a personal story.*

### Interaction 7.7: 4 Ps for a Perfect Speech (Connect)

Suppose you had to give a speech on the topic of "travel." Provide a creative, engaging example of how you would incorporate each of the four Ps for a perfect speech.

**Sample 4 Ps Applied to Speech Topic**

| CONNECTION | HOW WILL YOU? |
|---|---|
| **Probing Question** | |
| **Prop** | |

| CONNECTION | HOW WILL YOU? |
|---|---|
| **Physical Activity** | |
| **Personal Story** | |

Transitions are important to help your audience follow you from main point to main point, sub point to sub point, and even between your sources and connections. Between each speech element, be sure to explain that one point is complete, and then introduce the next point. Use visuals to supplement transitions between the main points so organization is clear to the audience. Literally display a slide with your points and indicate which is complete and which is next. This helps the different styles of learners to process your ideas, organize your words into the key points you selected. If the audience can't remember the points of your speech at the end, they did not get the message. Keep transition sentences simple—be clear about where you have been and where you are going, and avoid using this as an opportunity to go off on a rant highlighting your personal opinion.

### Transitional Phrases

All things considered...

As you can see from these examples...

As a matter of fact...

At the same time...

By and large,

Contrast that with...

Equally important...

Finally...

First...second...third...

Furthermore...

Given these points...

Generally speaking...

However...

In the final analysis...

In the long run...

In the same way...

In a like manner...

In addition to...

In any event...

In conclusion...

In essence...

In fact...

In light of...

Keeping these points in mind...

Let's begin with...

Likewise...

Moving right along...

My first point is...

My next example is...

Nevertheless...

Not only...

Not to mention...

Now let's consider...

Now that we have established...

Now that we understand...

Overall...

That brings us to...

The next point I'd like to make is...

Together with...

To say nothing of...

To summarize...

To sum up...

## Sample Speech: Listening Can Change Your Life

**Body**

I. What is listening? To understand what listening is, we need to explore the meaning of three key vocabulary words associated with listening: hearing, listening and active listening.

   A. Definitions:

   1. Source: Pearson, Nelson, Titsworth and Harter (2008) in the popular communication text book, Human Communication, define hearing as "the act of ear receiving sound." So, someone who is deaf cannot receive sound. They (Pearson, et al, 2008) go on to define listening as "the active process of receiving, constructing meaning from, and responding to spoken and/or nonverbal messages." Perhaps this why Harvey Robbins (1992) reports that listening is often a skill that is acquired. "Isn't it ironic, that the areas that we spend the most time, speaking and listening are the areas in which we are least trained? Listening is the most challenging of the communication skills and the most frequently ignored." (Display an abbreviated version with key words on a slide to support different types of learners—include all three words.)

| Key Word | Definition | Description |
|----------|-----------|-------------|
| Hearing | Act of receiving sound. (Pearson, et. al, 2008) | A deaf person ear drums cannot receive sound. Nephew Kyle = Amazing Deaf American Ninja Warrior! |
| Listening | Active process of<br>• receiving,<br>• constructing meaning from,<br>• responding to spoken and/or nonverbal messages"(Pearson, et. al, 2008) | Skill that is acquired (Robbins, 1985). |

   2. **Connection:**

   (Probe) How many of you have been in a situation where you heard a friend speak? When they finished speaking, they asked you a question or sought your advice, and you couldn't respond because you realized you had not listened carefully.

   (Personal) Personally, after I choose this topic I was trying to analyze my own listening skills. I clearly recall a recent conversation with my friend Zhenya. She was trying to explain a serious money problem that could cause her to have to move back to Russia. As she spoke, my mind wandered to other things. When she asked me for advice, I could not respond, because I had not listened to her. I was thinking about something else. I felt so embarrassed. I really did not mean to hurt her, but it looked like I didn't care.

**Transition:** Current research attempts to resolve this situation by highlighting the process of active listening.

Cornell University professor Judi Brownell (1985), the author of two books on listening, distinguishes active listening as "an intent to listen for meaning." It is a structured way of listening and responding to others." In this transaction, listeners' attention is focused on the speaker. For this focus to occur, listeners must suspending their own frame of reference and refrain from judgment to fully understand the speaker. As a result, Brownell points out, speakers will be free to fully express themselves without becoming defensive. The good news is that most anyone can learn to become an active listener with practice.

| Key Word | Definition | Description |
|---|---|---|
| Active Listening | • intent to find meaning<br>• structured<br>• focus on speaker<br>• no judgment<br><br>(Brownell, 1985) | Skill<br><br>Anyone can learn! |

**Transition:** Now that we understand these key words, I would like to share some common myths about listening.

**B. Myths:** Take a moment to review this list—are there any items on here that you believe to be true about listening

**1. Source**

| Common Listening Myths Steil, L. K., Summerfield, J., & De, M. G. (1985) |
|---|
| *Myth #1: Listening is largely a matter of intelligence.* |
| *Myth #2: Listening ability is closely related to hearing acuity.* |
| *Myth #3: Daily listening eliminates the need for training.* |
| *Myth #4: Our educational system taught us how to listen well.* |
| *Myth #5: Learning to read is more important than learning to listen.* |
| *Myth #6: People can will themselves to listen well when they want.* |
| *Myth #7: Listening is a passive activity and the responsibility is on the sender.* |

**2. Connection:** So which myth stood out to you? Michael? #1. I agree, many smart people have way too much to say! Anyone else? For me Myth #4 stood out. It made me wonder why our schools don't teach and require listening competency. What's the last course on listening you attended?

**Transition:** I will provide a copy of these myths for your review in my handout at the end of the presentation. For now, let's conclude this section by considering a few facts about listening.

C. Facts

   1. **Source:** *Get In Front Communications (Piombino, 2013)*, highlights some current facts about current communication. Let's see if you can determine fact from fiction! Have one slide that says Fact or Fiction. Place each of these bullets on individual slides (given that it is a game, cite on the last slide where you reveal the answers.)

      - We listen to people at a rate of 125-250 words per minute, but think at 1,000-3,000 words per minute.

      - Less than two percent of people have had any formal education on how to listen.

      - Images go into your long-term memory, whereas words live in your short-term memory.

      - 55 percent of a message's meaning comes from the speaker's facial expressions, 38 percent from tone and inflection, and seven percent from the actual words spoken.

      - The ability to communicate (listening is a vital part) is crucial for promotion, more important than drive or numbers (Harvard Business Review).

   2. **Connection:** (Physical) With slide displayed, ask audience to stand if they believe the statement to be a fact and to remain sitting if they believe it to be fiction. Alternative suggestion: Ask for three volunteers to join you on stage. Instruct the volunteers to move their body to right side of the room if they believe the statement to be a Fact and to the left if they believe it to be Fiction  Have the audience call out the statement. All are facts (if you want to put a false fact in—you can always do so). At the end share the whole list and explain that all are facts and provide the citation. Ask volunteers to sit.

      Look at list. (Probe) How can these facts affect your ability to listen? (Wait for a response—share my opinion…#1 helps to explain why it is difficult to truly focus on what another person is saying, our brain works faster than their mouth!

**Transition:** Given this information we have covered thus far, do you feel that you have a better understanding of what listening is? Great! Let's move on to our second question. Show Main points on PP.

II. **How can we improve our listening skills?**

   A. **Awareness, question your ability to listen.**

      1. **Source:** Judi Brownell (2015) states that the first step to improving our listening skills begins by questioning our own ability to listen. Listening is so important it is the basis of human interaction. As Susie Mitchell Cortright (2001) points out: "Listening makes our loved ones feel worthy, appreciated, interesting, and respected. Ordinary conversations emerge on a deeper level, as do our relationships. When we listen, we foster the skill in others by acting as a model for positive and effective communication."

2. **Connection:** (Personal) Believe it or not, I equate listening with respect. I have been in situations where I heard what the person is saying, but really was sending messages to wrap it up, so I could make my point. I realize, I can listen better. Awareness involves developing a personal awareness in regards to your own ability to listen. You must be willing to find opportunities to improve. Furthermore, you must have a desire to really hear what others say. We can always improve. Just think, do you feel respected when you're ignored, or someone pretends like they are listening, or seems anxious for you to shut up so they can begin making their own point? I don't. But, in the moment, it is easy to anticipate another's words to get to your point faster. I yearn to slow down and respectfully listen to others even more. How?

**Transition:** I was happy to discover some strategies in my research to improve my listening skills. The second thing we can do to improve our listening skills is to...

B. **Practice active listening skills.**

1. **Source:** Susie Mitchell Cortright (2001) describes 10 tips to practice active listening skills. Review this list! Which of these will be easy to master? Which will be difficult?

| Tip | Description |
|---|---|
| 1. Face the speaker | Sit up straight or lean forward slightly, using body language to show your attentiveness. |
| 2. Maintain eye contact | To a comfortable degree. |
| 3. Minimize external distractions | Turn off the TV. Put down your book or magazine, and ask the speaker and other listeners to do the same. |
| 4. Respond appropriately | Raise your eyebrows. Say words such as "Really," "Interesting," as well as more direct prompts: "What did you do then?" and "What did she say?" |
| 5. Focus solely on what the speaker is saying. | Try not to think about what you are going to say next. The conversation will follow a logical flow after the speaker makes her point. |
| 6. Minimize internal distractions. | If your own thoughts keep horning in, simply let them go and continuously re-focus your attention on the speaker, much as you would during meditation. |
| 7. Keep an open mind. | Wait until the speaker is finished before deciding whether you agree or disagree. Try not to make assumptions about what the speaker is thinking. |

| 8. Avoid letting the speaker know how you handled a similar situation. | Unless they specifically ask for advice, assume they just need to talk it out. |
| --- | --- |
| 9. Even if the speaker is launching a complaint against you, wait until they finish to defend yourself. | The speaker will feel as though their point has been made. They won't feel the need to repeat it, and you'll know the whole argument before you respond. Research shows that, on average, we can hear four times faster than we can talk, so we have the ability to sort ideas as they come in. . . and be ready for more. |
| 10. Engage yourself. | Ask questions for clarification, but, once again, wait until the speaker has finished. That way, you won't interrupt their train of thought. After you ask questions, paraphrase their point to make sure you understood. Start with: "So you're saying. . .?" |

2. **Connection:** Each day I have been practicing one strategy and have been amazed at the how my relationships have changed! It is as if there is another dimension added to my interactions. Just Tuesday, I was talking with Coach Steele about my speech—truthfully, I was really proud of it because I worked hard. Rather than the praise I expected, she offered critique on a section. When this happens in my life, my normal instinct is to deny or explain what I meant. Instead, I swallowed my words, consciously opened my ears, and practiced Mitchell's active listening skill #9. Guess what? After a moment, my ears did open, and I heard what she was saying. As a result, I eliminated two minutes from the speech. Now it makes more sense, and I am happier with it. Initially, I really wanted to defend my reasoning. If I had, I would have missed a valuable lesson. I wonder how many valuable lessons I've missed by trying to defend myself?

### Interaction 7.8: Body

Write the body for your speech topic, be sure to fill out the skeleton outline incorporating each element of the Speech Formula for the Body: Main Points, Sub Points, Source, Connection.

# Part 4: Introduction

*Note: Don't discuss your research in the Thesis—wait for the Body.*

No matter what type of speech you are delivering, your introduction is like a commercial or a movie trailer designed to "sell" your words and ideas. It is hard-core persuasion at its best. Ultimately, you must convince the entire audience that you, and your words, are worth their attention. People often seem to pay physical attention during a speech while their minds wander. Don't allow this scenario to occur—the audience sits there, you stand there blah, blah, and blah. Everyone's time is wasted! Convince the audience they would rather hear your words than listen to the voices in their heads. You must earn this privilege. Remember, the introduction is the most important part of the speech for the audience. Why? First impressions mean a lot! Once made, they are difficult to change. Capture your audiences' attention with carefully constructed words designed to get them onboard or to buy into the journey you advertise. What can you do to convince your audience that your message is so compelling they want to listen, indeed, are excited to hear your message? Complete each part of the Introduction as intended. The introduction includes three different parts; each serves an important role in capturing the attention of the audience. The Introduction only deals with the topic. Do not go into any specific points or details. Save the specifics for the body of the speech.

## Attention Grabber

Grab your audience's attention right here, now! You want to the audience with your first words! Whatever you do, be sure that it supports your purpose statement. Don't do something just because you can. In fact, do something vastly different from the rest of the speech. Recently, two people who were debating healthcare began the speech by telling a story. They brought up a male to represent Juan, a 70-year-old man with current Medicare benefits. They brought up a female to represent Jane, a young woman without insurance who takes advantage of the system. As one speaker described "Juan," they gave him props like a paper mustache pasted on a lollypop, a cane, a check to represent the money he made working at a grocery store and his Medicare card. As the other speaker described "Jane," she handed her props including a picture of her five children, keys to her pricey car, and a government check. This was a fantastic way to start this speech—the entire audience was spellbound by their creativity. Do something different than you will through the rest of the speech. Don't just use your voice or body by providing a statistic or quote or story—you will do all that and more in the body of your speech, jump out of the box for your Attention Grabber!

Think of all the ways you can be creative, you can use a short video clip, if you do it should never be over a minute and should never have someone else giving a speech about the speech you are going to give. You can use a skit or role play. Once a someone gave a speech on the importance of your personal brand. He looked really lethargic and almost uninterested. He was not dressed professionally, more like sweats that might even be considered pajamas. He started his speech really poorly. Until we realized it was all an act! He stripped off the PJ's and had a suit underneath. He literally demonstrated why positively promoting yourself matters.

### Thesis

Once you grab audience attention, keep it. How? By executing your persuasive strategy. Refer to Aristotle's insights on rhetoric and load your thesis with his three elements.

1. Relate (pathos): appeal to audience, ask questions.
2. State (logos): the logical argument or thesis statement.
3. Support (ethos): speaker credentials, authoritative quotations, statistics.

### Relate

In the Speech Formula, we will refer to these as "Relate, State and Support" because we are going to apply our Pathos, Logos and Ethos in a very specific way. Consider incorporating these three techniques as a boxing combination designed to completely knock out your audience! They are down for the count, completely convinced they want to listen to your message.

Relate (pathos): The **Relate** fulfills our Pathos by appealing to the audience, evoking emotion from them. There are many ways to appeal to an audience by using pathos. We are not going to use just any story or emotional evocation with our audience; we want to use the most effective type. (For our purposes, this is an appeal using questions to induce the audience to envision their own example.) This is powerful because personal experiences are almost always more significant than anyone else's. To accomplish this task, ask a series of carefully planned questions that take the audience on a very specific journey filled with imagery that leaves them curious, wanting more.

### State

This is the center of the speech, the reason everyone is here.

1. Refer to your Purpose Statement. "By the end of my speech my audience will listen more competently."
2. Replace the beginning phrase: "By the end of my speech the audience will..." with

   "Today, I would like to discuss with you how to..."

That is your thesis statement. After a stunning Attention Grabber, your thesis statement asks the audience "will you listen?"

Do not go into the specific points of your speech here (your main points, only address the topic copy this directly from your Purpose Statement. For example,

   "Today, I would like to discuss with you how to listen better."

That's it! Be careful! Don't go off on a tangent including an explanation or going into the points of the speech. Just introduce the topic!

**Support**

This is where you are seeking to establish your credibility as a speaker and tell the audience why they should trust you.

Use a quote from a famous person that supports the topic statement to deliver the final blow—the Upper Cut. The Knock Out! The audience learns that an "expert" believes the topic is important too! If you are the expert, hopefully someone else has introduced you and highlighted your qualifications. However, you can reference a study or experience briefly here. However, always add a quote by someone else, especially someone famous whose words emphasize what you are trying to accomplish in this speech. While quotes and statistics provide credibility in and of themselves, your delivery thus far does too. For instance, if you look the part, professionally dressed, obviously well-prepared, words intentionally spoken in a controlled manner designed to lead the audience on an important journey—if you can convey this message in your non-verbals, you will resonate with your audience and you will "earn" the needed respect or credibility necessary to continue with the speech. If you seem unprepared, unfocused and roll over your audience with the questions, you will not establish your ethos.

Ultimately, these persuasive appeals convince the audience that they should listen to your speech…and they can't wait to do so! Let's give them what they want.

> If you have an important point to make, don't try to be subtle or clever. Use a pile driver. Hit the point once. Then come back and hit it again. Then hit it a third time — a tremendous whack.
>
> *- Winston Churchill*

**Preview Main Points**

Your audience needs signposts and transitions in order to follow your path. This is the most important signpost of your entire speech. You always want to tell the audience what you are going to tell them (Preview), tell them (Body) and then tell them what you told them (Conclusion). This reinforces the main points of the speech. Hopefully, if you did this right and your points are clear, they will be able to recall the points you made. If they can do that, chances are they got your message because they are able to process the information in relation to the points.

1. Be consistent. Don't change the wording from the Roman numerals of your speech. Literally, copy and paste from the Roman numerals in the body of your speech. Begin with a statement, like  "There are two points I'd like to address…

2. Only state the points. Don't muddle the points with dialogue.

3. Emphasize the points. Use body language—show the number of points with hand gestures. Whenever possible, use a visual aid like Power Point to display these points to your audience. Connect with the audience by asking them to read one slide.

**Sample Speech: Listening Can Change Your Life**

**Introduction**

**Attention Grabber:** Movie clip from "Hitch" http://www.youtube.com/watch?v=-n6ehVRzA-s

**Thesis**

**Relate (Probe):** Think with me for a second…who is the best listener you know? Picture this person clearly in your mind. Okay, now think of the worst listener you know. Now, how do you think **you** rate as a listener?

**State:** Today I would like to talk to you about how to listen more competently.

**Support:** Many people have spoken wise words about listening. My favorite is a quote from Brenda Ueland, printed in a 1938 Ladies Home Journal issue: "Listening is a magnetic and strange thing, a creative force. The friends who listen to us are the ones we move toward. This is the reason: When we are listened to, it creates us, makes us unfold and expand."

**Preview Main Points:** Let's explore two questions, #1: What is listening? and #2: How can we improve our listening skills? (Display these two main points on a PowerPoint slide to accommodate different learning styles and emphasize key points.)

## Interaction 7.9: Introduction

Write the introduction for your speech topic.*
Thesis
    Relate:
    State:
    Support:
Preview the Main Points:

# Part 5: Conclusion

| Speech Formula | |
| --- | --- |
| **CONCLUSION: Remind them why they listened** | **Introduction Backwards** |
| Review main points *"Today we discussed…"* | Share main points, not sub points. |
| Review thesis. Include: Relate, State, Support | Return to each part. |
| Return to Attention Grabber. | Bring them full circle! |
| Call to Action<br>Include a persuasive appeal that is timely and specific. | **Only** persuasive speech. |

### Review the Main Points

Return to the Main Points of the speech. Don't muddle the water with extra words, or redoing the whole speech. Just be sure the audience can recall the points of the speech. Engaging the audience can be a great way to see if the audience got your points. You can reward those who respond to you, for example with candy or company merchandise—rewards are sure to liven things up and increase retention. But be sure to show the slides with the Main Points for complete audience retention.

### Thesis

**Support:** Return to the famous quote you shared in the beginning. "Remember how (famous person) said...(insert quote)." Be sure to insert a transitional statement that connects the statement to those words. "Hopefully now you too can ..."

**State:** Return to your thesis statement. Use a transitional statement and simply restate the thesis statement. "Hopefully by incorporating these skills discussed here today you can now, (insert thesis statement)."

**Relate:** Return to the questions you posed in the beginning.

**Attention Grabber:** Once again, transition from the relation to the audience and bring it back to where you began. Don't be concerned with being repetitive. Returning to this content allows the audience to rethink and compare where they began with what they now know. It allows them to feel complete. If you are playing a video, you may not have to play the entire video but just bring the audience back to the premise.

---

## Sample Speech: Listening Can Change Your Life

### Conclusion

**Review Main Points:** What were the two points we covered today?
(Reward audience/Show on PP)

What is listening? How you can become a better listener?

**Review Thesis** (Return to **each**)

**Support:** Remember how Brenda Euland points out that, "Listening is a magnetic and strange thing, a creative force. The friends who listen to us are the ones we move toward. When we are listened to, it creates us, makes us unfold and expand."

**State:** Thus by incorporating these skills in our lives, we can be the creative force that helps those around us expand by listening more competently.

**Relate:** And, in so doing you can avoid being someone who is a bad listener and perhaps. ..you can even be someone who listens like this.

**Return to Attention Grabber:** Replay Hitch video.

---

## Interaction 7.10: Conclusion

Write the conclusion for your speech topic.*

Review the Main Points:

Restate Thesis:

Support:

State:

Relate:

Return to Attention Grabber:

> You are not being judged, the value of what you are bringing to the audience is being judged.
>
> *- Seth Godin*

## Chapter 7 Review Questions

1.  What are the five parts to a dynamic speech?

2.  Describe the three different types of audience anayalysis.

3.  What are the five rules for writing a quality purpose statement?

4.  Which part of the speech is most important to you, the audience?

5.  Which part of the speech is most imporant to you, the author? Why?

6.  Who writes the speech?

7.  What order do you use to deliver the speech?

8.  In what order do you construct the speech?

9.  Suppose you were delivering a speech with this purpose statement: By the end of my speech my audience create a great personal brand. Identify three organizational strategies you could use. Which would work best?

10. How are the introduction and conclusion different?

11. How many times should you tell your audience your main points during the course of the speech?

12. Which quote from this chapter resonates with you the most?

## Sample Speech: Randy Pausch, Really Achieving Your Childhood Dreams

1. Watch Randy Pausch's speech, *Really Achieving Your Childhood Dreams*: http://www.cmu.edu/randyslecture/

2. Analyze his speech:

   a. Outline his speech (use an outline not an essay).

   b. Compare/contrast the outline of Professor Pausch's speech to the Speech Formula you used to write the speech in this chapter. Did Dr. Pausch follow the Speech Formula? What was the same? What was different?

   c. In your opinion what were the best moments of his speech? What were the weakest moments? Why?

   d. Consultation: Suppose you had the opportunity to consult with him prior to delivering his speech again to an even larger crowd, what advice would you offer him? What should he do the same? What should he do differently?

# References

Brownell, J. (1985). Building active listening skills. Englewood Cliffs, NJ: Prentice Hall.

Brownell, J. (2015). Listening: Attitudes, principles, and skills. Boston, Mass: Pearson/Allyn & Bacon.

Cortright, S. (2001, January 1). Ten secrets of good listeners. Retrieved December 13, 2014, from http://www.christian-mommies.com/special-features/just-for-moms/ten-secrets-of-good-listeners/

Hitch - a part of movie 2 [Video file]. (2005) Retrieved from http://www.youtube.com/watch?v=-n6ehVRzA-s

Llopis, V. M. (2015). The effect of an online speech preparation tool on public speaking associated anxiety: A pilot study. Unpublished manuscript.

O'Toole, G. (n.d.). When we are listened to, it creates us, makes us unfold and expand. Retrieved December 13, 2014, from http://quoteinvestigator.com/2014/06/13/listen/#return-note-9121-1

Pearson, J. C., DeWitt, L., Child, J. T., Kahl, D. H., & Dandamudi, V. (2007). Facing the Fear: An Analysis of Speech-Anxiety Content in Public-Speaking Textbooks. Communication Research Reports, 24(2), 159-168. doi:10.1080/08824090701304923

Pearson, J, Nelson, P., Titsworth, S, Harter, L. (2017). Human communication, sixth edition. Boston, Mass: McGraw-Hill

Piombino, K. (2013, December 30). Listening facts you never knew. Retrieved December 14, 2014, from http://www.prdaily.com/Main/Articles/Listening_facts_you_never_knew_14645.aspx

Robbins, H. (1992). How to speak and listen effectively. New York, NY: American Management Association.

Steil, L. K., Summerfield, J., & De, M. G. (1985). Listening—it can change your life: A handbook for scientists and engineers. New York: McGraw-Hill

# Chapter 8:
# Putting it All Together

Phase 1: Planning

Phase 2: Preparation

Phase 3: Construction

Phase 4: Delivery

Phase 5: Reflection

## Objectives

**By the end of this chapter you should be able to:**

1. Compare and contrast the two components of a great speech.

2. Explain the significance of the design of the message.

3. Identify the three stages involved in the design of the speech according to the Construction Checklist?

4. State the components of the delivery strategy?

5. Create an effective personal plan of action.

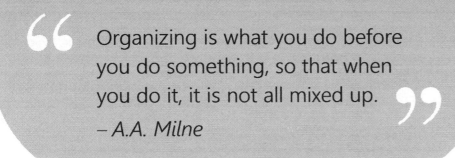

> Organizing is what you do before
> you do something, so that when
> you do it, it is not all mixed up.
>
> – A.A. Milne

## Chapter 8
# Putting It All Together

### The Process

Delivering a great speech involves an elaborately detailed process. A great speech is more than just writing clever words. A great speech is more than delivering with finesse. Without a strategic system to complete the process, balls are dropped and opportunities are missed. How many times in life do you have the opportunity to stand before a group of people and inspire them to act? When you have this chance, it is worth the effort to make your speech all that it can be. This chapter will guide you through the complete process. We will revisit parts we have already discussed as we put all of these ideas together. Follow this process and you will deliver your best speech ever.

As a reminder, as you go through this chapter, you are invited to log onto www.speechformula.com to use the speechwriting tool that will guide you through the process to create a fantastic speech. As you progress through each step of the speech writing process, you answer prompts from the tool. It includes videos to explain each main step and instructions for each sub step. When you reach the end, your speech, your cards and even your visuals are ready to use. The web application helps make the tedious speech writing process a breeze by guiding you every step of the way. Augment your process by following the guidelines outlined in this chapter and you are sure to be a master speechwriter in no time!

## Interaction 8.1: Brainstorm

Think about presentations you have heard or presented in the past. Consider all that you have learned about the speech writing process in this book. What do you think is involved in the following phases?

| | |
|---|---|
| Phase 1: Planning | |
| Phase 2: Preparation | |
| Phase 3: Construction | |
| Phase 4: Delivery | |
| Phase 5: Reflection | |

Let's compare your ideas and experience to the Speech Process. How did you do? Carefully explore the Speech Process to see what is involved in each stage of the process.

SPEECH PROCESS

**Table 8.1: Speech Process** (Read speech out loud 5-10 times.)

| Phase 1: Planning | Phase 2: Preparation | Phase 3: Construction | Phase 4: Delivery | Phase 5: Reflection |
|---|---|---|---|---|
| • Request<br>• Assessment<br>• Schedule<br>• Topic | Conduct research | **F4: Body (Write)** | **Before Speech** | **After Speech** |
| | **F1: Audience Analysis** | **Source:** Write source content - cite | • Read speech out loud 5-10<br>• Create your cards & visuals<br>• Practice deliberately with Plan of Action<br>• Practice reducing anxiety<br>• Time your speech<br>• A/V analysis<br>• Prepare evaluations<br>• 25 hour check—*Ready* | • Secure audience feedback<br>• Reflect upon your delivery<br>• Watch video<br>• Create an Improvement Plan<br>• Any opportunities to deliver speech again? |
| | **F2: Purpose Statement** | **Connections:** Incorporate the 4 Ps | | |
| | **F4: Body (Organize)** | **Transitions:** Guide between points | **During Speech** | |
| | • Select emotional and motivational appeal<br>• Select *best* Organizational Strategy<br>• Skeleton outline | **F3: Introduction**<br>**F5: Conclusion**<br>• Check Formula<br>• Sweeten It!<br>• Solicit feedback | • Reduce anxiety<br>• Arrive early<br>• Test A/V equipment<br>• Assess yourself<br>• Record speech<br>• Set the Stage – Do IT! | |

Note: F=Formula. F1: Audience Analysis; F2: Purpose Statement; F3: Introduction; F4: Body; F5: Conclusion

SPEECH FORMULA

## Table 8.2: Speech Formula

| Audience Analysis | Purpose Statement | Introduction | Body | Conclusion (Intro backwards) |
|---|---|---|---|---|
| **Primary:** Who is my audience? Not about topic! | **1. Use words,** "By the end of my speech my audience will..." | **Attention Grabber** Special, interesting & provocative have them @ "Hello!" | Which organizational strategy works BEST to support my purpose? **Select Organizational Strategy** | **Review Main Points** Last opportunity to ensure audience got your points! |
| Ask questions re: demographics, psychographics or behaviors. | **2. Dream!** GO BIG! What would you like to occur? | **Thesis** | **Create a Skeleton Outline:** I. II. A. A. B. B. | **Restate Thesis** |
| **Secondary:** WIFM, connects speaker, message and audience. | **3. KISS:** Keep it simple, 1 idea, no 'and's or conjunctions. | **1. Relate:** Ask probing questions | **Fill out Skeleton Outline** For each sub point break out: 1. Source 2. Connection | 3. **Return to Thesis Statement** |
| 1. Why is this topic important to them? | **4. Use active verbs—** something you can physically do! | **2. State:** State your thesis.Modify your purpose statement. | **1. Source:** Write what you will say to your audience about your sub point. Include quality research and be credible, cite. | 2. **Return to Thesis Statement** |
| 2. How will my audience benefit from my words? | **5. Do not share in this form with audience.** You will repurpose for your thesis statement | **3. Quote:** Use a quote written by someone famous to support value of speech. | **2. Connection:** For each sub point, make the information come alive by making it fun and interesting using the 4Ps Personal Story, Probe, Physical Activity, Prop 3D) | 1. **Relate:** Ask probing questions. |
| 3. Will they learn something new? | | **Preview Main Points** One sentence, literally copy/paste your Main Points! | **Transitions:** Create transitions to guide the audience from one point to another. | **Return to Attention Grabber** It's an art; bring them full circle! |
| **Formal:** Conduct a pre-speech questionnaire. | | | Write out source, connections and transitions for each sub point. | **Call to Action** (Persuasive speech only) |

# Phase 1: Planning

The planning stage is vital to the success of your speech and involves strategically thinking about what you want to accomplish with your speech and securing the materials necessary to do so. If you want to succeed, you must have a plan. Or, as Benjamin Franklin allegedly said: "If you fail to plan, you are planning to fail."

### Interaction 8.2: Will You Speak?

Create a list of situations where you might be asked to deliver a speech.

## The Request

Typically, a speech begins with a request or mandate to deliver. Let's explore the nature of these typical requests in the following table:

**Table 8.3: The Request**

| Type | Description | Considerations |
|------|-------------|----------------|
| 1. Development | Speeches or presentations are often required as a part of a course, workshop, or other knowledge based program. | Examine the rubric. Follow instructions. Create a system to ensure you included all requirements. |
| 2. Role | Your role requires you to represent an organization with a presentation or speech. | Expectations require you to fulfill your role, with consequences for not doing so. |
| 3. Expert | Developed expertise in a particular area and people want to learn from you. | Consider all the variables such as time, energy, effort, reward, opportunities, and threats. |
| 4. Leader | Represents an organization and is the face of it. | Part of the leadership role involves representing the group to your best ability. |
| 5. Driven | Desire to create change. | Be sure that your passion for the issue can endure other points of view and even criticism. |

### 1. Development

Speeches or presentations are often required as a part of a course, workshop, or other knowledge based program. Student in classes are often asked to give a presentation at some point during the semester. Why? A presentation is one of the best ways to learn and typically involves the most advanced level of learning which is to create. According to Bloom's Taxonomy used by educators since it's inception in 1956, lower level learning involves

> Our lives begin to end the day we become silent about the things that matter.
>
> *- Dr. Martin Luther King, Jr.*

"remembering" or recalling facts and basic concepts. As you move up the pyramid, learners are required to engage with content at different levels, including application and analyze. The top of the pyramid requires learners to evaluate and actually create or produce new or original work. In a classroom, what better way to require students to interact with content than to create a presentation where the learner can author their conclusions regarding assigned content?

Instructors or workshop facilitators usually outline the expectations. The expectations are usually tied to a learning objective. If you are going to be evaluated, you want to get the most from the effort you exert into the presentation, and it is going to affect your grade, it is a fantastic idea to refer the rubric change to "to refer to the rubric" the instructor is using. A rubric refers to the grading methodology used. It is a document that articulates expectations for an assignment by listing the criteria, or what counts, and describing levels of quality from excellent to poor. Ask for the rubric if it is not provided. If one is not available, use the guidelines to create your own. It makes no sense to complete an assignment that requires so much work and not fulfill expectations. Far too often, people just start working with no thought of guidelines. As a result, they receive a poor grade or complicate the process by having to revise their work repeatedly to meet expectations.

## 2. Role

Many situations in life have built-in expectations. At times, your role will require you to deliver presentations. Whether you face people who seek out sales pitches or become father-of-the-bride, your role may require you to stand and deliver a speech. Failure to do so can have consequences from demotions to disappointments. Do all that you can to meet the expectation of your role.

## 3. Expert

As a result of your experience in a given area, you may be seen as an expert.

- This can result from recognition for outstanding performance, for example as an athlete who wins an Olympic gold medal.
- It can be a result of years of work and experience in a field that endow you with insights others find valuable.
- It can also be a result of an unanticipated situation you handled well—for instance Captain "Sully" Sullenberger's emergency landing of US Airways flight 1549 on the Hudson River without the loss of life. He was celebrated for his heroic act and remains in demand as an inspirational speaker.
- Sometimes, particularly as a way to develop your business, you may be smart to brand yourself as an expert in your particular area. Event organizers or board members of organizations seek speakers with insights on a wide range of topics to educate members of organizations or attendees at an event.

*Note: Any of the situations can open doors for you to speak to others about your expertise. Keep in mind that your time is valuable. Consider the risks and rewards involved before accepting.*

### 4. Leader

A person who leads or commands a group of people in essence becomes the face of the organization. Leading an organization requires communication. A good leader needs to be an effective communicator in large and small settings. Part of being the leader involves leading and representing the group to your best ability. Leaders inspire and motivate. Articulate messages are needed to do both.

> " Anxiety is caused by a lack of control, organization, preparation, and action. "
>
> - *David Kekich*

### 5. Driven

A wide range of life circumstances may compel the most unsuspecting people to create change. Strategies for accomplishing this may from addressing the town council or school board, starting an organization, or even speaking up on a street corner when a public injustice occurs. Concerned citizens sometimes have a formal place to voice their opinions. Other times, the issue may be so compelling organizations ask or for a speaker to share their experience related to the cause.

### Assessment

Consider it an honor when you are asked or selected to speak to a group. Doing it right takes time, energy, and a desire to do well. If you cannot make this commitment, do not accept the responsibility to address the group. Before accepting the invitation, always ask yourself these two questions: 1. Should I be the one speaking to this group? Make sure you are the right fit—your "help" should match their "hurt." 2. Is this the right time?

As I was finishing writing this book, several different speaking opportunities arose. I felt honored, but every minute spent developing those presentations was time away from completing my book. Also, it made more sense for me to speak to these groups when I could offer them the book to help them grow as speakers.

Finally, consider the event itself. Does the event allow you to do your best? Perhaps your presentation requires an hour for full effectiveness, and twenty minutes doesn't give you the time you need to present your ideas. If the situation is not optimal, the best decision might be to hold off until a win-win situation presents itself.

Typically, someone from an organization will contact you with an invitation to speak. It is crucial that you ask this person key questions to help you deliver your best speech ever! Carefully review these seven questions, and next time you have a speech, use this as a guide.

**Table 8.4: The Talk Every Presenter Must Have Before the Speech**

| 1. Who is requesting you to speak? | What is their role in the organization? |
| --- | --- |
| | Are they your contact for any other questions/concerns? |
| | Why are they asking you? Did they have a topic in mind for that purpose? |
| | Are there any VIP guests? |

| | |
|---|---|
| 2. What is the event? | Are there any programs or advertisements for the event? Can you obtain a copy? |
| | What is the schedule? Can you have a copy? |
| | Are there other speakers? Who? |
| 3. What is the purpose of the event? | Is there a theme? What is it? Why was it selected? |
| | How do they get people to attend? |
| | Is this an annual event or new? If recurring, what was the best year and why and what was the worst year and why? |
| | Are there any materials from the last event? |
| | What do you wish for the audience to "get" from the speech? |
| 4. Who will attend? | Is there a guest list you can see? |
| | What do they know about your topic? |
| | How do they feel about your topic? |
| | What is their "hurt"? How can you "help"? |
| | Of what are they proud? How can you plug into that? |
| | Are you able to send a questionnaire before the presentation? If so when? How? |
| 5. What are the logistics? | What is the date? |
| | What time should you arrive? |
| | How much time are you allotted? |
| | What are specifics of room size, seating, and lighting?. |
| | Where will you be presenting?<br>    a. Is there a podium?<br>    b. Is there a microphone?<br>    c. Can you move around? |
| | What type of technology or presentation aids does the room feature?<br>    a. Do they have white board/chalk board?<br>    b. Is there an easel for brainstorming?<br>    c. Is there a projector? What is the quality?<br>    d. Is there a computer? Type/Connectors?<br>    e. Is the computer connected to the internet?<br>    f. Are there audio speakers?<br>    g. Is there someone to operate equipment?<br>    h. When can you test equipment? |

| 6. What is the budget? | Ask if they have a budget. |
| | Share your speaking rate and contract. |
| | Outline social media promotion expectations for the event. |
| | Inquire as to the process to be paid. (Becoming a vendor may be required and the process can be timely and extremely frustrating.) |
| | Submit an invoice per company guidelines. |
| | Follow up. |
| 7. If they do not have a budget what do they offer? | Dinner |
| | Contact information of their members. |
| | How will the event be promoted? |
| | Request specific social media promotion post event (Linked In, Facebook, Twitter, Instagram). |

## Schedule

The process of delivering a great speech takes time. Create a schedule to ensure that you don't procrastinate and let the audience down. When leaders of organizations are asked to speak to groups, they often have good intentions, but get busy with other things. Suddenly the speech is three days away and they don't have time to put the effort they intended into the presentation. They are however, expert and can speak competently about their topic. So they deliver a speech, but not their best. Have you ever been in the audience when this occurred? I consider it a lost opportunity, and I feel a bit disappointed. I really appreciate a great speech. I love to be plugged in to a presentation and get the most from it.

Here's the rule of thumb I recommend for scheduling and completing each phase.

Table 8.5: Schedule

| Phase | Completion |
|---|---|
| 1: Planning | Complete within 48 hours of the request. |
| 2: Preparation | Complete within 1 week of the request. |
| 3: Construction | Do this with as much focus and uninterrupted time as possible. Try to complete the written presentation in one sitting, two at the most. Do not spread out over a long period. |
| 4: Delivery | Be in delivery phase at least 48 hours before presentation. Do not go to delivery stage until the final week of the presentation. |
| 5: Reflection | Within 48 hours of presentation, review while it is fresh in your mind. |

> ## For every minute spent organizing, an hour is earned.
>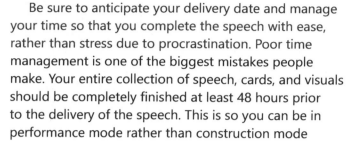
>
> *- Benjamin Franklin*

Be sure to anticipate your delivery date and manage your time so that you complete the speech with ease, rather than stress due to procrastination. Poor time management is one of the biggest mistakes people make. Your entire collection of speech, cards, and visuals should be completely finished at least 48 hours prior to the delivery of the speech. This is so you can be in performance mode rather than construction mode right before the presentation. Create a schedule that makes sense and allots ample time to implement your delivery plan.

### Topics

Topics are most often selected for you based on your expertise or the nature of the event. You should always modify or mold your topic to the direct needs of the audience. Special occasions like a wedding, funeral, or anniversary also dictate the speech topic. Obviously, in these instances your topic is the person. Your relationship with the person is your expertise. Local meetings (town hall or school board) debating an issue that matters to you might provoke you to share your thoughts on the issue, but once again the topic is predetermined.

Consider five situations when you might be asked to give a speech: Development, Role, Expert, Leader, and Driven—in all of these situations, the topic is predetermined by your relationship to the content. If you are in an Art History Class, you may be asked to give a speech about a famous artist or an art movement. Rarely are you asked to "pick a topic." If you are, focus on content that will interest your entire audience rather than just your own personal interests. Always consider your audience needs, not yours. Audience needs should be addressed when you refine your topic.

Be wary of speaking requests that could dilute your core competency. Unless contacts know you and your work well, their ideas about what you do are often unclear. Explore this territory; don't hesitate to clarify. When hashing out the details of the speech I have often felt pressured to change my core message or include too much content. Being the innate optimist, I used to be open to both these scenarios until I realized it hurt my product. My compromises diluted my message. My strength is speaking about public speaking! While I can speak about how to be a better communicator, why should I? After I learned to respect my core competency, I learned how to stick to my guns and provide a better product. I am always willing to adapt to the organization, but I cannot easily change my core competency.

## Phase 2: Preparation

### Conduct Research

The quality of the research you conduct will provide the necessary credibility for you to speak competently about your topic. Most speeches should incorporate credible sources like published articles, academic research, government publications, or legitimate news articles from respected periodicals. Google Scholar and your library are reliable resources. In most situations, the more current the research the better! An exception to this is going "old school," referring to the founding work in a given field, for instance Aristotle's Rhetoric, which provides the basis for "persuasion." Take the time to do the necessary research that will substantiate ideas you have. Use the Credibility Checker and, set standards for the quality of information you will use (See Table 7.5).

When I hear notable speakers like American biographer, historian, and political commentator Doris Kearns Goodwin, American academic, psychologist and popular science author Angela Duckworth, American broadcast journalist, best known as the anchor for Nightline, Ted Koppel, American radio host, environmental activist, author and attorney Robert Kennedy, Jr., French oceanographic explorer, environmentalist, educator, and film producer Jean Michel Cousteau speak, they all have something in common. They quote sources all the time! When I listened to Angela Duckworth, I started counting the references she incorporated into her speech. All my fingers and toes were used within five minutes! Be a credible communicator, even if you are the expert. Experts stay experts by staying current and relevant.

Some speeches, like a toast for a bride or groom or eulogy, call for personal experiences. Even in these instances, a well-chosen quote reflects positively on you and helps make your point. If you have conducted research yourself, do include results such as interviews, experiments, surveys, personal experiences, or anecdotes, but not at the expense of or in lieu of credible published research.

## Audience Analysis

Remember there are three different types of Audience Analysis.

**Primary Audience Analysis** explores who is in your audience. Identify six to eight questions you will use to familiarize yourself with who your audience is. These questions have everything to do with who your audience is, not about your topic. Like a marketer, use demographics, psychographics, behaviors, and geography get into the mind of our audience members.

*Note: Do not literally ask your audience these questions, these questions are asked to help you visualize the needs of the audience. If the coordinator is available do your best to secure basic demographic information and any other insider information about the audience members.*

**Secondary Audience Analysis** is all about how you think key items from your research will connect with your audience. Ask three key questions about your research:
- Why is the topic important?
- How will they benefit?
- What new information will they learn?

**Formal Audience Analysis** (Optional) should be conducted if you have the opportunity. Don't hesitate to send out a questionnaire to gain valuable insight into your audience. If you do use a questionnaire, be sure to include your finding in your speech.

## Purpose Statement

Remember, that your Purpose Statement is the most important part of the speech for you, the author. It provides a clear, guiding light as to what should go into your speech and what should not. Always follow the rules for creating a clear Purpose Statement.

**Body (Organize)**

Organization is key; or as Lynda Peterson said, "with organization comes empowerment." Let's examine how to go about organizing the body.

**Select Emotional and Motivational Appeal**

The first step to organizing your body is to determine how much appeal you want in your speech. You can appeal to your audience two ways: 1. How much emotional response do I wish to evoke? 2. How much do I want to motivate them to action?

The answer to these questions helps you to identify the impact you want your speech to have, the type of speech you will deliver and the strategies that best lend themselves to that type of speech.

Suppose you chose medium emotional and medium motivational appeal. Look at where your speech falls. There are many different types of speeches and general guidelines for the

Figure 8.1: Speech Type by Appeal

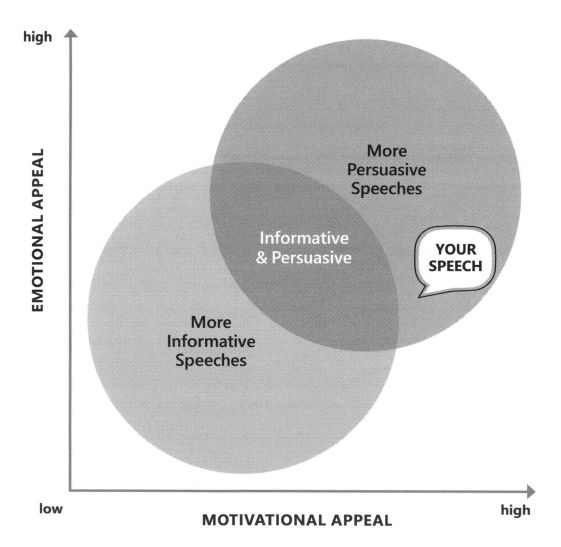

emotional and motivational appeal of each. Look at the breakdown of the various speeches shown in the Speech Type by Appeal chart.

### Select Best Organizational Strategy

Now that you understand how different types of speeches evoke different reactions based upon the appeal the speaker selects, we can explore the organizational strategy that will work best for your speech. Some organizational strategies are more effective for speeches that are more informative; some are more effective for speeches that are persuasive. Some are used for both. Explore this chart to see the array of choices at your disposal. After careful consideration determining the type of speech you want, you should identifythe strategy that will serve the purpose of your speech best. To best choose, identify three strategies you could use, then review your purpose statement and select the best strategy. By following this process, you design your message with an effective organizational strategy. Next, choose your sub points. Once again, an array of strategies is available. Choose the one that will best package the information you plan to share in your research. Sometimes the best option is just a topic strategy but other times these more specific strategies provide clearer points.

Here is an example:

> ## The way a message is designed is the determining factor that influences every interaction we encounter.
> *- J.R. Steele*

---

**Purpose:** By the end of my speech, my audience will listen better.
**Appeal:** Motivation High, Emotion Medium
**Organizational Strategies:** Problem/Solution, What it is/How to use it, Three Steps
The Best strategy is what it is (Structure)? How is it used (Function)?

**Create Skeleton Outline**
**Main Points:** Using this strategy, my main points become:
    I. What is listening?
    II. How can we become better listeners?

**Sub Points**
To create my sub points I need to think about how I respond to the Main Points and consider of all the research I have collected to determine what to include in my speech. My purpose and main points help me make that decision. In this instance after reviewing my list of strategies, I choose. Notice how each sub point, I can clearly identify a piece of research to support that point.
I. What is listening?
    A. Definition
    B. Myths
    C. Facts
II. How can we become better listeners?
    A. Do's
    B. Don'ts

---

This outline is commonly referred to as a Skeleton Outline. It contains just the logic. Never write a speech or a paper or respond to a message that matters without having a skeleton outline that make senses and supports your goal.

Never use full sentences to for your Main Points and Sub Points. Label them so they have a name and you and your audience can make better sense of the content.

# Phase 3: Construction

### F4: Body (Write)

Now you are ready to write the body of the speech. Essentially all you have to do is fill out the skeleton outline with 1. Source and 2. Connection for each sub point. Look at this example.

| Speech Formula |
|---|
| **BODY: Drives the speech. It is the reason for the speech as it reveals the crucial information about the topic.** |
| **Select the organizational strategies that best support your purpose statement to organize your main points and sub points.**<br>**Main points:** _____<br>**Sub points:** _____ |
| **I./II. Main Point** (must have two main points)<br>Breaks down topic. Category title for sub points. Should be easy to remember, organized. |
|     **A./B. Sub Point** (must have two sub points)<br>    Provides name (description) for your research like "Definition" or "Types." Breaks down Main Point. |
|       **1. Source:**<br>        Drives the speech; reveal "jewels" of information you have discovered.<br>        Share/cite source (display on PP cite orally/paper/PP). |
|       **2. Connection:**<br>        4 Ps = Super Speech (Personal Story, Probing Questions, Physical Activity, Prop) What type of connection will you select to engage your audience? The 4 Ps are crucial to help your audience make sense of the information. |
|     **Transitions/Connectors/Sign Posts**<br>    Act as a tour guide, explaining where you are and where you are going. Don't hesitate to **share** your organization. |

**Source:** Write source content. Be sure to include your citations. Add your research that provides the definition of listening, giving credit to the author.

I. What is listening?
  A. Definition
    1. Source: According to the Oxford Encyclopedia *(2015)* "Listening is. . ." Write the exact words you will say to your audience.

**Connections:** Now that you have supported your point with your research/source, connect it to your audience by incorporating at least one of the Four Ps: Personal Story, Probe, Physical Engagement, Prop 3D

> **There are three things to aim at in public speaking: first, to get into your subject, then to get your subject into yourself, and lastly, to get your subject into the heart of your audience.**
> *- Alex Gregg*

  2. Connection: "How many of you have ever. . ." Or a (Physical) "Stand up if you..."

**Transitions:** Guide the audience between points.

When you finish filling out the skeleton outline with the exact words you will use with your audience, add a transitional statement in between each main point and sub point. Act as if you were a tour guide, guiding your audience from one exciting location to another.

Your complete body now features a clear structure that supports your purpose. It provides credible information and is entertaining, engaging the audience at each point.

**F3: Introduction**

At this point, you can breathe a sigh of relief. This is going to be a great speech. No matter what type of speech you are delivering, your introduction is like a commercial or a movie trailer designed to "sell" your words and ideas. It is hard-core persuasion at its best. Ultimately, you must convince the entire audience that you, and your words, are worth their attention. People often give their physical attention during a speech, but **not** their minds. In other words they look like they are listening but they are day dreaming. Don't allow this façade to occur—the audience sits there, you stand there blah, blah, blah. . . time is wasted! Convince the audience that they'd rather hear your words than listen to the voices in their heads. This is a privilege you must earn. Remember, the introduction is the most important part of the speech for the audience. Why? First impressions mean a lot! Once made, they are difficult to change. Capture your audiences' attention with carefully constructed words designed to "get them onboard" or to "buy into" the journey you advertise. What can you do to convince your audience that your message is so compelling they want to listen, indeed, are excited to hear your message? Complete each part of the Introduction as intended.

**Introduction**

The introduction includes three different parts. Each part of the introduction serves an important role in capturing the attention of the audience. The Introduction **only** deals with the **topic**. Don't go into any specific points or details. Save the specifics for the body of the speech. Look at how to create an Introduction so compelling that it serves as an advertisement causing your audience to buy into your message!

  **1. Attention Grabber:** (Do something different that you will do the rest of the speech.)

  **2. Thesis:** (Incorporate these three persuasive appeals to gain the audience's interest.)

Relate: Ask probing questions to gain audience interest into your topic. State: State your thesis (reworded from your purpose) and credibility statement. Quote (Logos): Find a quote by a notable, famous person like Mark Twain or Maya Angelou. The statement should support your purpose statement. This is not the same or similar information you will use in your body to make the specific points of the speech.

**3. Preview Main Points:** Preview just the main points of the speech. Always show on visual if possible to help visual learners retain your message. Make them points not sentences.

### F5: Conclusion

The Conclusion is perhaps the simplest of all! Just write the Introduction backwards. Simply bring the audience back to your topic by touching briefly on each part—leave them exactly where you started. This will provide a feeling of completeness. The audience, now having the benefit of the points made in the speech, will appreciate the topic from a deeper, more informed perspective.

### Check the Formula

Each part of the Speech Formula serves a very specific function. Be sure that you followed the exact guidelines for each part. Review the Speech Formula chapter and follow use the grade sheet to evaluate each part of it. You can solicit the advice of a Speech Coach available on the website: www.speechformula.com if you want a direct feedback and analysis of your speech.

### Sweeten It!

Do you remember how to implement DP4: Sweeten It? What can you do to make the speech all that it can be? How can you use your voice? Are there any ways that you can creatively think outside the box and incorporate the audience's senses? Is there an engaging game or way to get the audience moving and engaged enjoying the content? Don't hesitate to solicit advice or ideas from other people. Sometimes their perspective can be a breath of fresh air, providing new energy and ideas.

### Solicit Feedback

Carefully read your complete speech aloud. Does it make sense? If you were in the audience, would you want to hear it? Check to be sure that it is in a logical order and that your supporting information actually makes the points you want to make. Consider whether your connections are supporting the idea or slightly off topic, diverting attention or focus from your intended point. Once you have completed your own review, solicit the opinion of a peer or friend. Request their honest feedback. Select someone who has enough discernment and willingness to provide feedback, rather than just say it is "good." Listen to their feedback and make adjustments accordingly.

Congratulations! You have now completed the Construction Phase. Now on to Delivery.

# Phase 4: Delivery

### Before the Speech Stage

As we have discussed, effective practice involves more than just reading through your speech. Use the following strategies to be fully prepared.

### Read Speech 5-10 Times

The first thing you should do is print out your final speech and read it aloud five to ten times. This creates a groove in your brain, building on the thought you put into writing the speech. Although you are not memorizing verbatim, you are embedding specific words and phrases in memory, placing them on the tip of your tongue during the speech.

### Create Cards and Visuals

Depending upon the type of speech and where and why it's being delivered, slides can add impact to your speech and help you audience get your message. Visuals, when used correctly,

**Figure 8.2: Sample Listening Speech Slides**

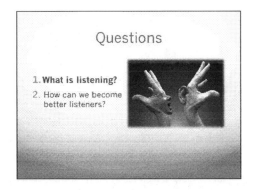

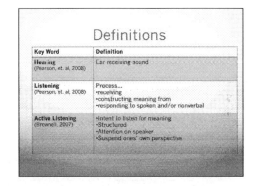

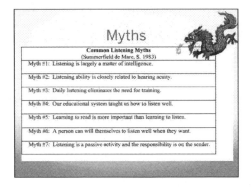

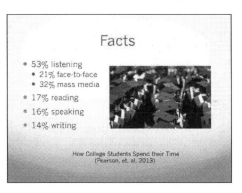

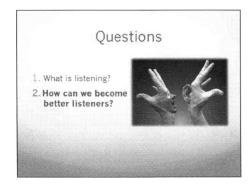

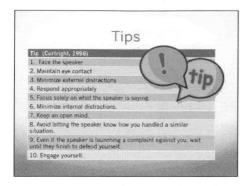

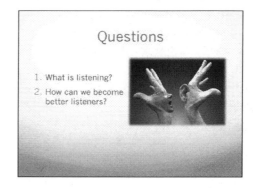

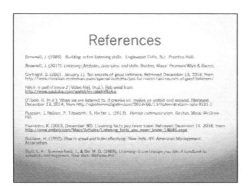

infuse your message with positive energy and clarify points. Creating and interacting with visuals is a skill. It does not just naturally happen. The Slides and Cards for the sample listening speech are displayed Figure Table 8.2 for your review.

### Cue Cards: Formula + Keywords

Your notecards should contain "Speech Formula" plus key words. Do not include any Slide content on your Cards. Depending upon the length of your speech, you may only need a few note cards (3-4 cards for a 10-minute speech). The biggest card-related mistake is to include too much information, too many words. During tense moments, even the most seasoned speaker will opt to refer to their cards too often and miss opportunities to connect with their audience. If you use full sentences on your cards, you will read from them.

### Slides

Your slides will contain your Main Points and your Source information. Follow the rules covered in Slides Do's and Don'ts, and fill out a C2ARES rubric for each slide. That will ensure that you remember your audience at all times and never do a boring slide show. Remember, when it comes to your slides most often, less is more.

### Practice Deliberately with a Delivery Action Plan

Create a Delivery Action Plan for any speech you deliver. The Delivery Action Plan identifies three specific personal performance goals that you want to achieve for this speech. As a reminder, use the resources below to identify worthwhile goals:

- The 10 Delivery Principles
- 4 Ps for a Super Speech
- C²ARES Method for Making Visuals Work for You

As you learn each of these techniques and tips, work to apply them to your delivery. Don't try to do too much. I recommend setting three goals for each speech. Assess how you did, then build on your progress and create new goals to further develop your technique. Using the 10 Delivery Principles, begin with the first three—Set the Stage, Speak Up and Control Your Energy. For each goal, identify three very specific steps that describe what exactly you will do to master the principle.

Table 8.6

| | Goal | How/Process (Steps |
|---|---|---|
| Goal #1 | Speak UP! Deliver from the diaphragm. | 1. Take a deep breathto fill up lungs to support my words. 2. Pull from deeper within and talk using diaphragm muscles rather than throat muscles. 3. Release your words; let each one hit the back wall. |
| Goal #2 | Bandwidth: Stretch the bandwidth of my speech | 1. Use a short video clip with just a little music proactive. 2. Choose which words to emphasize, practice to build with tone, pitch, volume to create the mood I envision. 3. Surprise my audience with fresh baked cookies. |
| Goal #3 | Control my energy | 1. Monitor the mood of my peers as I set the stage. 2. Capture the energy with my eyes, excitement. 3. Be optimistic, and pull the message from deeper inside. Think about how they will appreciate the cookies! |

As you can see, your Delivery Plan of Action requires you to assess yourself as a speaker and accurately incorporate the feedback of your audience in a systematic way that will help you improve. The purpose of a Delivery Plan of Action is to help you improve and grow as a speaker. Build off your strengths, but also be willing to identify opportunities for improvement too. Remember, we tend to be our own worst critics. When you review your delivery, focus on the strengths, then identify an opportunity to improve and focus intently on that.

When you practice, be sure to focus 100%. Allow no outside interruptions! When you are confident, secure an audience to rehearse the speech. Remember this has proven to be the best way to reduce anxiety. Get feedback from your audience. Finally, reflect and refine!

At this point, no book learning in the world will help you improve. You must actually stand and deliver. That's the only way you can assess what you are doing well and what strengths you can draw on. You can deliver a speech in front of stuffed animals, your pets, your family, and friends. I recommend that you record your delivery so that you can accurately assess your assets and work from there!

### Practice Reducing Anxiety

Remember there are some surefire ways to reduce your anxiety. As you practice your delivery, incorporate these tips so your confidence improves.

1. Imagine yourself nailing the speech!
2. Use your breath to control your nerves.
3. Think positively
4. Practice power poses
5. Dress professionally

### Time Your Speech

Your speech has a time limit. Know what that is and don't steal others' time. It is even possible that your time is reduced on the spot. It might be a good idea to discuss your minimum time requirements with the coordinator but ultimately if you are asked by the host organization to shave your time, do so. Eliminate content rather than rush the delivery. Be sure to establish your practice time and eliminate content or make modifications if necessary. Always respect the time you are allotted.

### Audio/Video Analysis

Once you grasp the concepts of delivering a speech, I strongly suggest you use your cell phone or a camera on a tripod to record yourself delivering the speech. Eric, a former student of mine, once explained the value of audio/video analysis, "It is like going on a date without looking in the mirror!" It is not easy to look at yourself on a video or listen to a recording, but it is worth the effort. Summon up your courage and face your fear head on! Remind yourself that the audio video analysis will show how you can immediately improve. It will enable you to make strategic adjustments based upon insights you've gained about delivery principles and improvement strategies.

### Prepare Evaluations

Is the organization conducting an evaluation for your presentation? If they are, ask to see the results. If they aren't, ask if you can bring your own form. Do not miss the opportunity to obtain feedback. It is also helpful to coordinate a conversation with the organization to secure direct feedback from the stakeholders. It is crucial that you secure feedback from your audience as a way to realistically determine how the speech was perceived by the audience. Here is a sample feedback sheet that can provide a nice amount of information. Often times organizations will have their own feedback sheets. Refer to Figure 8.3 Feedback Sheet.

### 24-Hour Check. Are You Ready?

One day before you deliver, be sure that you have all the materials you need organized and in one place. This includes your speech, evaluations, handouts, props, thumb drive holding your slides, your cards, rewards for the audiences, and any thing else you need to deliver your greatest speech. Plan your outfit. The last thing you want to be doing before a speech is running late. Do not wait to print things out...that almost guarantees a printer malfunction! Murphy's Law seems to target technology to add to your stress. Be proactive and prepare well ahead.

### Reduce Anxiety

As you make your way to the event, remember to again implement the tips to reduce anxiety. Dress professionally, practice visualization techniques, do your power poses, think

## Figure 8.3: Feedback Sheet

<The event logo goes here.>

# Conference Name

## Session Evaluation

Shade Ovals Like This

**Session Title:** *<The Session code and title is custom printed here.>*

### SESSION EVALUATION

**Overall session evaluation:**

| Excellent | Very Good | Good | Fair | Poor |
|---|---|---|---|---|
| 5 | 4 | 3 | 2 | 1 |

**This session will help me perform my job more effectively:**

| Strongly Agree | | Neither Agree nor Disagree | | Strongly Disagree |
|---|---|---|---|---|
| 5 | 4 | 3 | 2 | 1 |

**Information presented met my expectations:**

| Strongly Agree | | Neither Agree nor Disagree | | Strongly Disagree |
|---|---|---|---|---|
| 5 | 4 | 3 | 2 | 1 |

**Session was at the educational level I expected:**

| Strongly Agree | | Neither Agree nor Disagree | | Strongly Disagree |
|---|---|---|---|---|
| 5 | 4 | 3 | 2 | 1 |

**Session content matched description:**

| Strongly Agree | | Neither Agree nor Disagree | | Strongly Disagree |
|---|---|---|---|---|
| 5 | 4 | 3 | 2 | 1 |

**Session length relative to amount of content:**

| Too Long | Just Right | Too Short |
|---|---|---|
| 3 | 2 | 1 |

**Would you recommend this session to a friend or colleague?**

Definitely — Definitely Not

10 9 8 7 6 5 4 3 2 1 0

**Number of years in the industry:**

- Less than 1
- 1 - 3
- 4 - 6
- 7 - 10
- 10 +

**Your age range:**

- Under 25
- 25 - 34
- 35 - 44
- 45 - 54
- 55 and older

### SPEAKER EVALUATION

***If not already printed, please write the speaker name(s) clearly.***

| | | EXCELLENT | VERY GOOD | GOOD | FAIR | POOR |
|---|---|---|---|---|---|---|
| *<Speaker 1's Name is custom printed here.>* | | | | | | |
| **Speaker 1** | Presentation Skills | 5 | 4 | 3 | 2 | 1 |
| | Knowledge of Topic | 5 | 4 | 3 | 2 | 1 |
| | Content | 5 | 4 | 3 | 2 | 1 |
| | Speaker Avoided Selling | Yes | | No | | |
| *<Speaker 2's Name is custom printed here.>* | | | | | | |
| **Speaker 2** | Presentation Skills | 5 | 4 | 3 | 2 | 1 |
| | Knowledge of Topic | 5 | 4 | 3 | 2 | 1 |
| | Content | 5 | 4 | 3 | 2 | 1 |
| | Speaker Avoided Selling | Yes | | No | | |
| *<Speaker 3's Name is custom printed here.>* | | | | | | |
| **Speaker 3** | Presentation Skills | 5 | 4 | 3 | 2 | 1 |
| | Knowledge of Topic | 5 | 4 | 3 | 2 | 1 |
| | Content | 5 | 4 | 3 | 2 | 1 |
| | Speaker Avoided Selling | Yes | | No | | |
| *<Speaker 4's Name is custom printed here.>* | | | | | | |
| **Speaker 4** | Presentation Skills | 5 | 4 | 3 | 2 | 1 |
| | Knowledge of Topic | 5 | 4 | 3 | 2 | 1 |
| | Content | 5 | 4 | 3 | 2 | 1 |
| | Speaker Avoided Selling | Yes | | No | | |
| *<Speaker 5's Name is custom printed here.>* | | | | | | |
| **Speaker 5** | Presentation Skills | 5 | 4 | 3 | 2 | 1 |
| | Knowledge of Topic | 5 | 4 | 3 | 2 | 1 |
| | Content | 5 | 4 | 3 | 2 | 1 |
| | Speaker Avoided Selling | Yes | | No | | |
| *<Speaker 6's Name is custom printed here.>* | | | | | | |
| **Speaker 6** | Presentation Skills | 5 | 4 | 3 | 2 | 1 |
| | Knowledge of Topic | 5 | 4 | 3 | 2 | 1 |
| | Content | 5 | 4 | 3 | 2 | 1 |
| | Speaker Avoided Selling | Yes | | No | | |

**Please provide your comments on the speaker(s) and session.**

Speaker(s): ____________________

Session: ____________________

Conducted by ShowValue info@showvalue.com

**Figure 8.4: Feedback Sheet**

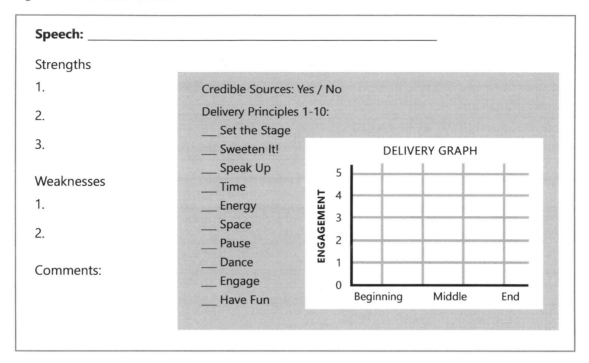

**Speech:** _____

Strengths

1.

2.

3.

Weaknesses

1.

2.

Comments:

Credible Sources: Yes / No

Delivery Principles 1-10:

___ Set the Stage

___ Sweeten It!

___ Speak Up

___ Time

___ Energy

___ Space

___ Pause

___ Dance

___ Engage

___ Have Fun

DELIVERY GRAPH

ENGAGEMENT

5
4
3
2
1
0

Beginning    Middle    End

positively, and **breathe**! Most importantly, think about your audience instead of your nerves. Visualize the audience getting your message.

### Arrive Early

Do not be late! Accidents can leave highways blocked for hours. Give yourself plenty of time and be familiar with alternate routes. You can arrive early and enjoy a beverage near the event location.

### Test Audio Video Equipment

Coordinate with the event planners to see when you can set up. Test the equipment, be sure that you always give yourself a Plan B and a Plan C should any technologies nightmares occur. Your slides should be on the cloud, on a thumb drive, and printed out so that whatever happens, your show can go on.

### Assess Yourself

Take a moment to take inventory. Is your face relaxed? Smile! Take a deep breath! Roll your shoulders. Do a power pose. Think positive thoughts. Visualize your audience. They should be arriving soon, if they aren't already there. Make a good first impression with your body language. Be open, friendly, approachable, and say Hi!

### Record Your Speech

Double-check to see that a representative from the organization is recording the speech for you, and be sure that you have enough memory on your device. Keep in mind that many devices today are capable of recording your speech: phone, tablet, laptop, MP3 player and cameras.

### Set the Stage

Your time has come! You are on! Remember to set the stage. Establish eye contact with individual audience members. Plant your feet on the ground. Stand confidently, poised for success. When the entire audience has focused on you, **project**—confidently say your first engaging words. DO IT! You have got this. Do your best—the audience always appreciates effort. You have worked hard and smart—they will respect you for your efforts.

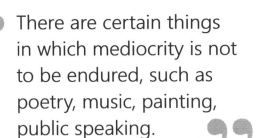

> There are certain things in which mediocrity is not to be endured, such as poetry, music, painting, public speaking.

*- Jean de la Bruyere*

## Phase 5: Reflection

### After Speech

Great! You delivered your speech. I hate to say this, but as hard as you worked, there are always opportunities. Dale Carnegie tells us, "There are always three speeches, for every one you actually gave. The one you practiced, the one you gave, and the one you wish you gave."

### Secure Audience Feedback

Obtain the feedback sheets from the organizers of the event as applicable. Review the sheets with an open mind. This can be very difficult to do. Don't be defensive. Imagine you are observing someone else receive feedback. Everyone's opinion matters. Their opinion doesn't make them right, but it is their point of view, and it's worth exploring.

Giving and receiving quality feedback is an art. The Three to One Rule of Feedback is a basic principle which suggests you give three positive feedbacks to every negative. Be kind. Follow this strategy when you provide feedback to other speakers or when you provide feedback to even yourself. You can even use it as the basis for the feedback sheets your create for your audience.

### Three to One Rule of Feedback

Any speech has strengths and weaknesses and presents opportunities for improvement and threats. Always consider both positives and negatives when you critique a speech. I recommend using the Three to One Rule of Feedback. For every opportunity, highlight three strengths. This is good advice to heed! Did you know relationship expert, John Gottman *(1999)*, identified a "Magic Ratio" of feedback for romantic relationships—we must hear five compliments for every criticism. Marriages fall into the danger zone of divorce when the ratio of positive to negative interactions dips below five to one. It isn't that arguments can't occur. Happy couples manage to deliver positive emotional messages even when they don't see eye to eye. Many believe the same "Magic Ratio" should be applied in parenting, the classroom, and business. Business research reports positive reinforcement engages employees far more than negative feedback. You get more results with candy than coal!

In any situation that evokes stress and anxiety, which is certainly the case when we critique a speaker, we should always be kind! Always provide more positive feedback than negative. In their paper, *Bad is Stronger than Good*, Baumeister, Bratslavsky & Finkenauer (2001) found, "Bad emotions... and bad feedback have more impact than good ones, and bad information is processed more thoroughly than good. The self is more motivated to avoid bad self-definitions than to pursue good ones. Bad impressions and bad stereotypes are quicker to form and more resistant to disconfirmation than good ones."

**Reflect Upon Your Delivery**

Think about the speech that you delivered. How did you do? Graph your speech out. What were the best moments and why? What were the weakest moments, why? Review your Delivery Plan of Action. How did you do? Did you reach your goals? Complete the Self Reflection Journal.

- How well prepared were you to deliver your speech?
- How well did you feel that you did delivering your speech?
- What feedback did you receive from your audience?
- How similar or different was your audience feedback from you own opinion? How distorted were the two versions?
- Create a Delivery Action Plan

**Watch Your Video**

Now that you know what you think and you know what the audience thinks—let's see what really happened. Watch the video. Evaluate. Congratulate.

**Create an Improvement Plan – Plan of Action**

Considering all the feedback, identify three stretch goals you will focus on in your next speech.

**Any Opportunities to Deliver the Speech Again**

Chances are you worked really hard on this presentation. Are there any opportunities to present it again to another audience? If so, why not explore those possibilities? This can help grow your business, as well as helping you grow personally.

There are always three speeches, for every one you actually gave. The one you practiced, the one you gave, and the one you wish you gave.

- *Dale Carnegie*

## Chapter 8 Review Questions

Since this chapter incorporated many of the ideas we built on from the rest of the book let's see how much you know. Answer these questions to see if you are ready to design and deliver Your Best Speech Ever!

1.  What are the five phases of the speech writing process?

2.  True or False: You should always accept a speaking engagement.

3.  How often do speakers have the opportunity to speak about whatever they want? Why?

4.  List five different types of reasons people are requested to speak.

5.  List several questions you should ask the coordinator prior to the event.

6.  Explain how to schedule your time to prepare ideally for a speech.

7.  Should every speech have credible research? Why? Why not?

8.  According to Benjamin Franklin, how much time is earned for every minute spent organizing?

9.  What are the three different types of audience analysis? How do they differ?

10. How do your emotional and motivational appeal differ?

11. How should you determine the organizational strategy for your main points?

12. What is a skeleton outline and how does it differ from a regular outline?

13. True or False: You should only write key words not full sentences when you write your speech.

14. Which part of the speech is most important to the audience? Why?

15. Compare and contrast the Introduction versus the Conclusion.

16. What should your cards contain?

17. What is the biggest mistake speakers make in regards to their cards?

18. What rubric should you use to be sure you make your visuals work for you?

19. What is involved in creating a deliberate practice?

20. How can you create a Delivery Plan of Action?

21. What are five things you can do to reduce your anxiety?

22. Which phase do you think will be the easiest to master? Which phase will be the most difficult? Why?

23. Explain the 3 to 1 rule of feedback.

24. True or False: You should always record your speech.

25. What questions do you have?

26. Which quote from this chapter resonates with you the most?

Made in the USA
Lexington, KY
29 December 2017